CALLED 2 LOVE

DEVOTIONS FOR COUPLES

CALLED 2 LOVE
DEVOTIONS
FOR
Couples

David & Teresa
Ferguson

TYNDALE
MOMENTUM®

The nonfiction imprint of
Tyndale House Publishers, Inc.

Visit Tyndale online at www.tyndale.com.

Visit Tyndale Momentum online at www.tyndalemomentum.com.

TYNDALE, Tyndale's quill logo, *Tyndale Momentum*, and the Tyndale Momentum logo are registered trademarks of Tyndale House Publishers, Inc. Tyndale Momentum is the nonfiction imprint of Tyndale House Publishers, Inc., Carol Stream, Illinois.

Called 2 Love Devotions for Couples

Previously published as *Never Alone Devotions for Couples* under ISBN 978-0-8423-5386-1 and as *The One Year Devotions for Couples* under ISBNs 978-1-4143-0170-9 (sc) and 978-1-4964-2530-0 (LeatherLike).

Cover designed by Libby Dykstra

Edited by Lynn Vanderzalm

For information about special discounts for bulk purchases, please contact Tyndale House Publishers at csresponse@tyndale.com, or call 1-800-323-9400.

ISBN 978-1-4964-4281-9

Printed in the United States of America

26 25 24 23 22 21
8   7   6   5   4   3

How to Get the Most Out of This Book

We believe that marriage is one of the most exhilarating relationships God has created. But sometimes marriage can be exhausting because it takes work to keep a marriage alive and flourishing. However, we can tell you—from personal experience and from our observations of others—that it's well worth the effort it takes to deepen the intimacy of marriage.

God has uniquely called a husband and wife to meet each other's "aloneness" needs. When God created Adam, He said that it was not good for him to be alone, so He created Eve to fill his emptiness. We believe that God calls husbands and wives to be His companions in meeting each other's needs for things like acceptance, affection, appreciation, approval, attention, comfort, encouragement, respect, security, and support.

What Will This Book Help Me to Do?

This daily devotional tool will help you grow in your ability to join with God in meeting your spouse's needs. We have divided the book into fifty-two themes, each one covered in a seven-day block. The themes are arranged alphabetically. For example, the meditations for January 1 through January 7 address the theme of acceptance, and the meditations for January 8 through January 14 discuss admonition (constructive feedback). We have arranged this book this way because we believe that studying an aspect of marriage for a seven-day period will help you to understand more fully the things that make a marriage all that it can be.

What Are the Themes Covered?

During the course of a year, you will cover these themes in seven-day blocks:

1. *acceptance*
2. *admonition*
3. *affection*
4. *appreciation*
5. *approval*
6. *attention*
7. *care*
8. *comfort*
9. *compassion*
10. *confession*
11. *consideration*
12. *counsel*
13. *courting*
14. *deference*
15. *devotion*
16. *discipline*
17. *edification*
18. *encouragement*
19. *enjoyment*
20. *entreaty*
21. *exalting*
22. *exhortation*
23. *forgiveness*
24. *freedom*
25. *gentleness*
26. *grace*
27. *happiness*
28. *harmony*
29. *honor*
30. *hospitality*
31. *instruction*
32. *intimacy*
33. *kindness*
34. *leadership*
35. *love*
36. *mercy*
37. *peace*
38. *praise*
39. *prayer*
40. *protection*
41. *rebuke*
42. *reproof*
43. *respect*
44. *security*
45. *service*
46. *support*
47. *sympathy*
48. *teaching*
49. *tolerance*
50. *training*
51. *trust*
52. *understanding*

When you finish the year, you will have spent focused time learning how to deepen your intimacy through each of these areas.

How Should I Approach the Book?

Each day includes a *Scripture verse,* a *meditation* that often builds on a personal story from our marriage and family life, a *prayer,* and a *commitment question* that will help you put into practice what you have learned through the meditation. The best way to go through this book is to read it together as a couple, but not everyone will choose to do that. You and your marriage can grow even if only one of you reads the book. We suspect that as you practice what you learn in these pages, your spouse will notice the difference and may even ask to join you in reading the rest of the book. Then, when you finish the book on December 31, start again on January 1 and deepen your understanding of how to partner with God in what He wants to do in your marriage.

Encouragement for the Journey

As you read through this year-long devotional, you will see real struggles in marriage—in our marriage, in the marriages of people we know, and maybe even in your own. But you will also see real and lasting triumphs. You will see that God gives us everything we need to deepen our marriages in the way He wants to shape them.

As you begin, we want to give you a final word of encouragement. We want you always to remember that marriage is God's idea, and as such, He is the one who knows what it takes to help marriages not only survive but also flourish. God wants to bring you deeper intimacy with Him and your spouse through your marriage. Lend Him an ear, and let Him do what it takes to bring you that intimacy.

JANUARY

acceptance
admonition
affection
appreciation
approval

A Deliberate, Unconditional, and Positive Response

Accept one another. Romans 15:7, NIV

My (Teresa's) ability to show acceptance of another is contingent upon my deep knowledge of a loving and accepting Christ. If I am to accept my spouse as Christ has accepted me, then I need to understand His wonderful love for me.

God, please help me to "look beyond" my spouse's flaws and imperfections and unconditionally and deliberately love this person, just as You have unconditionally and deliberately loved me.

God made a deliberate choice to allow Christ to die on my behalf. It wasn't a convenient or easy choice, either. It was a choice that prioritized the relationship between my heavenly Father and me, His child. Christ took the initiative when He came to "seek and save the lost" (Luke 19:10). He didn't wait for me to "get my act together." Rather, He looked beyond my actions and sins and accepted me as I was. This acceptance is unconditional and permanent. There is nothing I can do to earn it or lose it.

God demonstrated this unconditional acceptance when He looked beyond my faults to see my need. He didn't excuse my sin but instead gave the best He had as a remedy for that sin.

This kind of "looking beyond" makes marriage work, too.

Accepting my spouse as Christ has accepted me means making a choice. It won't be convenient or easy. It will mean taking some initiative. It may mean being the first to say, "Honey, I love you." It may mean not waiting until he changes to tell him how glad I am to be his wife.

Unconditionally accepting my spouse means looking beyond differences, disagreements, and disputes. It means looking beyond irritations, personality flaws, and idiosyncrasies. It even means looking beyond wrongs and sins committed—not to excuse these things, but to see his worth in spite of them.

In what ways can you daily demonstrate your deliberate
and unconditional love for your spouse?

Acceptance Begins with Him

Accept one another, then, just as Christ has accepted you,
in order to bring praise to God. Romans 15:7, NIV

My wife is so different from me. I (David) am laid back and tend to go with the flow, while she's very punctual, even to the point of being compulsive about being on time. I'm flexible—maybe even a little oblivious to details—while she's a perfectionist. I'm quiet and reserved, while she's outgoing and likes lots of attention.

When my life gets stressful, these differences between us can make my wife seem—from my perspective—impatient, critical, and loud. Those character traits are difficult for me to accept.

Lord, may my gratitude for Your unconditional acceptance of me prompt within me today a joyful acceptance of my spouse.

I have learned, however, that acceptance doesn't mean condoning someone's behavior. It simply means looking deeper than someone's actions to see that person's true worth, just as God does with me when He sees my sin. Christ looked beyond Zacchaeus's selfishness and greed and offered kindness and warmth. Jesus separated Peter's impulsiveness and cowardly betrayal from his worth. Christ talked with the woman at the well, a woman who lived year after year in habitual sin, and offered her freedom because He saw her need for unconditional love.

Have I ever been selfish or greedy in my marriage? Undoubtedly! I've even cheated my wife out of undivided attention and stolen her joy at times. Have I ever acted without thinking or spoken without caution? Absolutely! Have I ever betrayed a confidence or trust? Are there sins I live with year after year? Yes!

And yet, despite these imperfections and sins, God still accepts me and offers me kindness and compassion.

As I look beyond Teresa's manner, my gratitude for her as a special and loving helpmate continues to grow. But that happens only as I remind myself of how Christ accepts me despite my own shortcomings.

In what ways can you continually remind yourself of your
spouse's true worth, despite that person's imperfections?

I'm a 10!

For by one offering He has perfected for all time those who are sanctified. Hebrews 10:14, NASB

I (Teresa) had always been critical of myself—and of everyone else, for that matter.

Lord, help me put down the tally sheet and magnifying glass I hold over my spouse.

The way I understood God, He was up in heaven with a great big magnifying glass and tally sheet, inspecting every move I made. When I went to church or did a good deed, He'd make a mark on His tally sheet. But on that same sheet, He'd make a mark for every blunder, sin, or imperfection. I believed that my net number of "good" marks determined how much of God's love and acceptance I would receive.

This faulty perception of God had a huge impact on my marriage. I believed that since God was constantly inspecting me and looking for faults, then surely I should inspect my husband just as closely. In the midst of one of my inspections, I said some really hurtful things to David. Immediately, I knew I needed to confess this sin to God and ask for forgiveness.

In times past, as I confessed my sins to God and told Him how bad I'd been, I would have expected a halfhearted response: "Okay, Teresa," I could hear God reluctantly saying. "I'll forgive you. I'll mark your confession on the tally sheet, and we'll let it go this time."

But this time, my heavenly Father very gently said, "I know what you've done. You're forgiven, Teresa."

When I heard God's truth—that He already knows my sins and accepts me anyway—a burden was lifted. I realized that God doesn't hold a magnifying glass and tally sheet over me. Instead, He holds the crown of thorns that His Son wore and the nails that pierced His hands and feet.

I saw God as He really is: the heavenly Father who sees me as one being perfected because of the Cross.

How have your wrong perceptions of God affected your relationship with your spouse?

Acceptance in a Sycamore Tree

Zacchaeus, come down immediately. I must stay at your house today. Luke 19:5, NIV

Zacchaeus—a hated tax collector, a traitor to his own people, and a thief—was no doubt often ridiculed and attacked for his sins. Lonely and curious, he climbed a tree to get a good look at this "Messiah." He had to wonder if Jesus would notice him. And if He did, would He too reject him?

What a miracle Christ's call must have been to this outcast!

God, remind me to look to You as my example as I respond to the imperfections of others.

Our Savior called Zacchaeus to fellowship with Him by the sharing of a meal, which was one of the most intimate social settings of the day. This was a deliberate offer of welcome, reception, and loving relationship.

In the midst of Zacchaeus's failures, Jesus offered compassion, companionship, and acceptance. It's interesting to note what Jesus didn't do that day: He didn't attack the tax collector's behavior, point out things that were wrong with him, or even give helpful advice. He didn't remind Zacchaeus of what he should be doing or criticize him for not taking more responsibility. Jesus didn't quote Scripture to Zacchaeus or make comparisons with other tax collectors in town. He didn't try to manipulate change or withhold affection.

I (Teresa) want to respond to David the way Christ responded to Zacchaeus. As I encounter David's inevitable failures, I want to be free from the impulse to be critical and give advice. I want to say words that are tender and welcoming, rather than judgmental and comparing. I want to make certain that the "welcome mat" is always out. To be like Christ will mean that I consistently invite David to fellowship with me.

I want to respond to David with words and actions that invite him to "come down out of the tree." After all, it gets awfully lonely up there!

What steps can you take today to replace words of judgment, comparison, complaint, and criticism with words of unconditional acceptance and love?

Welcome Home!

Anyone who welcomes you is welcoming me, and anyone who welcomes me is welcoming the Father who sent me. Matthew 10:40, NLT

When Jesus returns to His hometown with His disciples, they file into the back of the Nazareth synagogue where He had worshiped as a child. The priest has just finished his closing remarks, and the musicians begin to lead the people in a song of worship: "Praises to Jehovah! Hosanna to the Lord our God!"

Lord, remind me daily to welcome You by welcoming the spouse You have sent to me.

The Savior is overwhelmed with feelings of joy and gratitude. He is in the company of His family and friends, and together they are worshiping the one true God.

Before anyone has a chance to move, Jesus begins to speak. He teaches with uncommon boldness and clarity about the God they have just studied in the Scriptures.

When Jesus finishes teaching, the people leave the synagogue a little bewildered. A few of the neighbors come to shake His hand. Some of the synagogue officials extend to Him an uncomfortable, "Thanks for being with us today." But the Savior reads their hearts, which are filled with questions such as, "Who does He think He is? Isn't He just a carpenter's son?" Scripture puts it this way: "And they took offense at Him" (Matthew 13:57, NASB).

Can you feel the rejection? Jesus is in His hometown, the place where He should be most accepted, yet His friends and neighbors take offense at Him and in their hearts put up a sign that clearly reads, "Unwelcome."

Would you have offered Jesus acceptance and welcome in that situation, or would you have put up the "Unwelcome" sign? Before you answer that question, think about these words of Jesus: "Anyone who welcomes you is welcoming me."

When I (Teresa) accept my husband, I am accepting Christ, who sent him to me. Every time I welcome David, I am saying, "Welcome" to the Lord.

In what ways can you daily accept and
welcome your spouse into your life?

Just As I Am

Why do you look at the speck of sawdust in your brother's eye and pay no attention to the plank in your own eye? Matthew 7:3, NIV

I (Teresa) grew up in a family that valued routine and schedules. However, my husband's family was much more laid back. Both of his parents worked, and their routines were never the same each day.

Because of this difference in upbringing, when David and I married, our expectations clashed like brown shoes with a tuxedo. For example, I'd cook David's favorite dishes for dinner, just certain that he'd come through the door promptly at 5:30 each day, kiss the kids and me on the cheek, and sit down to a family dinner. But on more nights than I care to count, I'd end up with a tapping foot, a disgusted look on my face, and a cold dinner in the oven as I waited for my husband to come home.

God, help me accept my spouse as he or she is, focusing instead on the changes I need to make in my own life.

Looking back, I have realized that I didn't respond well to the situation. In fact, I was pretty intolerant. I had come to view David's seeming lack of appreciation for my cooking as absolutely unacceptable. But God showed me that this wasn't necessarily David's problem. In His gentle voice, He prompted me with these thoughts one day: *Teresa, could it be that the intolerance you have for David's schedule has actually become a "plank in your eye"? Don't worry about the speck in his. Your lack of acceptance of David's differences is a part of the conflict between the two of you.*

I still need David to keep me informed about when he's coming home, and I need some "thank you's" every now and then. But each late dinner is a reminder to me to accept David as he is rather than trying to change him to be like me.

What changes might God be trying to make in you, using your spouse's flaws and shortcomings as the tools to make those changes?

Accepting an Imperfect Person

God demonstrates His own love toward us, in that while we were still sinners, Christ died for us. Romans 5:8

This verse tells us that Christ died for us even though we were sinners. The best word in this verse is "while." He died for me *while* I (David) was still rebellious and hostile to the things of God.

Heavenly Father, keep me aware that real love is an unconditional commitment to an imperfect person.

We are to love our spouses in the same way Christ loved us. We are to love them even though they are imperfect and sinful. How do we do that, you ask? By reflecting on the fact that He first loved us.

Most couples go through several stages in their marriage before they reach the ability to commit to loving a real and admittedly imperfect person. It takes a while for some couples to stop trying to change one another and to choose to accept one another WHILE both are still sinners.

Which stage are you in?

Romantic Stage: You see your spouse as perfect, as everything you need.

Bargaining Stage: Your spouse surely isn't perfect, and you will change if your spouse does.

Coercive Stage: You will change your spouse, whether or not he or she likes it.

Desperation Stage: You give up trying to change your spouse, believing that person will never change.

Romantic Realism: You are finally at a point where you can live out Romans 5:8 and love your spouse, who sees and admits his or her own imperfections. This stage of marriage is summed up with this kind of vow:

"I take you to be my spouse with full knowledge that you will sometimes disappoint me gravely and hurt me deeply. In spite of all your weaknesses and failures, I commit myself to loving you. I am able to do this because of the acceptance of Christ, who loved me and died for me while I was still a sinner."

In what ways can you demonstrate unconditional
love for your spouse?

admonition

Constructive Guidance

Do nothing out of selfish ambition . . . but in humility consider others better than yourselves. Philippians 2:3, NIV

Admonition: constructive guidance in what to avoid; warning.

That definition of admonition has a positive feel to it. But I (Teresa) must admit that my admonitions have not always sounded so positive. I readily confess that I'm a take-charge kind of person. David has called this my "whip and drive" mode of operation, and it has at times been a point of contention in our marriage. No matter how good my intentions may be, sometimes my tendency to "whip and drive" overshadows my well-meaning attempts to give constructive guidance.

Heavenly Father, help me work on the way I present my constructive guidance. Give me the right words, tone of voice, and timing.

I certainly had the best intentions when I warned David about the speed traps lurking around the next turn in the road. I really didn't want to see him get another ticket. But, unfortunately, David didn't receive my admonitions as positive or constructive guidance. I suppose my technique needed some work. I don't think I used the most positive words when I said, "David, slow down! Didn't you see the speed limit sign back there? You're going way too fast for this neighborhood."

David might have sensed that I was sharing these words because of my own agenda. I didn't want to hassle with the insurance company. I didn't want to be stopped by the police and embarrassed once again. I didn't want David to have to be gone another Saturday for a defensive-driving course.

I must admit, my attempt at admonition that day was all about me. Me! Me! Me!

I finally decided to stop trying to control David's driving and let God do the admonishing. When I did that, I soon discovered that not only was he more responsive to my warnings, but I was freer to focus on all the things he does right.

That's what true admonition looks like!

What steps can you take to be certain that your motivation for admonishing your spouse is true care and concern for him or her?

Admonition in the Garden

The day that you eat from [this tree] you shall surely die.
Genesis 2:17, NASB

Remember God's admonition to Adam? What an act of love it was for God to warn him!

A few years ago, I (David) would have never been able to say that it was "loving" of God to warn Adam about the tree. Instead, I saw this warning as God depriving Adam, as dangling the proverbial carrot in front of the man then yanking it away.

Father, help me to examine my motives before I speak admonitions to my spouse.

I have since come to realize that God's warning was an act of profound love for humankind.

The truth is that God created an incredible paradise for Adam and provided generously for his every need and desire. He placed only one limitation on mankind: There was one tree in the midst of the garden that Adam was not to touch, for God knew that if Adam ate from it, he and all the generations to follow would be destined for pain.

God put the tree in the garden because He wanted the man to choose a relationship of mutual love. Had there been no "forbidden tree," there would have been no choice, and the man would have obeyed God simply because there was no alternative. God warned Adam about the tree because He didn't want him harmed or separated from Him. What an awesome God!

As we travel the narrow path that leads to life, we must remember that God's admonitions are always clear and in our best interest. His warnings serve to protect us, to shield us, and to defend us from harm, not to place limits on us.

Our admonitions of one another should be the same.

When I feel prompted to admonish Teresa, I must first thoroughly check my heart to see that my motivation is right. I have to ask myself if I'm motivated to speak out of her best interest and a concern for her well-being, or if I'm speaking out of my own selfish desires for convenience, retaliation, judgment, or accusation.

How can you be absolutely certain that your heart is truly in the right place when you feel the need to admonish your spouse?

A Voice of Admonition

You also are full of goodness . . . [and] knowledge, able
also to admonish one another. Romans 15:14

Like the proverbial sheep, I (Teresa) tend to wander among the conflicting pulls on my life. For that reason, I rejoice often that I've not been left without God's admonitions.

I have a tendency to be self-reliant and stubborn. I sometimes ignore God's guidance, thinking all the while that I can handle my problems on my own. And just when I've needed it the most—and when I've finally admitted it—God has been there to lovingly see me through.

Father, make my heart sensitive to Your admonishing voice and to the voice of my spouse, whom You involve to bring me warnings and correction.

I know others of God's sheep who have a tendency to blatantly ignore the admonitions of the Shepherd. They take risks, almost seemingly "daring" God to save them at their most dire moment of need. Still other sheep have a mind-set that says, "What's the point of following God's guidance? I don't know that He cares about me one way or another."

All of these sheep—including me—have the wrong idea about God. The Great Shepherd has promised that He will guide and direct us through His Spirit and His written Word. Our only responsibility is to pay heed to His wonderful guidance and direction.

God has also provided us with other sheep who can serve as voices of His guidance. Among those "other sheep" He has provided are our spouses. Because Jesus lives within the heart of my husband, God actually uses him to guide me and instruct me.

The Bible says that because David has a relationship with Christ, he is "full of goodness and knowledge." Therefore, I want to hear the admonitions for me that God has laid on my husband's heart.

What factors can keep you from heeding words of admonition that come through your spouse? What can you do to overcome those factors?

Who Needs Admonition?

I do not write these things to shame you, but to admonish you as my beloved children. 1 Corinthians 4:14, NASB

"Sweetheart, do you really want to go down the interstate?"

It was an innocent enough question. Teresa was just trying to help us make our social engagement on time. So what was my response?

"I'll get us there," I replied sharply and sarcastically.

Why did I (David) react with such quick anger? Because although I need admonition, I tend to resist it. To me, constructive guidance implies that I don't know everything, that my way is not perfect. That truth is hard for me to swallow.

Father, please grant me a heart that is soft and receptive enough to receive loving admonition from my spouse.

At that moment, I began to reflect on how God had encouraged me to relate to my children. I had warned them about climbing on the stairs and crossing the street. I had admonished them about their attitudes with teachers and motives with friends at school. Did I do those things because I wanted to make my kids miserable or spoil their fun? Of course not! Did I say those things to expose my children's ignorance? No way! My motivation for these admonitions was love. I didn't want my kids to get hurt or to hurt others.

My next thought was the most sobering. As I examined my interactions with my kids over the years, I realized that they have had a much more teachable spirit than I've had. For the most part, they have received and followed my instructions and warnings.

I wondered if I could cultivate this same willingness to receive instruction, if I could have a more teachable spirit.

At that moment, I asked God to make me more childlike in spirit and more willing to receive admonition from the spouse He had lovingly placed in my life.

What steps can you take to allow your heart to be receptive to the admonition God brings through your spouse?

Warning: Trouble Ahead

*He guides the humble in what is right and
teaches them his way.* Psalm 25:9, NIV

There are many warning signs in life. Signs that read "DO NOT ENTER,"
"DON'T WALK," "CAUTION," or "DANGER AHEAD" are put in place to
help us avoid dangerous situations.

I (David) must confess that I have a difficult
time heeding warning signs. I see "CAUTION—ICE
ON BRIDGE" and speed on, only to slide out of control. I see "DON'T WALK" and think, *Oh, I'll ignore
this warning just this once!* I see "DANGER AHEAD"
and barrel on through, oblivious to the hazards that
lay ahead.

In His written Word, the Bible, God has given
me plenty of warnings to help me avoid danger zones
in my marriage. I have to admit that there have been
times when I failed to pay heed to those warnings as
well. For example, in Ephesians, He tells me to "let no
unwholesome word proceed from [my] mouth," but
only those that "give grace" (4:29, NASB). But I have
to wonder how many fights with Teresa I could have
avoided had I only paid attention to this warning. In
1 Timothy, God tells me to avoid the foolish pursuit

*God, let me
approach Your
Word with
openness and
with humility
in spirit. Make
me teachable
and receptive to
the guidance and
warning signs
within that Word.*

of money (6:9-10). But I wonder how many conflicts I could have avoided
had I given priority to my relationship with my wife and not to money.

The Word of God gives us all the guidance we need to keep our relationships—relationships with imperfect people, including our spouses—on
the right track. It is in that Word that we find not just encouragement to do
what we should, but warnings against what we should avoid.

In your reading of God's Word, what admonitions have
you seen that you can apply to your marriage?

Where Do Your Loyalties Lie?

Guard yourself; always remain loyal to your [spouse].
Malachi 2:16, NLT

My (Teresa's) family had just left after the holiday celebration. The house was finally quiet, but David seemed unusually withdrawn.

"Sweetheart," I asked, "what's bothering you?" David began to tell me about how he felt left out and unprioritized during my family's visit, and about how he was the last to receive my attention whenever my relatives were around. He spoke with gentleness, but his words cut to the bone as he said, "Teresa, I just need to know that you care about me, even when your family is around. I need to know that I'm your top priority."

God, help me to remember that aside from my relationship with You, I am to place my relationship with my spouse above all others.

I listened intently, but I had a hard time receiving his words. My immediate response was defensive: "You've always had a hard time fitting in with my family. I just pay a lot of attention to them because I don't get to see them very often." I could see that all my excuses wouldn't make the hurt in his eyes go away.

I called a friend that evening to talk about my predicament. "Amy," I said, "several of my brothers and sisters are hearing impaired, so there are many times when most of the communication is in sign language. David doesn't know sign language, so it's tough to involve him in everything. Besides, isn't he just being oversensitive?"

My friend listened for a while and then gently reminded me that my husband needed me to be his wife first, and a daughter or sister second. She reminded me that he needed the reassurance that I thought of him first, before my relatives. He needed me to sit beside him and include him in family conversations. He needed me to make sure *his* glass of tea was filled and that I carefully prepared *his* pumpkin pie.

What acts of love can you perform to assure your spouse
that he or she is your number one earthly priority?

Admonition to Agree

Can two people walk together without agreeing on the direction? Amos 3:3, NLT

Agreeing on where you're going is essential to oneness in a relationship. This kind of unity can start with the simple rule that neither spouse makes a commitment involving the other without discussing it first. It can also include things such as a weekly family night, remodeling plans, or vacation ideas. Each of these encourages "walking together" as a couple or family.

Think about the satisfaction you feel when you've checked each and every item off your "to-do" list, or about that sense of accomplishment that comes with achieving a larger goal. Setting goals for marriage and family can have the same effect. Accomplishing these goals can also bring a deep sense of togetherness and unity.

God, may the unity between my spouse and me be a testimony of Your work in our marriage.

Assess the following areas of marriage and family as you consider how closely you and your spouse are "walking together":

Finances: savings, tithing, debt reduction, retirement planning, investments, college preparation

Child rearing: overall discipline, potty training, driving privileges, curfews, dating, family devotions, relating to adult children

Holiday traditions: Whose house? how often? how long?

Housing decisions: remodeling, yard, and decorating projects

Vacation ideas: Who decides location? alone or with another family? hotel or camping?

Ministry: To church families? focus on outreach? ministry to extended family? ministry beyond our local church?

Health and fitness: meal planning, exercise routines, eating out vs. cooking at home

Individually, these categories for agreement may not seem like such a huge deal. But when taken as a whole, they can spell the difference between unity and division in your marriage.

In what areas do you and your spouse find yourselves in agreement? In what areas do you disagree, and why?

affection

Communicating Closeness through Touch

Greet one another with a holy kiss. Romans 16:16, NASB

Of the five senses, touch is the one we need most in our relationships. Studies have shown that lack of physical touch hinders development in newborns and that plenty of affection actually stabilizes the physical development of infants. Caring touch not only nurtures security in a child, it communicates worth and value to adults.

Lord, help me to remember the importance of sharing warm and tender greetings, particularly with my spouse.

Jesus often used physical touch as a way to demonstrate His care and concern for people. For example, He accompanied miraculous healing with physical touch. Christ could have just spoken a word, but He touched a blind man's eyes, a leper's skin, and a young girl's hand.

As I (Teresa) have learned to love David in the way that he longs to be loved, I have discovered that as I initiate affection, his fears decrease. Each time I reach over and hold his hand or rub his hair, he is reassured of my love for him. He doesn't have to wonder, "Does she still love me?" My initiative to give to David in these tender ways deepens his trust in our relationship.

One of the practical ways we've practiced the art of affection is through our good-byes and greetings. As we leave one another each morning, David and I make sure to start the day with a hug. We'll give one another a hug and usually include a group hug with the kids. Greeting one another with a kiss at the end of a long day has also paid big benefits. It has taken concerted effort to stop what I'm doing or shake off the kid clinging to my leg. But with each greeting, David and I reestablish our commitment to one another.

The message in these actions is clear: "Our relationship is important, and these simple gestures remind us to cherish one another."

At what times during the day could you begin making
it a point to share physical affection with your spouse?
What would stop you from doing that?

Affection in the Upper Room

Leaning back on Jesus' breast . . . John 13:25

The time of His departure is near, and Jesus has just revealed the troubling news about His betrayal. In utter shock and disbelief, the disciples listen as the Lord says, "One of you is going to betray me." Having heard that announcement, they stare at one another in silence.

Peter motions to John and encourages him to ask the Master for more information: "Find out who the traitor is," Peter requests. John asks the question that Peter suggests, but in a much more caring manner. John has no idea exactly how to handle the situation, but he draws closer to Jesus. Finally, he asks, "Lord, who is it?"

Father, sensitize my heart to my spouse's need for gentle, caring touch.

Scripture tell us that at that moment, John leaned close to Jesus, even to the point of leaning back against Him. This is a warm, caring, compassionate gesture on John's part. John seems to sense Christ's agony, and he shows the love and concern for his Teacher through genuine, appropriate affection.

John wanted more than anything to solve the problem at hand. But how in the world could he have helped the Savior of the universe? How could he have done anything that would make a difference? Apparently, John was quite aware of his inability to fix the problem, so he simply cared for Jesus with a simple touch.

I (David) wonder if I could take a few hints from John.

There are times when I'm not exactly sure how to help Teresa or support her when she's in pain. And if I can't fix the problem, then I'm often at a loss for what to do. It's at those times that I shouldn't minimize the value of simple affection. It may seem inadequate to solve the problem, but my touch tells my wife, "I care, and I'm here for you."

During times of trouble and pain, there's no greater message than that.

What steps could you take to learn to show simple affection to your spouse during troubling times?

Afraid of Affection

Perfect love casts out fear. 1 John 4:18, NASB

This may sound strange, but there was a time when I (Teresa) actually *feared* times of affection with David. I have since realized that one source of that fear was my own upbringing. I have always known that my mom and dad loved me, and they demonstrated that love the best way they knew how. Mom cooked our meals and Dad went to work. I had all my physical needs met, but I missed receiving physical affection and hearing the words "I love you."

God, help me find and deal with any hidden hindrances to enjoying affection with my spouse.

Because of this, it was very difficult for me to receive affection from David and even more difficult to give it. He came home wanting a hug, but I wanted to show my love by cooking him a roast or a pie, much the way my mom had done for me.

A second source of my fear was the unhealed hurts that occurred when David and I were first married. To become affectionate with David meant that I would have to become tender and vulnerable, and that meant there was a great risk of being hurt again, a risk I was reluctant to take.

God started to heal my hurts from childhood. I was able to admit that while my parents did the best they could in raising me, it still hurt deeply to have missed the physical and verbal expressions of love.

At the same time, David and I also began to heal the hurts between us. Ever so slowly, my fear of affection has melted away. And it has been God's love demonstrated through David that has cast out my fears.

Affection seemed unnatural to me at first, but now I not only enjoy it but actually *need* it. God has changed me in ways that have profoundly deepened my relationship with David.

Do you truly enjoy physical affection with your spouse?
Why or why not?

Affection: Why Waste It?

The Lord said to me, "Go, show your love to your wife again."
Hosea 3:1, NIV

"Claim me when we're out in public!" "Show other people that we're married and that you like the idea!"

Those were some of Teresa's complaints early in our marriage. I admit that when we were in a social setting, I (David) would often withdraw to a quiet corner with a colleague or escape into a conversation with friends, leaving her to fend for herself. Teresa felt rejected and ignored when I did that, but for the longest time, I saw it as her problem. I saw her as being too insecure or clingy.

Lord, help me to know how to show affection to my spouse in the ways that will bless him or her.

However, God showed me differently.

The Lord reminded me through the prophet Hosea that I am called to love my wife just like Hosea loved Gomer. The Lord told Hosea to return to his wife and love her again. But in order to do that he had to redeem her from slavery. He had to step into a public arena and buy his wife (Hosea 3).

As I read this passage, the Lord seemed to say, "David, Teresa needs to sense that you are ready to stand in any public arena and loudly, unashamedly proclaim that she is your wife. Your wife needs to know that you will stand with her and never leave her."

All those times before, I had thought I was "wasting" my affections on Teresa. I wondered what good a public show of affection would do. But I realized I had missed an incredible opportunity to express my love.

Now I realize that my displays of affection yield an incredible reward for me and my wife. Each time that I give her my arm or hold her hand in public, I remind her of my love and reassure her that I am glad she is my wife.

In what ways can you appropriately express your
affection for your spouse in a public setting?

Can a Zebra Change Its Stripes?

Greet one another with a holy kiss. 1 Corinthians 16:20, NASB

As I (Teresa) mentioned before, I'm not naturally affectionate. My husband, David, is just the opposite. He likes to hold hands and give hugs. He always has lots of "sugary" words to say. My words often sound stunted, rather than sugary, and holding hands is sometimes a little too mushy for me.

God, remind me of the ways that You have actively expressed Your love to me and motivate me to do the same with my spouse.

You might think David and I are a bad match, but I assure you we are a great match. That's because God has provided me with a very affectionate husband who can encourage change in me. The Lord has used David to help me grow comfortable with my feelings and with expressing them toward others.

It has been a process for me. I started off by writing a few sentences in a card to express the best I could the love I felt for David. Next, I worked up to writing a whole letter in which I told David all the feelings that were inside of me. I became comfortable doing that because I could take the time to write, rewrite, and edit anything that wasn't just right. Finally, I graduated to actually saying tender words of love to David, who is patient and listens attentively simply because he knows it isn't always easy for me to communicate those things.

Am I a superaffectionate person now? No, but I am a lot warmer now than I would have been if I had married a male version of myself. I now reach for David's hand before he reaches for mine. Sometimes I even hug him before he hugs me. To some, that may not sound like much, but it's been a long journey for me and my husband.

In what specific ways will you show affectionate physical touch to your spouse today?

Reach Out and Touch

One day some parents brought their children to Jesus so he could touch them and bless them. Mark 10:13, NLT

I (Teresa) am a people watcher. I especially enjoy watching married couples in restaurants. It's amazing how they interact. You can see couples who have obviously drifted chasms apart or the ones who struggle just to maintain a conversation. Couples such as these look awkward just making eye contact and touching minimally.

I've also watched what appeared to be newly married couples. They talk in lively, involved tones. They find any excuse to touch one another. They hold hands across the table or place hands on the other's leg as they sit close together. These couples make as much eye contact as possible. They smile and laugh together.

Lord, in simple ways, help me be vulnerable in my marriage and reach out to my spouse with a loving touch.

We all know that the early years of love are ignited with new discoveries, but the later years don't have to be filled with complacency and distance. David and I have made a commitment to make "date nights" a priority in our schedule. At least twice a month, we schedule nights when we go out together—just the two of us. During those dates, we decide ways we can act like newlyweds. I'll make a special effort to hold his hand as we watch the movie together. David might lean over to kiss me after we bless our meal. We both make conscious efforts to communicate and display our love for one another.

Our purposeful affection has increased the intensity of our love for one another. It's made our date nights more fun and our marriage more loving. It's those simple gestures of care that have prompted tender moments of compassion, vulnerable sharing, and passionate times of intimacy.

What can you and your spouse do today to bring the tenderness and passion back into your relationship?

Three Kinds of Touch

You have made my heart beat faster with a single glance of your eyes.
Song of Solomon 4:9, NASB

Sarah and Andy sat with Teresa and me expressing a common struggle. Sexual intimacy had become a huge battleground for them. Andy portrayed Sarah as being frigid, and Sarah accused Andy of being a sexual maniac. What had started out as one of the best parts of their marriage had deteriorated to nightly conflict.

Lord, give me extra sensitivity to the sexual needs and desires of my spouse.

We first spent a great deal of time healing the hurts from the past. Each started by confessing their sins to God and then to one another. Then Sarah made an insightful observation when she said, "It seems like the only time Andy touches me is when he wants sex!" We could now address this common issue by expanding their understanding of affectionate touch.

A balanced relationship includes each of these three kinds of touch:

Spiritual touching: Holding hands to pray communicates spiritual agreement. Touch in church, embrace each other at times of great joy, and hold hands as a family at the dinner prayer.

Soul touching: Embrace each other as you depart for the day. Kiss one another as you reunite. Hold hands while you walk through the mall, walk arm in arm as you stroll through your neighborhood, give one another a back rub, and hug one another—even in public.

Sexual touching: Soft touching is usually preferred over grabbing and mauling. Kiss tenderly as well as passionately.

Before Andy and Sarah concluded their counseling time, we talked more about what sex was and was not. We pointed out to them that sex is not something you manage or bargain with and not merely another activity that you count. Sex is something you *share*. It is the freedom to share all of yourself—spirit, soul, and body—with your spouse.

What can you do today to increase the amount of touching within your marriage?

Gratitude in Words and Feelings

I praise you because you remember me in everything.
1 Corinthians 11:2, NASB

Appreciation means saying, "Thank you!" It means saying that I've noticed something good you have done. Appreciation means recognizing effort and expressing gratitude for that effort. It means communicating with words and feelings that I am grateful for you and to you.

Here are some ways you can show your spouse some appreciation:

- Praising your spouse for demonstrating a positive attitude or character trait.
- Publicly praising your spouse for a positive deed. Bragging about him or her in front of others.
- Calling attention to what your spouse does right, rather than what he or she does wrong.
- Saying, "Wow, honey! I really appreciate your hard work in the yard. It looks terrific!"
- Saying, "Thank you for being such a good hostess to my family. I know you worked very hard during their visit."
- Sending an e-mail or thank-you card in the mail.

Father, remind me often of my spouse's strengths. Remind me of the reasons we fell in love.

David and I have often had trouble seeing each other with appreciative eyes. At times our focus has been on the negative: what we don't like, what we don't have, or what we don't do for one another.

Sometimes it has helped us to "think appreciatively" about one another. That means taking time to remember the positive character traits that first brought us together. I liked David's daredevil tendencies combined with his ability to "go with the flow." He liked my spunky attitude and easy spontaneity. When we think about it, we remember the things we liked about each other when we first got married.

It's amazing how remembering what made us fall in love in the first place sparks gratitude and hope.

What are some things your spouse is or does that you can praise him or her for today?

One of the Nine?

Was no one found to return and give praise to God?
Luke 17:18, NIV

Ten men—their flesh rotting and their extremities gone—were united by a common tragedy: leprosy. In desperation, these lepers cried out, "Jesus, Master, have mercy on us!"

Lord, remind me that each time I show my spouse appreciation, I am showing You appreciation as well.

Jesus showed mercy, and a new beginning was underway for them. He instructed them, "Go and show yourselves to the priest." As they set out, the lepers were healed. As their flesh became whole before their very eyes, these men must have been flooded by many emotions such as bewilderment, ecstasy, and hope. But one man's heart was overwhelmed by one emotion: appreciation.

The other nine continued on their way to the priest, but one reversed direction. He ran back to Jesus, fell at His feet, and with a loud voice praised and thanked the One who had made him whole. At this moment, his heart was fixed on one thing: expressing appreciation to Jesus.

In the next few words of this exchange, we gain a glimpse into the Savior's feelings as well. As Jesus gladly received the man's thanks, we hear disappointment as well. "Were not all ten cleansed? Where are the other nine?"

Did Jesus really wonder if the other nine had been cleansed? Of course not. Was this a trick question for the grateful leper? No. Our Savior's words reflect His disappointment and sadness. He had given renewed life and freedom to ten men, yet only one came back to show his appreciation.

It saddens me (David) to think about Christ miraculously blessing ten men and only one returning to show his appreciation.

Then I realize that I am doing the same thing every time I neglect to show appreciation to my spouse, whom God has given me.

What can you do today to show your spouse appreciation?
What would keep you from doing those things?

Opposites Attract

Fulfill my joy by being like-minded, having the same love, being of one accord, of one mind. Philippians 2:2

David and I (Teresa) are opposites in almost every way. He is laid-back, easygoing, and an "I'll deal with it later" type. I'm compulsive, a "let's deal with it now" person. There were a lot of years when I couldn't see David's personality traits as praiseworthy, much less share appreciation for them.

Our opposite natures surfaced when it came time to discipline the kids. My greatest fear was that David wasn't involved enough. He wasn't there all day with the kids, so how could he possibly know the circumstances? I was terrified that my "I'll deal with it later" husband would leave me alone to deal with misbehaving kids.

Father, I am grateful for Your wisdom and divine plan in giving me a spouse who complements me as a parent.

David saw his passiveness with the kids as a way to bring balance to my severity. The more strict I would get with the kids, the more laid-back he would become. This led to me and our kids feeling insecure, and David feeling trapped. Something had to change.

My husband and I needed to be like-minded and of one accord. In order for that to happen, I had to share my fears with David and then trust God to prompt him to be more involved with the kids. David had to tell me how his own father had been terribly strict and how that had produced incredible hurt for him. He had to tell me he didn't want that same pain for our kids and then trust God to prompt me to be caring and comforting with him and the kids.

David and I make a good team when we work together—united in mind, heart, and love. And I dare say that when that unity occurs, we bring joy to the Lord.

What are some of the differences between you and your spouse that can cause conflict, and what steps can you take to overcome those differences?

Appreciation for Irritations

And we know that all things work together for good to those who love God. Romans 8:28

It's been said that opposites attract. But why? I (David) know a lot of couples who've raised that very question. But it's usually because they feel so frustrated by how different they are from their spouse. I felt that way myself for many years, as Teresa and I were like two very strong magnets who "repelled" one another.

Thank You, God, for knowing my needs and for giving me a spouse who helps me to work on my weaknesses.

Teresa seemed so rigid. "Nip it in the bud, and do it now!" was her motto. My philosophy for living life was usually, "When in doubt, don't!" At my first sign of procrastination, her diligence and compulsivity was on me like a bulldog. I remember thinking, *God, why do I have a wife like this? What were You thinking?*

Over time, I came to see the answer. God knew I needed a wife just like Teresa. Although her diligence irritated and frustrated me, I could see clearly that my procrastination and passive resistance were weaknesses. Without Teresa, I would never get some of the most simple (but important) things done. That pesky parking ticket would probably sit on my desk for six months, incurring major financial penalties. Those license tags wouldn't be renewed until I got a ticket for their expiration. The list goes on and on!

God has used Teresa's strengths to convict and change me. He's not finished with me yet, but what I once saw as a "thorn in my flesh," I now appreciate as a vital part of God's plan. I regularly give God appreciation for those little irritations.

What character flaws or weaknesses do you think God wants to change in you today? How do you think He can involve your spouse to make those changes?

Thanks, I Appreciate That!

Her children arise and call her blessed; her husband also, and he praises her. Proverbs 31:28, NIV

We all want appreciation. I (David) forget that sometimes.

When I come home from a long day at work, I am often preoccupied with my own concerns and worries, and I may overlook what Teresa has done that day. She's kept the Ferguson family running smoothly for over thirty-five years, but there are days when I hardly notice. I take it for granted that my shirts will always "magically appear" neatly pressed in my closet. I barely notice that the kitchen is always clean and the bills are in the mail on time. There are days when I don't even give a cursory thanks for the dinner she cooks or the coffee she brings.

Lord, give me extra sensitivity to my spouse's efforts. Help me praise him or her daily.

I know there have been too many times when I have missed the hurt and disappointment in her eyes when I failed to express my appreciation for what she does.

The flip side can be pretty powerful, though. On the days when I really let Teresa know that I not only notice but greatly appreciate all she has done, her spirits lift, her step quickens, and the smile returns. It only takes a few seconds to express gratitude for the errands she runs with, "Sweetheart, thank you so much for getting my license tags renewed. I know it was a hassle to do and very time-consuming. I know your time is valuable, and I appreciate your help." It only costs two minutes of time to send her a note that says, "Thank you, Teresa, for taking our grandkids to the zoo and making dinner for our guests—all in one day! Your ability to get it all done with grace and style is amazing."

God has definitely given me a woman who is worthy to be praised. I need to be reminded to rise up and call her blessed.

What things—errands, chores, and the like—does your spouse do daily that you can express your gratitude for?

You're the Best

I am so glad . . . that you always keep me in your thoughts.
1 Corinthians 11:2, NLT

I (Teresa) am usually not one to get emotional at weddings, but one ceremony David and I attended recently was different. The groom had been widowed a few years prior, and he was thrilled to be marrying a new young bride. They were clearly in love, but seeing the mix of pain, admiration, and genuine affection was heart wrenching.

Lord, let me never take for granted the gift You've given in my spouse.

After that wedding, I started asking myself some questions about my relationship with David. How would I respond if something happened to him? Is there anything that I would regret or wish I'd done differently? I came to this conclusion: I think I would want to have told David how much I appreciate him more often.

That day I wrote down all the things I appreciated about my husband. The list was long. It included his commitment to work hard and provide for our family, his leadership in our church and our community, how he loves to play with his kids and grandkids, his generosity and gentle spirit.

As I ended my list, I was struck with how often I fail to recognize these qualities in David. Sometimes I'm too preoccupied with my own agenda to notice his uniqueness. At other times I am too easily preoccupied with my complaints. I was saddened by how infrequently I verbalize my "thank you's."

I gave my list to David that evening. "Sweetheart, I just want you to know how much I love you and how much you mean to me and this family." He beamed from ear to ear.

I know I met an important need for David that night. He still keeps that list in his briefcase. In fact, I noticed the tattered edges of the paper the other day.

What would be on a list of ten things you
genuinely appreciate about your spouse?

Appreciation in a Journal

How can I repay the Lord for all his goodness to me?
Psalm 116:12, NIV

During a challenging family time several years back, the Fergusons began journaling in what we called a "Blessing Book." It was a particularly faith-stretching time for our family, but it became almost fun to see how God creatively provided for us.

Teresa found an attractive, lined journal, in which we recorded individual and family blessings. That year, Teresa was grateful for the huge brisket that was a surprise gift from a local restaurant owner. I was thankful for the opportunity to work at Robin and Eric's school, which provided for us financially while giving me an opportunity to see more of my kids. These exchanges helped us focus on the positives, rather than the struggles, and brought us together with grateful hearts.

Lord, I want to reflect on all Your benefits today. Help me to see how You've blessed my life in innumerable ways.

Now Teresa and I regularly take the time to do a "blessing search" with one another. We each name ways the other has blessed us, and then we express our appreciation. For example, I wrote, "Teresa, I've been particularly appreciative of your forgiving spirit. This week you've had plenty of reason to hold grudges and yet each time I've found your heart receptive to my confessions." Teresa wrote, "David, I've been especially thankful for your attentiveness. You've noticed that I needed help in the kitchen or with the kids and you've taken initiative to help. I never had to ask for you to pitch in!"

Another part of our blessing search includes sharing our gratefulness for what God has done in our lives. We pay close attention to the often-overlooked blessings of health, life, creation, and salvation. A final step in our blessing search includes praising God for His specific answers to prayer.

It never fails—after each blessing search we are more grateful to the Lord and more appreciative toward one another. Praise and thanksgiving are contagious.

In what specific ways has God involved your spouse to bless you today? What can you do to show your appreciation for that blessing?

Approval through Thoughts and Words

This is My beloved Son, in whom I am well pleased. Matthew 3:17

Approval means thinking and speaking well of another person. It means commending another person because of who that person is, possibly apart from what he or she does. It means affirming the fact of and importance of a relationship. Let's see how the Father met the Son's need for approval.

Father, thank You for loving me for who I am rather than what I do. Let me concentrate on how You have approved of me, so that I in turn will be able to give approval to my spouse.

Jesus is standing in line with the rest of the followers waiting to be baptized by John the Baptist. John raises his hand and announces that "Jesus of Nazareth is to be baptized today." As Jesus comes out of the water, an unusual thing occurs. The heavens open up, and the Spirit of God descends like a dove. And, out of nowhere, a thundering voice announces, "This is My beloved Son, in whom I am well pleased."

With these simple words, the heavenly Father is essentially bragging about His Son. The word *beloved* shows just how deep the sentiment goes. It's also important to notice that the Father initiates this contact. Jesus didn't have to ask for it. And one final thing to notice: The Father approved of His Son before the Son had *done* anything. This blessing came before Jesus had performed any miracles or healed or converted anyone. The Father gave His Son approval because of who He was, not for what He had done.

As the Father approved of the Son, so He approved of me. Knowing that, I (David) can do no less to those around me, particularly the one who holds such a special place in my life, my spouse.

What are some ways you can show approval to your spouse for who that person is and apart from what he or she does for you?

Approving Father vs. Prodigal Son

Put a ring on his finger and sandals on his feet. . . . For this son of mine was dead and is alive again. Luke 15:22-24, NIV

No doubt you know the parable of the Prodigal Son. I (David) would venture to say that it's been talked about from every pulpit and Bible classroom in the country. It goes something like this: Kid takes trust fund and blows it on wine, women, and song, and winds up in pigsty, then returns home to beg for food and employment.

The most gripping scene in this biblical account is the father waiting for his wayward son. We see the yearning on the father's face, the anxiety mixed with anticipation. Then one day, the father glances toward the road and sees his son.

Lord, help me to show my spouse unconditional approval, even when he or she "blows it."

Reflect for a moment on your life. Have you had any "pigsty" moments? Have there been times when you're just sure the Lord has had it with you, when you're scared that even begging His forgiveness won't help? I certainly have. There have been plenty of times when I've just flat-out blown it, badly.

Reconnect with your feelings during your "prodigal" moments: ashamed, sad, guilty, insecure, lost, anxious, and disconnected. Now picture in your mind the scene of the prodigal—you—coming home. You're coming down the road toward home. What do you see? It's your father, and he's running toward you with outstretched arms. His face is relieved, rather than strained or angry. He reaches you, embraces you, and holds you close to tell you how much he loves you. He's proud to call you his child. He's excited to see you. His love is unending and unwavering. What feelings would that prompt in you? Gratefulness? Amazement? Humility?

That, my friends, is approval—a loving father affirming the importance of the relationship with his son. The father affirmed the value of who the son was—apart from his behavior.

That is the kind of approval we must daily show our spouses.

In light of the unconditional acceptance God shows you each day, what keeps you from showing that same acceptance to your spouse?

The Look and Sound of Approval

Give, and it will be given to you. Luke 6:38, NASB

Lord, make me sensitive to my spouse's need for approval. Alert me to opportunities to show him or her—in deed and in word—approval.

In my years as a seminar speaker, I (Teresa) have met many women who never receive their husband's approval. Instead, they have been criticized—for their size, the way they dress, how they keep house, or for their cooking. These women would all tell you how terribly it hurts to receive nothing but disapproval from their spouses.

On the other hand, I've also seen men who long to hear some approving words from their wives. Their wives make sure to point out the slightest flaw or imperfection in their performance. Their wives' words and attitudes have wounded these men deeply.

David has set the standard in our family in this area. He never puts me down, criticizes me, or picks over my faults. Instead, he makes it a point to approve of me in his deeds and in his words. And that has proved to be contagious. The more David honors me by showing his approval, the more I've wanted to do the same for him.

Here's what showing approval might *look* like:
Displaying photos of your spouse on your desk or in your home.
Taking photos or videos of your spouse's important life events.
Wanting your friends or coworkers to meet your spouse.

Here's what giving approval might *sound* like:
"I'm so proud to be your wife. I am so thankful that God brought us together."
"I'm proud of you. It was such a blessing to sit in the audience tonight and know that I'm married to that wonderful woman up there!"
"I am so glad to be married to your son or daughter. He or she is God's precious gift for me" (said to spouse's parents).

What can you do and say today to show your spouse
the approval he or she needs from you?

FEBRUARY

approval
attention
care
comfort
compassion

Never Enough

Blessed are those who mourn, for they shall be comforted.
Matthew 5:4, NASB

Dad was a Marine drill instructor, and approval was scarce when I (David) was growing up. There were things such as bed inspections to confirm the tightness of the sheets, and the words "I'm proud of you" were hard to come by.

Father, show me ways that I might help restore my spouse's heart.

I know now that I married Teresa hoping—even expecting—to receive from her the approval I had missed out on as a child. At first, when Teresa didn't automatically meet my need for approval, I just tried harder to get it. I would work longer and longer hours, hoping to hear her say, "Honey, you're a terrific provider." I would buy my wife the most expensive gifts I could afford, while all along, I wanted to hear the words, "David, I'm so proud that you're my husband."

When Teresa didn't get the hint and meet my need for approval, I would become angry and withdrawn. Rather than becoming vulnerable and telling her what I needed, I tried to *earn* her approval. It was the only way I knew to express my needs, but I was on a vicious treadmill of "never enough." The more I tried, performed, or bought, the worse things got.

Finally, after fifteen years of marriage, I put my finger on what was missing. I talked openly with Teresa about how I longed, especially as a child, to hear words of praise and approval. I talked about the pressure I felt to earn my father's approval and how no amount of effort seemed good enough. Teresa comforted me, and a wonderful healing began as I sensed her understanding.

Through many more times of comfort, those wounds have been healed, but approval is still very important for me. I'm happy to report that God continues to involve Teresa in further restoration.

In what ways can you openly communicate your
need for approval to your spouse today?

Medals of Approval

Commend those who do right. 1 Peter 2:14, NIV

My (David's) dad was an officer in the Marine Corps during World War II. During his service, he received numerous medals for duties he performed exceptionally well. Obviously, the Marines approved of my father, and the medals were statements of that approval.

The Marines award medals only for action above and beyond the call of duty, and never for solid character or because they value your relationship with the Corps. There is no medal for doing one's duty adequately.

As married people, we have the opportunity to decorate our spouse's "uniform" every day.

As each day begins, I have the chance to commend Teresa for her tremendous character. She deserves a medal for her forgiving spirit and devotion to family. And I would gladly award her a medal in recognition of her diligence and loyalty.

God, please help me cover my spouse's "uniform" with medals of approval. Let me see my spouse as You would see him or her.

Teresa also deserves medals of commendation for her service to a great cause: our marriage. She works hard to keep any hurts healed and important issues discussed. She is forthright and direct, and always with a heart full of love.

My wife should also receive a medal for the way she is always available to provide support to me in our busy ministry. I can always count on her to pitch in and lend a hand. These qualities have brought great security to our marriage.

My dad worked hard to give the military his best, and he received a lot of recognition for his efforts. Our spouses often work just as hard to make marriage loving and enjoyable. They need our commendations as well.

If your spouse had a medal for every word of approval, how full of medals would his or her uniform be?

What actions or attitudes your spouse demonstrates deserve your commendation—verbally or otherwise—today?

Safe and Secure at Home

*Anyone who serves Christ in this way is pleasing to
God and approved by men.* Romans 14:18, NIV

A few years ago, David and I traveled through a Middle Eastern country. At that particular time and in that particular country, some of the local citizens were very hostile to American tourists.

*God, thank You
for the approval
You give me and
for the approval
my spouse
gives to me.*

One day, we walked slowly through a small marketplace and turned down a very crowded street. People, animals, and merchandise were jammed into this narrow side street. Tensions began to rise as people began bumping into one another. As David and I worked our way toward the exit, the crowd shifted, and we were suddenly forced into the oncoming traffic of people. We stumbled as we attempted to regain our composure, but bumped into several "ladies of the city," who cursed at us and gave us hateful looks. One of the women actually shoved me back into place and yelled something hostile at David.

After those moments of insecurity overseas, all I could think about was how I wanted to be back home with David. I realized then that I had taken for granted how safe I felt at home.

Marriage is supposed to be a place of safety. No matter what you run into on the outside, you should feel the approval you need when you get home. No matter how people treat you "out there," at home you should feel confident that God and your spouse are pleased with you.

What a secure place to be—at home with God and with my spouse! That's the kind of environment we all need to create for our spouses. It's the kind of environment that produces true security and true marital intimacy.

What can you do today to help create a home environment in
which your spouse will feel safe and secure in your approval?

Praise for Your Spouse's Best

This poor widow has put in more than all the others.
Luke 21:3, NIV

I (Teresa) looked through Scriptures the other day to find examples of Jesus giving His followers His approval. I found one example in the book of Luke, which contains an account of Jesus teaching in the temple and looking up to see a widow put two small, copper coins into the treasury box. Jesus gives this woman an incredible compliment. He voices His undeniable approval when He says, "This poor widow has put in more than all the others, because she gave all she had."

Father, make me generous with praise for my spouse, who gives me the best he or she has.

I was impressed with the Lord's words of approval, but also with His technique. We don't know if the widow heard the words the Lord spoke about her that day, but we can be sure the disciples and the others at the temple did.

I began to wonder if I should follow the Savior's example and speak words of approval about David to other people? Should I tell his mother how much I love being David's wife? Should I say some affirming words about him in front of his staff?

I was also struck by this thought: There have been times when I've compared David to other women's husbands, times when I have been stingy with praise because I'm looking at what other husbands do for their wives.

The Holy Spirit took me aside that day and began to convict me and remind me to praise my husband for giving me what he can: "He may not be as good a handyman or mechanic as other husbands, but could you praise him for giving all he has? I know those aren't big deals, but sometimes that's all he has. It's those times when he's giving you more than all the others."

What things—even seemingly small, insignificant things—does your spouse do for which you can praise him or her today?

Entering Another's World

[All] the members should have the same care for one another.
1 Corinthians 12:25

Christ's journey from heaven to a manger in Bethlehem is the model for me (David) in my daily life. He left His world and entered mine. He left the security and sanctity of heaven and entered my chaotic, unfamiliar, sin-filled world.

Jesus, thank You for leaving Your world and entering mine. Remind me daily to do the same for my spouse.

Giving attention in marriage sometimes sounds just as hard. It often means leaving my safe, secure, familiar world and entering the uncomfortable world of my spouse.

To give attention means doing things with my spouse that she enjoys doing. Giving attention means listening without interrupting so that I can understand her and her world. It means asking about my spouse's day and really *wanting* to hear the response. It means cooking a favorite meal or buying a favorite flower. Finally, attention means spending time alone with my spouse. It means giving focused, purposeful effort to spending time just with her. All of these send the message to her that I know and remember "your world."

My world includes meetings, appointments, conferences, and phone calls. I'm an indoor person who doesn't like to sweat. In order to meet Teresa's need for attention, I must leave my world, which often means going outdoors. She loves to go for walks and sit on the porch swing out in the backyard. Teresa loves to watch any kind of animal, so to spend time doing things she likes to do, we can't be on the living-room couch.

I've discovered that as I leave my world, we share a deepened sense of oneness. As I share her world, our friendship grows and there's an increased fondness in her eyes that I'd never trade for a million meetings.

What specific areas of your spouse's world can you enter and share with him or her today?

Entering Your Spouse's World

Being found in appearance as a man, He humbled Himself.
Philippians 2:8, NIV

Christ took the initiative and humbled Himself in order to enter my (David's) world. He didn't just think about His own concerns; He thought of me.

In order to meet Teresa's needs, I have to be willing to be humbled. I can't think only of my interests; I must consider her world. When it all comes down to it, that's the issue I struggle with the most. It's not just that I'd rather stay in the air-conditioning than sweat. The fact is, I have trouble being humble.

Teresa and I have learned that when each of us longs for attention from the other, we must be humble in our presentation of that need. We must express our needs in a way that shows our vulnerability and humility yet leaves out criticism. For example, if I attack Teresa by saying, "You've been shopping with your friends every weekend. You're a mother and a wife too, you know!" she's not likely to be able to hear the need behind those words. But if I say, "Sweetheart, I want you to enjoy your time out of the house, and I also want to spend time with you on weekends," then she's more likely to respond positively.

God, remind me how important it is for my spouse that I "enter" his or her world from time to time.

Similarly, I'm likely to miss Teresa's need for attention if she complains, "You've worked every night this week, and I'm sick of it." But if she says, "David, I know how hard you've been working at the office, and yet at the same time I am lonely, and I need you," I'm more likely to respond to the need she has communicated.

Compare these two approaches. Which would you rather hear?

How can you humbly and effectively communicate your
need for your spouse to be part of your world today?

Let's Go Outside!

Let us not give up meeting together, as some are in the habit of doing, but let us encourage one another. Hebrews 10:25, NIV

I (Teresa) love to be out in my yard. I always have. In fact, some of my fondest childhood memories are of things that took place in our backyard.

During one of our conferences, I began to reflect on some of the positive memories of my childhood. As I was growing up, my family always went outside in the evening. Mom worked crossword puzzles, Dad watered the yard, and we kids played in the yard. Those were special times because that was when I had Mom and Dad's attention.

Lord, help me see my spouse's need just to spend time with me.

Suddenly, it hit me: Because I had enjoyed those times outside with my parents, I came to associate being outside with my need for attention. I enjoyed being outside for the sake of being outdoors, but there was also an important emotional component. When I was outside, I felt loved, valued, and cared for. In reality, when I asked David to come outside and work with me, I was really expressing the need to receive the kind of attention and feel the kind of feelings I felt as a child.

Understanding this connection helped me see that David could spend time with me in ways other than going outside. He could meet my need for attention in ways such as going for a walk with me in the mall, taking me to a movie, or taking me out to a quiet dinner.

Now David and I can both enjoy being outside. I can putter around the yard while he reads or writes, because my real need is to be close to him. I've realized that my husband's willingness to be with me has confirmed within me God's love, which He manifests through David. And as the years have gone by, what we're doing seems less important than our just being together.

What plans will you make today just to spend time with your spouse?

Showing Interest

*Each of you should look not only to your own interests, but
also to the interests of others.* Philippians 2:4, NIV

Nine-year-old Jason's temper tantrums were becoming extreme. Jason's father, Doug, brought him to me (David) for assessment. It didn't take long for me to see the problem.

When Doug entered the playroom, he noticed a Velcro dartboard on the wall and began throwing the darts while Jason retrieved them. This lasted about three minutes, then Jason noticed a Ninja Turtle play set on the floor. "Daddy! Daddy! Let's play on the floor with Leonardo!" Jason excitedly asked the same question of his dad several times. Doug refused.

God, let me consider my spouse before I consider myself. May my interests be secondary to Yours and to his or hers.

Jason's temper began to rise. His face flushed and his fists clenched. At his wit's end, Doug pleaded, "Don't cry, Jason! Don't get mad! Just relax! If you'll just calm down, I'll take you to a basketball game!"

Nowhere in our session had Doug really showed an interest in his son's world. Jason's world wasn't darts or basketball games; it was on the floor with Ninja Turtles. Jason needed his dad to enter his world and give him his undivided attention.

I have to wonder, how many times have I done the same thing? How many times have I selfishly looked out for my own interests while ignoring those of my wife? I've asked Teresa to go to professional conferences with me and patted myself on the back for being such an attentive husband, even though Teresa was left to entertain herself while I attended meetings. I've even chosen birthday gifts and Christmas presents that may have been trendy or financially good investments but weren't even close to the interests of my wife.

I need to take the time and effort to step into my wife's world and take an interest in what interests her.

What specific steps can you take today to involve
yourself in the interests of your spouse?

Attention Assessment

Let the wise listen and add to their learning. Proverbs 1:5, NIV

I (David) completed a painful assessment the other day. I started to ask myself how I was doing at meeting Teresa's need for attention, more specifically, her need for me to listen. I started to consider this question: Do I give Teresa individual, undivided, and unlimited attention?

God, may You prick my heart every time I am tempted to be slack in listening to my spouse.

Take a moment to do your own personal assessment in different areas of attention. The results may surprise you.

Individual Attention: Do I purposefully talk and listen to him or her when we are alone? Just being in the house by ourselves doesn't count. In order to give individual attention, I must actively pursue a conversation with my spouse—when no one else is around—and be a willing participant.

Undivided Attention: Do I give my spouse undivided attention? Do I make an effort to try to talk with him or her away from any potential interruptions? Do I concentrate on the conversation, or do I daydream or disengage? Do I dominate the conversation or encourage my spouse to talk about his or her day?

Unlimited Attention: Does my spouse sense my patience and willingness to give plenty of time to discuss difficult subjects, or do I give off signals that I just want to "get to the point"? Does my spouse know that I am available to listen to him or her without giving advice or criticism? Does listening to my spouse include a caring heart and loving attitude?

After doing such an assessment, I was sobered by the results. I realized that there were improvements that needed to be made in my life.

What changes can you make today in how you communicate with your spouse, specifically in how you *listen* to him or her?

Unhindered Attention for Your Spouse

Lord, what is man, that You take knowledge of Him? Psalm 144:3

Our son, Eric, was irritable and restless. He complained that he was bored, and he picked on his sister more than usual. After a little probing, we discovered that all Eric really wanted was more attention from Mom and Dad. He needed some uninterrupted time with us, time when our eyes and ears were only for him. Helping him to recognize his needs that day helped us to encourage him to ask directly for our attention rather than act out to get it.

Lord, remind me to take the time— no matter how busy life gets— to give my spouse my undivided attention.

We need and want our spouse's attention, too, but sometimes we're no better at communicating that need than our son was that day. Instead of asking directly for attention, we start picking on each other like children—eliciting negative attention rather than the more productive kind.

It's easy for couples to fall into a pattern of not giving each other enough attention. There's always a list of events and errands that seems to expand rather than reduce: The kids demand attention, the boss demands attention, and even the church demands a great deal from families these days.

In order to prevent some of the "childish" behavior, David and I have learned to set aside some time just for us each week. We make sure that the time is quiet and unhurried, so that we can catch up with each other's lives. It's a time when we can talk, share, and listen to one another.

We both look forward to giving each other our full attention during this time, and we end up understanding each other better because of that time.

When would be a good time and where would
be a good place for you to spend uninterrupted,
unencumbered, one-on-one time with your spouse?

Marriage Staff Meetings

I will seek the one I love. Song of Solomon 3:2

Developing and maintaining an intimate marriage requires a consistent investment of time and emotional energy. Our intimacy increased and marriage relationship dramatically improved when we began to "seek the one we love" through what we call our weekly "marriage staff meetings."

Lord, remind me of the need to consistently invest time with the most important people in my life—You, my spouse, and my family.

We didn't leave the meetings to chance. For a while we had lunch on Thursdays, and then for a time we met Tuesday nights after the kids were asleep. We made this time together a priority. We made it as inviolate as possible. We gave thought to distractions and interruptions and chose a place that was the most quiet and protected.

Consistency was important, but the emotional benefit of prioritizing each other encouraged our closeness. As I (David) heard Teresa turn down engagements with friends or negotiate appointments so that we could keep our marriage staff meetings, my heart was incredibly blessed. I was reassured that she cared for me and was thinking about me. When Teresa saw that I didn't even take my cell phone into our staff meetings, she felt loved and reassured that I had concern for her and our marriage relationship.

It may be intimidating to think about spending this kind of time alone with your spouse. You might be thinking, *What in the world would we talk about?* Here are some topics you might want to try:

Coordinate calendars: discuss kids' schedules, church attendance, and community events.

Family goals: discuss financial savings, vacation ideas, landscaping plans.

Parenting plans: discuss discipline issues and spiritual training.

Listen to one another: talk about feelings, latest devotions, ideas, questions.

Affirm one another: share appreciation and approval.

What benefits do you think you and your spouse could derive from planning weekly "marriage staff meetings," starting today?

Providing for Another's Needs

He went to him and bandaged his wounds, . . . brought him to an inn, and took care of him. Luke 10:34

The Savior tells the story of a man who is robbed and left for dead on the side of the road. Two religious men of the day walk past the injured man without offering help, but a man from Samaria takes pity on him and offers aid. The Samaritan bandages his wounds, takes him to an inn, and provides for his continued care.

Father, remind me to care for my spouse in the same way You have selflessly cared for me.

What did the Samaritan man have that the religious leaders lacked? What motivated him? I (David) think it was that the Samaritan had encountered the miraculous love of God and that he had never "gotten over" the wonder of God's abundant care for him. He was forever mindful and grateful for what God had done for him, and that motivated him to care for others.

Are we still grateful for what God has done for us? Though we were still in sin, God selflessly gave His Son. Christ humbled Himself and left heaven to become a servant on our behalf because His provision and care were exactly what we needed. He gave forgiveness, acceptance, love, and purpose in life.

Like the Samaritan, I can become genuinely sensitive to the needs of others—particularly my spouse—by being mindful that I am a blessed recipient of God's abundant provision.

It's sobering to think that I hold within me the "provisions" Teresa needs: acceptance, security, comfort, and other things a spouse is called to provide. To share these blessings with her is to care for her. On the other hand, to withhold these provisions or to be insensitive to her needs is to behave just like the religious men of the Samaritan story, who ignored the needs of the injured man and thought only of themselves.

In what specific ways might God want you to care for and provide for your spouse today?

Whose Side of the Road?

Be kind and compassionate to one another. Ephesians 4:32, NIV

Christ is the ultimate Good Samaritan. He cares for the neglected, is concerned for the unnoticed, has compassion for the wounded, and generously provides for those in need.

Heavenly Father, keep me attuned to opportunities to move from my side of the road and genuinely care for my spouse.

I (David) am so glad that Jesus didn't "pass by on the other side of the road" as I lay there in helpless, hopeless pain. I'm so glad He didn't just shout, "Take care of it yourself," or "Sorry, but I can't stop now. I'm in a hurry."

Leaving my side of the road to come to yours is what caring is all about. I learned that too long after I got married. For too many years I didn't participate enough in parenting our children. From my selfish perspective, raising the children was Teresa's side of the road. I was ready to bark orders or criticize Teresa's parenting, but not to do anything helpful. I was also too busy to leave my side of the road when it came to helping out around the house. In my mind, doing dishes was Teresa's side of the road. Instead of helping her, I would hurry after dinner to my place on the sofa and take care of my paperwork.

Through a great deal of stress and painful talks, God began to get my attention and change my attitude. Slowly, I began to join Teresa in parenting our children and managing the daily tasks of our household. I moved to her side of the road and worked with her on a plan to encourage our kids to do their chores. I moved to her side of the road when I cleared all the dishes from the table and loaded them into the dishwasher.

In what specific ways will you move from "your side of the road" and care for your spouse today?

A Stocked Refrigerator

*What is man that You are mindful of him, and the
son of man that You visit him?* Psalm 8:4

David's counseling practice was booming. He was booked from 8 A.M. to 6 P.M. every day of the week. It was tough for him to take a rest-room break, much less go out for lunch. I (Teresa) became worried about David missing lunch every day.

I was so concerned about this that I bought him a small refrigerator for his office. I even went out of my way to keep it stocked. I'd fill it with his favorite snacks and quick-to-fix lunches. I was very proud of myself for thinking of my husband and caring for him in such an important way. But my pride turned to frustration when I realized that David still didn't stop during the day to eat anything from the refrigerator.

*Lord, remind
me daily of Your
caring provision
for me.*

I was about to rip the refrigerator out of the office, when the Lord impressed me with these thoughts: *Teresa, I know it's frustrating to see David passing by your generous provision. But just remember, I provide you with an equally generous opportunity each day. I offer you fellowship and a divine visit every moment of every day. Some days you take the time to visit with Me, but on other days you're too busy to receive My provision. Why don't you give David the freedom to receive your care?*

I kept stocking that refrigerator, but I also tried something new. Every now and then, I'd call David and ask to meet him at the office for lunch. This touch of personal involvement gave David a feeling of being truly cared for, and we enjoyed some great lunches together. I had come to understand that David appreciated my efforts to provide for him, but what made him stop and receive what I had provided was my offer of personal involvement.

In what ways can you add some personal involvement
to your acts of caring for your spouse today?

Care in the Little Things

Put [your] religion into practice by caring for [your] own family.
1 Timothy 5:4, NIV

My day had begun with an early meeting, and I (David) was squeezing in phone calls along the way. An afternoon of three more sessions stretched before me. I didn't have much to look forward to but a long day and long drive home after dark.

Thank You, Father, for the simplicity of caring. Help me to look for the little things that communicate big messages.

I began to feel disconnected from my family and emotionally sapped from the tensions of the day. As I rushed past my message box, I checked for more phone calls, but I was greeted instead by "manna from heaven." My box contained a soft drink, my favorite crackers, and a short love note—all from Teresa, who had thought of me and passed through the office.

Her initiative and sensitivity spoke volumes. My whole perspective changed. I realized, "I've been thought of! I'm important! I'm loved!" As I walked back to my office, I told everyone who would listen how my wife had so lovingly cared for me.

That night I was reminded of how the little things make such an impact. Turning down her side of the bed at night says, "I'm thinking of you." Taking her a cup of coffee in the morning communicates, "You matter to me." These small gestures let your spouse know that you consider his or her needs and care enough to meet them.

There are a million little ways to care for your spouse. Here are some examples:

- Buy her favorite bagels at the store.
- Fix and serve her dinner plate first.
- Open her car door for her—like you used to do when you were dating.
- Pick up the video of the movie she's been wanting to see.

What "little things" can you do today to communicate to your spouse that you care?

Books of Care

Therefore, as we have opportunity, let us do good to all people, especially to those who belong to the family of believers. Galatians 6:10, NIV

I (David) love to study. During one phase of our marriage, I had enrolled in a seminary course through an extension program in our city. I was thrilled to be applying my love for study to the Bible.

Part of my research for the class was the use of a particular set of Bible commentaries. I envied the guys in my class who could afford to purchase these books. It was quite a hassle to have to check and recheck these books from the library every week, but finances were tight for the Fergusons that year, and the books were simply beyond our budget.

God, help me to care deeply about the things that matter to my spouse.

Our seminary course was about to conclude for the semester, but I knew I would need the commentaries next semester as well. So I searched the bookstores hoping to find a used set of commentaries. I came away from that search empty-handed.

The Christmas holidays sped by, and on Christmas morning the family opened gifts. Teresa and I opened the presents we had bought for each other, and guess what I got? That's right—those Bible commentaries! Teresa knew how much they meant to me, and she bought me a set.

What's the big deal about a set of books, you ask? Just the fact that Teresa cared enough to listen to the desire of my heart. She met my need because she cared about me and about what was important to me. Those books were her way of saying that what mattered to me mattered to her.

Those books still mean a great deal to me, and I will keep using them, even if they become obsolete.

What can you do today to meet a need or desire that, while it seems insignificant to you, truly matters to your spouse?

Surprised with Care

He cares for those who trust in Him. Nahum 1:7, NIV

The times when God has surprised me (Teresa) with His loving care have been some of my greatest reasons for praise.

Lord, help me to know my spouse's needs and to meet them without being asked.

For example, I remember the time I lost a fifty-dollar bill in an airport. I was terribly distraught over losing what was to me a large sum of money. But the following week, in a completely different location, I found a fifty-dollar bill literally lying at my feet. There was absolutely no one around to claim it or any place to turn it in. Even though I had never asked the Lord to replace the money I had lost, I know God put that money there just to remind me of His watchful care.

Another example of this surprising care is the time when David and I took a trip to Africa, where we had the privilege of touring on a safari. I had always been fascinated with animals, so this particular trip was sheer pleasure for me. The tour guide for our safari explained in amazement that we were seeing animals on that trip that he had not seen in several years. We saw animals that even the *National Geographic* photographer had not seen in his twelve years of experience. I never thought to ask the Lord for His abundant provision on the safari. I think He just wanted to show me how much He cared for me. I was incredibly grateful.

It feels good when someone cares enough to know what makes us happy and does it without being asked. Those can be some of the more blessed moments in marriage.

Ask yourself what would make your spouse feel cared for and loved. What would keep you from doing that very thing today?

What could you do today—without being asked—that would let your spouse know that you care genuinely and deeply?

Love Notes Say "I Care!"

*How beautiful is your love, . . . my bride! How much better
is your love than wine!* Song of Solomon 4:10, NASB

I (Teresa) know it may sound corny or completely over the top, but writing love letters is one of the best ways to show you care. It may seem silly, illogical, or irrational to write a note to someone you see every day, but this kind of romantic gesture helps keep love alive.

Here are some ideas that can warm your spouse's heart as they communicate your love in creative ways:

Write this note on the bathroom mirror: "You are important to me."

Place a note in a briefcase or purse that reads, "I'll be thinking about you today."

Write a note on the driveway with chalk that says, "Somebody loves you!"

Send an electronic card or e-mail message that spells out, "You are my sunshine!"

*Lord, remind me
often of the beauty
of my spouse's
love and help
me express my
gratefulness for
that love.*

Pick out a card at the store, write your own message of love, and mail it to your spouse.

Spell out "I love you" with her favorite candy or a new set of golf balls for him.

Write your spouse a poem and read it to her during a quiet moment.

Change the words of a familiar love song and show him your "personalized" rendition.

Write complimentary phrases that begin with the letters of your spouse's name.

These kinds of reminders communicate that you trust your spouse with your heart and with your vulnerable expressions of love. They can bring joy to both your hearts and carry you through until you are together again.

What creative reminders of your love can you leave
for your spouse today?

comfort

The Look of Real Comfort

Comfort one another with these words. 1 Thessalonians 4:18, NASB

Comfort is an expression of the heart. It means responding to a hurting person with words, feelings, and touch. Comfort means hurting with another person. It means showing compassion for another's pain or grief.

Father, as the God of all comfort, I pray that You will show me how to comfort my spouse in a loving, compassionate way. Show me how to respond when this person is enduring hurt or disappointment in his or her life.

A person who is hurting feels emotions such as sadness, disappointment, and rejection. That person doesn't need a pep talk like, "Come on! Cheer up! It's a beautiful day outside!" He or she doesn't need words of correction or teaching such as, "The reason this happened is . . . Next time, why don't you . . . ?" When someone needs comforting, don't give advice such as, "If I were in your shoes, I would . . ."

It's important to learn a "vocabulary of comfort." Here's what true comfort might sound like: "I'm so sorry that you're hurting. I'm so sad that you're going through this. I'm on your side, and I'm committed to helping you get through this difficult time."

It's also important to convey comfort through gentle touch. Holding hands, a warm embrace, or just sitting quietly and crying with someone conveys compassionate care. Putting your arm around someone who is enduring painful emotions shows that you are concerned and care about that person's hurt. Wiping a fevered brow or holding your spouse while he shares his heart brings comfort and consolation.

Comfort means expressing through words and actions what you feel for another person as you share in his or her pain. It means becoming vulnerable, too.

What are some ways you can bring true comfort
to your spouse when he or she needs it?

Tears of Comfort

Jesus wept. John 11:35, NASB

The Gospel of John recounts a beautiful example of Christ's compassion. Jesus receives the heartbreaking news that His close friend Lazarus has become very sick. Jesus travels with the disciples to visit Lazarus, and upon their arrival, Jesus finds Lazarus's sisters, Mary and Martha, mourning the death of their brother. Scripture tells us that when Jesus saw Mary weeping, He was deeply moved and that when He traveled to see the tomb where Lazarus was laid, He wept openly (John 11:1-35).

God, remind me of how deeply moved You are when you see me hurting. Then, as I receive Your care and comfort, let me share that with my spouse when he or she needs it.

It's important to note what Jesus *did not* do when He visited the two sisters. As the Son of God— the One who knew past, present, and future—Jesus certainly knew that Lazarus was going to live again. Christ approached Mary and Martha with the full knowledge that He was going to restore their brother's life and set everything as it was.

Even though He possessed this knowledge, Jesus didn't give the sisters a pep talk, an explanation, or a sermon on faith. Instead, upon seeing the sadness of their hearts, He wept. The Savior was so moved with compassion for His friends that He shed tears.

That's the kind of comfort we need in marriage. Even if we know a situation will turn out right, we must share in our spouses' pain if they are sad or disappointed. Even if we're sure that God will work on our behalf, if our spouse is hurting, we must express compassion for the hurt he or she is enduring.

If your spouse were in a deeply painful, disappointing situation at this very moment, in what ways would you offer comfort to him or her? What would you *not* do to offer comfort?

Comfort for a City

Blessed be the God . . . of all comfort, who comforts us . . . that we may be able to comfort those in any affliction. 2 Corinthians 1:3-4, NASB

Christ's reputation as a healer and teacher has spread across the country. So as He rides a small donkey down the winding trails, people begin to recognize Him. A crowd gathers and joyfully begins to praise God. For the first time in ministry, He is being publicly praised. Then something odd occurs. He reaches a certain point on the path to Jerusalem and begins to cry.

God, give me a heart like Yours: a heart that hurts for my spouse when he or she is in pain.

Cry? On a festive occasion such as this? What would prompt the Savior to cry?

Jesus looked down upon Jerusalem—past her regal palace, past her standing as a strong military force and a hub of commerce. Jesus looked past all that and saw the people. He came upon the city, looked into the future, and saw the people's hurt. His heart's response was to cry.

How has my heart responded when I (David) have "come upon" Teresa and seen her hurting? I can recall being unbelievably insensitive to her hurts early in our marriage. If I found Teresa sad or tearful about one of life's inevitable daily hurts, I had little things to say such as, "What's wrong with you now?" or "Well, next time you can handle it differently."

But then I began to ask myself, "What does God feel for Teresa when she is in pain?" The answer came back: "He feels sad for her. He hurts for her." With that in mind, I thought that maybe—just maybe—it's okay for me to feel sad and hurt for her too. Maybe it's okay for me to say things such as, "Sweetheart, I can see that you're really upset, and I hurt for you."

What words of compassion could you speak today to convey a heart that hurts for your spouse when he or she is hurting?

Share Hugs, Not Advice

I saw the tears of the oppressed—and they have no comforter.
Ecclesiastes 4:1, NIV

During one of our conferences I (Teresa) met with a woman who was going through a time when she was in need of comfort from her friends. Darla told me how hurt she was by the breakup with her boyfriend. He had treated her badly, yet she somehow wanted to be with him.

When I asked if she had a close friend to share her hurt with or a family member she could confide in, Darla just sighed and said, "All I get is advice, and some of the advice hurts more than the breakup. Advice like, 'Just dump him,' and 'Don't you dare crawl back to him.'"

God, help me to recognize times when my spouse might need comfort.

It saddened me that Darla was hurting, particularly since she was pretty much going it alone. What she needed more than advice was to be comforted. Darla needed someone to listen to her, talk with her, and put an arm around her.

I gently told her how sorry I was that her friends didn't understand her pain or her need to have someone listen without trying to give advice. I held her hand and prayed for God to continue to bring people into her life who would be able to give her true comfort. Darla hugged me on the way out.

We must learn to recognize when people around us need comfort. We must not only recognize the need, but we must be willing to minister to them. People need comfort when they've been rejected or disappointed, when they are physically ill, when they are under stress, when they are unemployed, or when they've lost a loved one or endured other tragedy.

Comfort is so simple, yet so profound. It is often needed, but rarely shared. We should all strive to be givers of comfort, and we should start with our spouses.

At what times in your spouse's life might he or she
be in especially acute need for comfort?

Learning to Walk

But I would strengthen you with my mouth, and the comfort of my lips would relieve your grief. Job 16:5

Our granddaughter, Madison, recently learned to walk. It was fun watching her as she went through the various stages of crawling, pulling up, standing, taking a step, and falling again and again. Thank goodness babies' bottoms are so well padded!

Lord, continue to teach me to comfort my spouse the way You would have me.

Just as a baby struggles in learning to walk, you may struggle with learning how to give comfort. It may feel as if you've fallen on your backside every time you've tried to speak comforting words with your spouse. If so, then don't fear! Learning how to give comfort takes time and practice.

I (David) remember how difficult it was to share comfort with Teresa at first. I couldn't get past my tendency to want to "fix" or "explain" things for my wife. The teacher in me would spring into action, and I would tell her how to solve the problem or why the problem occurred in the first place. As you may have guessed, Teresa was not blessed by my responses.

I have learned that there is a subtle simplicity to giving comfort that is easy to overlook. God has shown me that in order to give Teresa comfort, I must allow the Holy Spirit to help me look beyond myself, to understand that I don't necessarily know what to do or how to fix the problem. I must ask the Lord to give me His heart for Teresa—to show me what He feels for her—then give me His compassion for her when she is in pain. Then, once I have a true sense of His heart for her, I talk with Teresa about her hurt.

It's that kind of comforting that relieves my spouse's pain and brings the blessing that comes with comfort.

What steps do you think you need to take today in order to be a better "comforter" for your spouse?

The Bitter with the Sweet

Pleasant words are like a honeycomb, sweetness to the soul and health to the bones. Proverbs 16:24

As I (Teresa) reflect over the years of our marriage, I am struck with this irony: It's been at some of the most painful times that I have most strongly sensed God's abundant care *and* David's genuine love.

For example, I remember the weekend I lost my father. We had moved my mother from north Texas down to Austin to live with us for a few weeks so she could recover from some surgery. Things were going well with my mom, but I was also concerned about my father. He had decided to stay home and take care of the house.

Lord, give me Your words of comfort as I see my spouse in pain. Help me to bring sweetness to his or her soul with my words of compassion.

I went out one evening and then returned home to the news that Dad had died in his sleep of a heart attack. He had passed away at home—alone. I was heartbroken myself, and it was excruciating to have to break the news to Mom. We grieved and cried long into the night.

I remember how that time was filled with sadness, but I also remember how David was right there, sweetly comforting me in my grief. God used him—as He so often does—to comfort me during a painful time.

I also remember the nights in the hospital after my hysterectomy. When I awoke from surgery, David was beside me, wiping my forehead. Just seeing him was a comfort. He held my hand and told me the doctor said I would be fine. In the midst of the physical pain, David's sweet words and gentle touch helped bring relief and comfort.

Comfort from a spouse can mean the difference between a crisis that overwhelms us and a crisis in which we sense God's care and provision.

What opportunities do you see to provide comfort to your spouse?

Comfort with Emotion

Mourn with those who mourn. Romans 12:15, NIV

Lori tearfully described her disappointment at Sam's forgetting her birthday. As Lori sat next to him, hurting deeply over the rejection she felt, Sam finally responded: "I had such a busy week, and the kids' schedules kept us out every night. I'll make it up to you." While Sam meant what he said, his words didn't comfort Lori.

Father, help me to be sensitive to actions and words that can hurt my spouse.

When emotion is involved, logic, reasons, and facts don't help. Emotional hurt is not healed with explanations, criticism, or reminders of our own hurt. Nor is it healed through quoting Bible verses or through giving pep talks. When someone expresses emotion, he or she needs to have emotions given in return.

For example, Lori needed to hear Sam's emotional response, not any of these responses below:

"You're just being too sensitive. It's not that big of a deal."

"Cheer up, honey. I'll make it up to you next weekend."

"I know that I missed your birthday, but this is a time when I need your forgiveness, not your judgment."

Sam needed to first consider how Lori felt—disappointed, rejected, unimportant, devalued, taken for granted. Next, Sam needed to consider what feelings were prompted as he thought about his wife's pain. Sam needed to ask himself, "My wife is hurting, but do I care?"

After exploring his feelings about his wife's pain, Sam was able to communicate a more comforting message. He said, "Lori, I can really see that you're hurting, and I genuinely regret my part in hurting you. I deeply care about you and love you. Will you forgive me?"

Lori was able to receive Sam's confession and comfort, and that freed them to heal the conflict between them and reestablish intimacy.

What can you do today to be certain that your response to hurting your spouse—however unintentional it may be— is one that will heal those hurts?

To Suffer with Another

I have compassion for these people. Matthew 15:32, NIV

Compassion means caring when another is hurting, and taking action. It means having a heart response to another person's pain, and it means being sensitive to what it must be like to be in his or her situation.

The Gospel of Matthew contains an account of Christ expressing His compassion for the multitudes. The Savior climbed one of the hills that surround the sea. A great multitude came to Him, and He performed great miracles of physical healing that day.

The Lord also began to sense another physical need of the people: hunger. Jesus called His disciples and explained, "I have compassion for these people; they have already been with me three days and have nothing to eat. I do not want to send them away hungry, or they may collapse on the way" (Matthew 15:32, NIV).

Lord, remind me often of Your compassion toward me. Help me to share that same compassion with my spouse.

It's important to consider some questions as we read this story. First, how did Jesus know the people were hungry? Undoubtedly, He knew the people were hungry simply because He is God. But the Savior also knew the people were hungry because He was human.

Now, what could have prompted Christ's compassion? Yes, He is God, and God is compassionate. But Jesus had actually experienced physical hunger Himself. In fact, He knew what it was like to feel desperate hunger. Remember that several years before this event, Jesus had spent forty days in the wilderness without food. Christ felt compassion for the multitudes because He knew the pain of hunger Himself.

Christ's compassion wasn't based on the people's performance. His compassion wasn't contingent upon how well they had treated Him or how much they had given Him. He felt compassion for the people because He saw their pain, a pain He had felt Himself.

In what areas have you suffered that give you the ability
to extend compassion to your spouse today?

God's Endless Compassion

He will again have compassion on us. Micah 7:19, NASB

My (David's) compassion tends to run out, but God's never will. He will have compassion on us again and again. We can be assured of God's compassion when we look at Christ, who can have compassion for us because He has suffered Himself.

God, remind me of Your endless compassion. Your compassion never fails because You have known what it's like to hurt.

Reflect on these areas of suffering. They are all a part of life's journey, and they are also evidence of Christ's ability to hurt for us. He has endured every one of these emotions:

Disappointment and Loneliness: In Matthew 26, Jesus vulnerably shares a need with His closest friends. He knows that He is about to die and is praying to the Father in the Garden of Gethsemane. Christ asks the disciples to pray with Him for an hour. Three times, He asks for their support and three times they fall asleep.

Sadness and Loss: In Matthew 14, Jesus' cousin, John the Baptist, is beheaded by the king. Jesus leaves the crowds of people and withdraws to a lonely place.

Ridicule: In Matthew 9, when Jesus was about to heal a ruler's daughter, the crowds laughed at Him.

Forsakenness and Abandonment: In Matthew 26–27, after Jesus was arrested, all the disciples left Him and hid out of fear. Peter denied even knowing Him. On the cross, Jesus felt the abandonment of His heavenly Father when He took on our sin. He cried out, "My God, My God, why have You forsaken Me?" (Matthew 27:46).

What does it do to your heart to know that we have a Savior who can empathize with us, who can hurt for us because of His love, having felt the deep pains of this life? What emotions does that prompt in you? Gratefulness? Appreciation? Humility? Blessing?

What kinds of hurt and disappointment do you and
your spouse need compassion for today?

It's All Right

The Lord is very compassionate and merciful. James 5:11

We were eating in a coffee shop when I (Teresa) discovered that I'd lost the fifty-dollar bill we were going to use to pay our check. I panicked, but David's words were just what I needed. He was so gentle and compassionate as he said, "Teresa, accidents happen. We can pay the bill. Everything's going to be fine."

I was so thankful for David's response that day. I needed David's reassurance after that incident. But I also felt especially sensitive because of a similar incident as a child.

Father, thank You for giving me compassion when I need it.

When I was a girl, my mother had given me money to go buy supplies for a Girl Scout outing. Somewhere along the way, I lost the money. I felt so bad coming home empty-handed. I knew that money was tight at our house and I regretted my mistake. Instead of compassion and understanding, I received criticism and was sent back—alone—to find the money.

In both incidents, I needed someone to understand my hurt and to extend compassion to me. I needed someone to reassure me that everything was going to be all right.

Right after the coffee shop incident, the Lord reminded me that "as a father has compassion on his children, so the Lord has compassion on those who fear him" (Psalm 103:13, NIV). I thanked the Father for being a compassionate parent. I reflected on the hurts that resulted when my own parent had difficulty giving compassion, but I felt extreme gratitude for the confidence I had in the Lord. Secondly, the Lord took me to a passage in Jeremiah in which the Lord tells Jeremiah that He would have compassion on the people of Israel (Jeremiah 30).

I reflected on what a good God we have. I thanked Him for healing my heart and bringing restoration through David's comfort and compassion.

In what areas do you find it difficult to extend compassion and understanding to your spouse?

MARCH

compassion
confession
consideration
counsel
courting

Compassion Follows Comfort

*He departed from there by boat to a deserted place by Himself.
. . . And when Jesus went out He saw a great multitude; and He
was moved with compassion for them.* Matthew 14:13-14

I (David) have often wondered about the times when Christ withdrew from the crowds and spent time alone with the Father. I can't help but think that as Christ spent time with God, His Father showered compassion and love upon His Son. I'm just certain that the Father spent some time comforting His Son, telling Him how much He hurt that Christ was burdened by the cares of the world. It's those exchanges that must have empowered Christ to have compassion on the multitudes. It seems that compassion follows comfort.

God, please comfort me that I may be able to share compassion with others.

In order to have compassion for one another, we must first have received comfort for our pain.

Sandy brought her husband, Richard, to see us after twelve years of marriage. Sandy complained that Richard often seemed cold and callous toward her hurts. She knew he didn't intend to hurt her, but Richard's tendency to minimize his own pain left him insensitive to his wife's. Sandy told us that when Richard's mom died five years earlier, he had never really mourned her death, even though they had been very close. Sandy suggested that Richard's inability to grieve was just one example of his calloused heart.

We suggested that Sandy tell him how sad she felt over his loss and the loneliness he must feel, rather than point out his shortcomings. Sandy held his hand and poured out her sorrow for him. Richard wept openly as years of pent-up grief flooded out. Over the next few months, as Sandy continued to share words of comfort with Richard, he began to learn how to reciprocate. Richard became more sensitive and compassionate toward his wife. God began to bless Sandy with what she had longed for—more of Richard's heartfelt compassion.

What areas of hurt (in you or your spouse) need God's comfort?
How can you share compassion with your spouse?

Where's Your Plimsoll Mark?

*And be kind to one another, tenderhearted,
forgiving one another.* Ephesians 4:32

In 1876 the British government, at the urging of Samuel Plimsoll, passed a law requiring ships to bear a visible mark above the waterline to make sure the ship wasn't loaded with excessive cargo. When the so-called "Plimsoll mark" went below the waterline, the ship was carrying too much cargo and some of it had to be removed.

God, help us be compassionate about the burdens we each bear and help us stay afloat when life is stormy.

Part of compassionately loving your spouse is making sure you keep an eye on his or her "Plimsoll mark." That's the mark that appears—or disappears—when the burdens of life have pushed your husband or wife below his or her own physical, emotional, and spiritual waterlines. When you see that happening—and in time you will certainly learn to identify that mark in your spouse—you will need to ask a few important questions: Is my spouse's "load" too heavy at this time? Can I do anything to lighten the load? What worries, concerns, or burdens can we toss overboard to get his or her "Plimsoll mark" back above the waterline?

Real love means looking out for our spouses before we look out for ourselves. So the next time you meet your spouse at the doorway after a long day, check that "Plimsoll mark." Then think about how you can help lighten the load by either eliminating it or taking some of it on yourself.

Being kind and tenderhearted toward your spouse begins with such simple things as noticing when he or she is on overload, then taking initiative to express interest and care for burdens he or she carries. Finally comes the challenge to now fulfill the "law of Christ," the law of love, by "[bearing] one another's burdens" (Galatians 6:2).

Which of the burdens your spouse carries today can
you take on yourself or eliminate altogether?

In Sickness and in Health

*I . . . will comfort them, and make them rejoice
rather than sorrow.* Jeremiah 31:13

Teresa and I have both been blessed with great health. Teresa works diligently to keep herself healthy, and I credit my health exclusively to good genetics. We've therefore not had many opportunities to be of comfort to one another during times of sickness. Our experiences of deep comfort for one another have come during times of loss. We've each had both parents go to be with the Lord during our years of marriage, so our lessons in compassion have come during these times of sadness.

*Lord, help me show
the compassion
my spouse needs
to face life's ups
and downs.*

Recently, as we reflected on our ability to provide comfort, we both commented on how we had done a better job over the years, particularly in how we handled the death of family members. In years past, we would have escaped into activity or given spiritual pep talks. We would have tried to ignore the pain of hurtful times by avoiding even the mention of our loved one's name. Teresa and I were left empty during all of those times of sadness. There was something missing in our exchanges of the past. We needed something besides busyness, pep talks, and advice. We needed the compassionate heart of our spouse.

Gradually, as Teresa and I received compassion from the Lord, we came to a place where we were able to share a part of God's compassion with one another. Instead of escaping into busyness, we actually began to insist on time to hurt together. Instead of avoiding the topic, we initiated times when we talked about fond memories of the one we had lost. We learned to take turns, with one of us sharing sadness, the other giving comfort. In recent days, it's been the Lord's compassion flowing through us that has turned sorrow into joy.

How will you demonstrate God's tender compassion
and relieve your spouse's sorrow?

Selflessly Compassionate

Therefore, as the elect of God, . . . put on tender mercies.
Colossians 3:12

Hurts, irritations, unmet needs—life is full of them. How ironic it is that marriage often magnifies these things. For example, we might quickly forget a passing critical comment from a coworker, but we remember the same comment for days—or longer—if it comes from our spouse. And if a casual friend shows a lack of interest in our conversation, we probably think nothing of it. But if our spouse fails to give us undivided attention, look out!

Father, extend Your compassion to my spouse— through me!

We often ask questions that make our spouse's hurts worse, such as, "Why is my spouse feeling this way?" "Is my spouse overreacting?" or "Would I feel the same in an identical situation?" when we should be asking, "How could I be more compassionate toward my spouse when he or she is upset, sad, or anxious?"

For many years during our marriage, I (David) applied a simple-but-flawed approach to understanding Teresa's reactions to certain situations. My approach was to ask this "rational" question: "If the same thing that happened to Teresa happened to me, would I react the way she is reacting?" The way I saw it, if I would not have been disappointed, then she should not, and if I would not have been hurt, then she shouldn't be hurt. Because of this, I was not tender in my responses to Teresa's hurts, so there was little or no caring connection between us. In fact, my responses only made matters worse.

Over time, the Holy Spirit pierced my heart in the midst of my questions with this painful and convicting truth: "David this is not about *you*, it's about *Teresa* and *her pain*. Will you let Me care for her *through* you?"

What can you do today to show true, selfless compassion
to your spouse?

confession

Open Acknowledgment of Sin

Confess your trespasses to one another. James 5:16

Some of the most dramatic changes in marriage occur when the couple becomes willing to examine how they may have hurt one another and as they ask themselves questions such as, "Have I rejected my spouse? Have I been disrespectful or insensitive? Have I hurt him or her with selfishness or skewed priorities?"

Then, each spouse can spend time alone with God, confessing (acknowledging) any wrong committed. What emerges is a godly sorrow, a heart broken by the sobering knowledge of Christ's death and God's forgiveness. Now grateful and contrite, each spouse feels a divine urgency to seek the other's forgiveness.

Father, bring me to You often to acknowledge my wrongs; then send me, grateful and forgiven, to confess to my spouse.

The Lord often reminds me of how long it took for me to understand what true confession is. I understood the word *confess* to mean "say the same" as God says, to agree with Him. But one day—as I sat in my church study, convicted of my self-centered actions that morning toward Teresa—God began a deep work within me. I paused to pray for a moment—trying to "shake" the Holy Spirit's conviction so I could get on with ministry that day. I recall praying, "It was wrong of me to be so selfish and insensitive toward Teresa." Then came the Spirit's clear reply: "David, do you really want to 'say what I say' about your sin?"

Before I could respond, the Holy Spirit's quick follow-up broke my heart and changed forever how I view confession: "David, I say that your sin this morning is part of why Christ had to die." Deep sorrow flooded my spirit and then was pushed out by unexplainable assurance that He had cleansed and forgiven me.

That day changed how I approach confession: to God and to my wife.

Are there areas of sin you need to confess to God
and to your spouse today?

Confession Isn't Easy

He was wounded for our transgressions; He was bruised for our iniquities. Isaiah 53:5

Many couples who come to our conferences complaining of a lack of love and an abundance of hurts in their marriage are in that situation because they don't practice genuine confession with one another. Instead, many offer meaningless platitudes like, "If I've hurt you, I'm sorry." Others use apology manipulatively this way: "I'm sorry I lost my temper, but I just get tired of your . . ." And many others don't bother to confess or apologize, thinking that time alone will make the hurt go away.

Grant me, O God, a clean heart, and then prompt me to make it right with my spouse.

Confession is one of the most difficult biblical requirements to carry out, and it's all the more difficult when a couple doesn't understand what true confession is. I (David) believe we can better understand true confession when we personalize this important part of our faith and our marriage.

The provision of Christ at Calvary has become so familiar to us as Christians that it has lost its personal impact. How sad it is that the pivotal point in human history has lost that impact. This has motivated me to memorize Scripture and meditate on it, making sure that I don't take for granted its intended personal relevance and impact. For example, "He was wounded for *my* transgressions; He was bruised for *my* iniquities." Changing "our" to "my" brought more of the Holy Spirit's intended impact on my life. My flesh argued for *our* sin; He argued for me to see *my* sin.

Confession is from two Greek words meaning "speak the same." If I have been selfish, critical, unloving, or disrespectful, I must first "speak together" with God (1 John 1:9) and then to my spouse (James 5:16). But I must be ready to accept the pain and sorrow of Christ's death for my sins—I've been a part of killing Him! Our hearts must first be broken so that the forgiving, healing ministry of marriage reconciliation can begin.

What will you do today to begin the process that will lead to confession in your marriage?

Wrong? Who, Me?

*I acknowledged my sin to You, and my iniquity
I have not hidden.* Psalm 32:5

Christians love the Psalms for the openness and vulnerability they display. But the Psalms also reveal for us the "games" we play with God. In this verse, the psalmist demonstrates the directness and personal responsibility we need when we confess our sin.

God, confessing my sin to You and to my spouse keeps me in right relationship with You and with my spouse.

The psalmist's choice of the words "my iniquity I have not hidden" is interesting and telling. Isn't it amazing that we think we can hide our sin from God? Just imagine the created hiding something from an all-knowing Creator! This verse shows us that our first step to true confession is to stop trying to "hide" our sin—from God and from our spouses.

Around ten o'clock one morning, David and I were in his office planning our evening. I was going to pick him up after work so we could meet our son, Eric, for dinner. David said he'd be finished at 6:30. Well, because of our past experience, I just *knew* he would be late, so I told him—very sarcastically—that I'd be there around 7:00. When I left him at the office, I realized I had sinned, and I knew I needed to confess my wrong attitude to God and to David.

Most of us don't like to confess our mistakes. Most of us don't even know how. But confession is simply agreeing with God that our actions, attitudes, or behavior is not in line with His plan for our lives.

I first confessed my sin that day to God and then to David. I confessed that my attitude and words were wrong and asked for forgiveness. I didn't enjoy having to confess those things, but I was grateful to God for helping me keep the lines of communication and intimacy with David open.

What keeps you from routinely confessing your sin to God
and to your spouse?

The Path to Humility

He who humbles himself will be exalted. Matthew 23:12

Paradox is one word that describes much of God's truth. For example, "Lose your life and find it," "Love your enemies," and "Happy are those who mourn." The Bible is filled with a divine logic that is unlike ours. As the prophet Isaiah reminds us, God's ways are not our ways and His thoughts are not our thoughts (Isaiah 55:8).

Thank You, heavenly Father, for teaching me that when I am humble I am strong in You.

Among these divine paradoxes is God's plan and promise for exaltation of those who accept His challenge to humble themselves. Embracing humility is exactly what my (David's) "self" doesn't want to do. On the contrary, my "self" wants to hang on to my pride and my own sense of self-worth. Only the Spirit of God can produce a work of true humility, and one of His avenues of producing that work is true confession.

There's no quicker path to humility than confession. Confession turns the searchlight of God's truth upon our wrongs, and having seen them, we can openly acknowledge them and seek forgiveness first from God, then from others—like our spouse.

Harsh words, broken promises, or hurtful actions are all sins that require confession—to God and to our spouses. And when we humble ourselves and confess our sins, then God can exalt us and exalt our marriages. When we are broken before God, then He can pick us up, forgive and cleanse us, and bless us.

Confession is a powerful paradox. I've seen many a husband gain his wife's respect by confessing in brokenness his wrongs toward her. You see, from brokenness comes strength of character. From admission of inadequacy comes true, God-centered adequacy.

Such vulnerability can be scary, but it can be rewarding, too, for the exaltation of a humble and forgiven heart is priceless.

In what areas of your life are you most in need of confession—
to God first, then to your spouse?

Love Means Never Having to Say You're Sorry?

I will declare my iniquity; I will be in anguish over my sin.
Psalm 38:18

Remember the movie *Love Story*, starring Ali McGraw and Ryan O'Neal? Millions loved it, but it included a painfully misleading message, and that message is contained in the ludicrous line, "Love means never having to say you're sorry."

Love—true love—means saying "I'm sorry" all the time. Why? Because, as fallen human beings, all of us mess up from time to time, and the only remedy for those mistakes is to honestly acknowledge our error, ask for forgiveness, and dedicate ourselves to God's work of repentance.

The false premise behind this *Love Story* line is that if we truly loved one another, such confessions would not be necessary. However, in today's verse, the psalmist makes commitment to confession. Confession is in many ways simply a declaration of what's true.

God, please help my spouse and me to confess wrongdoing to one another, ask for forgiveness, and truly dedicate ourselves to Your plans for change.

"I'm sorry" are two of the most important words we can say when we err. Teresa and I have found that "I was wrong" may be even better. These words of confession are part of the humbling process that God uses to make us more mature as believers and as marriage partners.

Please keep confessing your sins to your spouse, and please keep giving reassurance that with God's help you will do better. Don't buy the *Love Story* notion that saying "I'm sorry" somehow means you don't really love each other deeply enough.

Confession is important to married love because it acknowledges wrongs committed. It's also important, I believe, because it powerfully states to your spouse, "When you hurt, I care."

What steps can you take today to overcome your reluctance to utter the words "I was wrong" when they are needed?

Open Confession

He who covers his sins will not prosper, but whoever confesses and forsakes them will have mercy. Proverbs 28:13

"Robin, you are so weird!" I (Teresa) heard my son tell his sister.

"Eric, please come here," I said. "You are not to talk to your sister like that again. Do you understand?"

"But, Mom," he replied, "you don't always talk nice to Daddy."

God, bring our sins—all of them— out for my spouse and me to see so that we can confess them openly.

Ouch! That really hurt. God had brought out into the open that which I thought I'd hidden from my children. I realized I had been sending Eric mixed messages, saying one thing with my words and teaching another with my behavior. I could see now which one he had adopted.

I hadn't realized the impact of some unkind things I had said to David. Through my son, God showed me how hurtful I'd been to my husband. I knew it was time for me to confess and ask for my husband's forgiveness. I went to David and said, "Honey, I'm sorry for treating you so unkindly." He hugged me and gladly offered his forgiveness.

David and I then talked with the kids about what had happened. We wanted them to understand that it wasn't enough to know you had done something wrong. We tried to help them see that true sorrow for doing wrong means openly confessing the wrong done.

Covering our sin is an all-too-human response when we are confronted with it. However, God's commitment is to truth, which sets us free to love. It's His commitment to us and to our freedom that prompts Him to expose our sin. He will go to whatever lengths are necessary to prompt confession and change.

What sins—in word, in deed, in attitude—have you been hiding that need to be confessed and forsaken today?

Healing Hurts: Confession and Forgiveness

But if we confess our sins to him, he is faithful and just to forgive us and to cleanse us from every wrong. 1 John 1:9, NLT

Teresa and I hurt each other. We don't mean to, but we do. And those hurts don't simply go away on their own. Time doesn't spontaneously heal resentments. We need to confess the sin behind the hurt and ask each other for forgiveness.

It's sobering to realize that my selfishness, my unloving attitude, and my abusive words are the kinds of sin that sent Christ to the cross. Experiencing His redemption and forgiveness frees me to confess my sin to my wife and ask her to forgive me.

Lord, break through my justifications to help me see and then confess how I've hurt this special one.

As God's Spirit challenges me to look at how I've hurt Teresa and to grieve my hurtful action, He also promises me that because He has forgiven me, it is safe for me to confess my sin to the person I love most. It's still hard for me to say to my wife, "Teresa, I realize that my sharp tongue has hurt you. I was wrong. Please forgive me." But I know it is the first step to the freedom of forgiveness. When Teresa says back to me, "David, thank you. And I forgive you," I feel cleansed.

I encourage you to practice confession and forgiveness with your spouse. In fact, I suggest that both of you take time alone to list ways in which you may have hurt the other. Ask yourself, "Have I been selfish, critical, negative, insensitive, disrespectful, verbally abusive, or unsupportive?" Then, take your list and confess each item to God and receive His forgiveness. Then come back together and share your lists and request forgiveness from each other. Experience the freedom of forgiveness—from God and your spouse.

What step will you take today to acknowledge your sin against your spouse and then to confess it to God and to him or her?

consideration

Taking into Account Another's Ideas, Feelings, and Needs

Julius treated Paul kindly. Acts 27:3

Doctor Luke tells us of the apostle Paul's journey to Rome as a prisoner. Luke recorded how at the port city of Sidon, Paul received favorable treatment from a Roman official, Julius, who allowed him to "go to his friends and receive care." Julius gave *consideration* to Paul's need for friendship and support.

Thank You, God, for my unique, special partner and for giving me the ability to give him or her consideration only a spouse can give.

In the marriage context, consideration means looking beyond someone's status or position and discerning the unique needs of that specific person. It involves taking the initiative to express care to a person based on what you know of him or her. Consideration in marriage is based upon becoming a lifelong "student" of your spouse—seeking to understand that person so that you can best love him or her.

The apostle Peter referred to this when he encouraged husbands to "live with your wives in an understanding way" (1 Peter 3:7, NASB). Proverbs encourages a wife to "[look] well to the ways" of her household (31:27, NASB). This kind of understanding paves the way for loving consideration of one's spouse.

I (David) can show Teresa consideration like no one else because I know her so well. For example, I know to buy her flowers and not candy. I know the colors she likes and the brand names of her favorite perfume and soap. I know she likes to socialize but not stay out too late. I know she prefers me to drive, but with caution. I know she likes me to open doors for her. She likes to "people watch," shop, and drink coffee—decaf after five o'clock in the evening.

I "consider" all these special things that make Teresa *Teresa*—and I love her.

What things can you do for your spouse today
that only you would know to do?

Consideration Requires Sacrifice

It is more blessed to give than to receive. Acts 20:35, NIV

Love is not real love without sacrifice, without giving of oneself. Our lives would be empty had not God provided us an example of sacrificial love when He gave up His own Son for us. He made the ultimate sacrifice in our behalf, also providing us with an example of the blessing we receive in giving.

Receiving is where the human focus tends to be. Each of us has about us a measure of the Prodigal Son's self-centered perspective of "Give me!" (Luke 15:12). Such focus can be related to the fear that "unless I look after me, no one will." But embracing the gospel truth of God's sacrificial love can free me from such fear. It assures me that someone is looking out after me, and it's God! Such sacrificial love is contagious.

Today, Lord, grant me an openness to listen to my spouse, to consider his or her ideas, feelings, and needs, and then lovingly give of myself.

But what does our sacrificial love entail? To genuinely give consideration to another's ideas, feelings, and needs, I (David) must be willing to lay aside my own. Many times I've asked Teresa how she wants to spend a free afternoon, hoping all the while that we would do what I wanted. Not exactly showing real consideration, is it?

Focusing on another's needs requires sacrifice, but it can also bring inexpressible joy. It gives God the opportunity to bring forth the greater blessing that comes when we give of ourselves.

Giving consideration does not mean that I can't have ideas, feelings, and needs of my own. But I know that God will look after me as I put my spouse's desires ahead of my own. God can be trusted to take what I have given, press it down, shake it together, and give it back to me overflowing (Luke 6:38)!

In what ways can you lovingly consider your spouse's desires over your own today?

Home Alone

Let us consider one another in order to stir up love and good works.
Hebrews 10:24

In today's Scripture text, the writer of Hebrews shares relevant wisdom for all believers, and that includes countless married couples. He encourages us to simply make it our goal to "consider one another" in the confidence that this consideration will "stir up love and good works."

Father, help me to always be considerate of my spouse's needs.

The promise within this verse gives fresh hope to every married couple, and it should prompt us to have as our goal truly considering one another. But how specifically should we "consider" one another?

To me (Teresa), this isn't so much a matter of finding specific ways to "consider" David but a matter of making our considering one another a daily mind-set and way of life. Here's an example of what I'm talking about:

David was working on another degree and needed to spend a week in Tennessee. His plane reservations required him to stay over the weekend, so he flew me out to meet him. I looked forward to having quality time with him, but a weekend away from home was not my choice. You see, David and I travel quite a bit, especially on weekends. For the past few years, I have spent almost every weekend away from home. While most people regard a weekend away as a treat, I see it as something of a burden.

But there was no question in my mind what I was going to do. Meeting David's need to see me brought me more joy than being home alone. I was grateful that he wanted me to share time with him, and I was happy to "consider" his desire for me to travel so that we could be together.

What kind of opportunities does God present you on a regular basis to "consider your spouse"? How can you best take advantage of those opportunities?

Keep Me in Mind

*[He] is able to do exceedingly abundantly above
all we ask or think.* Ephesians 3:20

Long before I (David) ever saw my need, God had already taken it into consideration. Long before I acknowledged my need for His Son, He had provided Him as my substitute. Long before I knew I needed forgiveness for my sins, the Lord had made a way for that forgiveness to become reality. Before I had even drawn breath, my heavenly Father had taken me into account in His plans for eternity. Even now, He is attentive to my every need.

Father, keep me looking beyond the routines to see the real needs.

Genuine consideration is just like that. Genuine consideration considers another's needs and lovingly responds—even without being asked in advance. It considers another's past and responds with acceptance. It gives sensitive attention to the present and makes provision for the future. Taking into account another's needs or point of view—that's what God's love is all about.

Our Scripture passage expands on the truth of God's extravagant care for us and on the fact that He took thought of us before we even knew we had need. No one can even dream of the goodness He has in mind, the care He has in store.

Just contemplating such love can prompt "freely giving" to those around us (Matthew 10:8), beginning with our spouse. Extravagant care in marriage is an attractive possibility, one that my wife and I both enjoy.

It means a lot to me when Teresa takes note of an extra-busy week and fills it with special and tender touches of love such as a favorite meal after a long day, pampering me in my easy chair at home, or a comfortable embrace at bedtime. When she does that, I know she has *considered* me, and that feels great!

In what ways can you "consider" your spouse
today without his or her having to ask?

Consider This

She carefully watches all that goes on in her household.
Proverbs 31:27, NLT

Have you ever gone out on a double date with another married couple and humiliated your spouse? You know, by overreacting to something in a way that embarrassed him? Or by cutting her off when she was talking so you could make your own opinions heard? Or by just not behaving in a mature, loving way toward your spouse?

God, help me be considerate toward my spouse no matter where we are or who we are with.

I know I (Teresa) have. Sometimes I am so concerned about whether or not the couple we are out with is having a good time, I forget to be sensitive to David. I'm so afraid that if the other couple isn't enjoying themselves, they won't like us or want to go out with us again, so I focus my attention on them, and David gets lost in the shuffle.

David isn't the kind of person to complain when that happens, but I know it hurts him—and with reason. That kind of behavior sends the message that he isn't the most important person in my life, that the couple we are with is more important. This isn't really how I feel, but actions truly do speak louder than words.

Whether you are on a double date, alone, or with the kids, do what's needed to let everyone around you know that your spouse's feelings and needs are of utmost importance to you. That is the kind of consideration we need to give to one another.

Our Scripture passage exhorts wives concerning this focus. We all need to ask ourselves if we are looking to please others or to meet the needs of our spouse.

What could you do today to go out of your way to let those around you know that your spouse's feelings and needs are your priority?

You Matter to Me

In lowliness of mind let each esteem others better than himself.
Philippians 2:3

Even though Don professed to be a Christian, he told his wife, Kathy, that he would not be going to church. He said he didn't see the need for it, and he made it clear that he didn't want to be nagged about it. Every Sunday morning Kathy would get up, prepare breakfast, and dress herself and their three children—while Don sat reading the paper. Kathy and the children attending church was fine with him, if that's what they chose to do. But he chose the Sunday paper.

God, help us to show consideration to each other in all possible ways, especially through respecting each other's choices.

Kathy was convinced that Don's problem stemmed from the fact that his parents had dropped him off at the church door every Sunday but never set foot there themselves. So, though she felt frustrated at her husband's lack of interest in church, she was determined to raise her children in the church.

Don was impressed with Kathy's behavior. He admired her efforts to get herself and the children to church and often felt guilty as he watched her hurry around on Sunday mornings. Although Kathy disagreed with his choices, she never complained or nagged. She was at times tempted to criticize him in front of the children or to "forget" to cook his Sunday breakfast while preparing everyone else's. But God gave her the strength to resist those temptations and the confidence that she was doing the right thing by "esteeming" her husband, despite his choices.

One Sunday, Don jumped out of bed as the alarm went off and hurried to wake the kids. In disbelief, Kathy asked, "Hey, what's going on?" Don replied, "Sweetheart, I want to help you because you are doing the right thing. We need to raise our children in the church, and you have lovingly shown me how."

How can you show esteem for your spouse today in a
way that sets a good example for him or her?

Considering Your Spouse's Needs

How much more will your Father who is in heaven give good things to those who ask Him! Matthew 7:11

The heavenly Father is our example of "much more" in giving. There's no way we can out-give Him. He takes initiative in giving first. He doesn't wait around to see if I move first before He gives. Marriage provides us an opportunity to model His example of giving.

Help me, Father, to give in ways that are not the most familiar.

For too many years Teresa and I seemed to play the waiting game, which goes something like this: "I'll do better at giving to your needs *after* you begin giving to mine." Because of this, we missed out on many of God's "good things." But He gradually taught us about His kind of giving.

Use this exercise to help you and your spouse get in touch with this type of "consideration"—giving, in other words. Check the items that most appeal to your spouse and those that appeal to you.

APPEALS TO MY SPOUSE	ACTIVITY	APPEALS TO ME
	Holding hands	
	Taking a shower together	
	Going for a walk together	
	Being served a favorite meal	
	Getting a back rub or massage	
	Being told "I love you"	
	Being praised for achievements	
	Helping with the kids	
	Having a quiet conversation	
	Being approached sexually	

Compare lists, then *give!* Don't wait until your spouse gives first. Most couples don't have more than one "consideration" in common. This is all the more reason to consider these things highly, and often.

In what ways not listed in this devotional can you give "consideration" to your spouse today?

Reflection and Wisdom Lovingly Shared

Listen to counsel . . . that you may be wise. Proverbs 19:20

Meeting the need for counsel in marriage is challenging for both the one giving and the one receiving. Giving counsel means I (David) must share my reflections in a loving manner, when given permission to do so. God also wants there to be an openness to my spouse's counsel, and therefore at times I must humble myself and ask her to share her reflections with me. What a call to maturity!

Heavenly Father, grant me the wisdom to seek the counsel of others who care— beginning with my spouse.

In a maturing relationship, we must seek counsel from one another in dealing with our marriage, our children, and our work. We need to ask these questions: "Next time I notice you feeling so (frustrated, withdrawn, sad), what response from me would help most?" "You seem to be more patient than I am when the kids begin to (procrastinate, talk back). What suggestions for me would you have?" "Why do you think I have such difficulty getting along with my boss? Is there a part of me that needs to grow?"

Wisdom is the payoff from listening to counsel. I grow in wisdom as I ask for and receive Teresa's input. She alone knows me well enough to share the truth I need to hear. By listening to her words, I gain insight and a wealth of knowledge that causes me to become more Christlike. By listening to her counsel, I am more equipped to make right decisions and more adequate in my ability to relate to others.

Teresa and I think of it this way: God views us as "two becoming one." Because of that, input from the "other half" of me seems wise indeed!

In what area could you gain wisdom from your spouse's counsel? When will you ask him or her for that counsel?

Counsel from the Book

The counsel of the Lord stands forever. Psalm 33:11

Wise counsel has its roots in the One who is forever wise. Counsel based only on personal experience or impression will be flawed by human weakness. It's God's counsel, extracted from His Word and lived out in human experience, that will stand the test of time and be perfect in its wisdom. Couples seeking the wisdom of Scripture together find unity as they look beyond their individual desires and submit their hearts to God's eternal truth. Couples who search the Scriptures together find oneness as they trust God for direction in their spiritual pilgrimage.

Heavenly Father, thank You that Your Word gives us light for our path.

Turning aside to consider His counsel takes the focus off my prejudices. As Teresa and I have sought the Lord's counsel on child-rearing issues, business decisions, and money management we've come away with a renewed sense of unity. Without fail, God and His Word have remained faithful to provide us with direction and guidance for every issue. Even when we began our search with a difference of opinion, the simple practice of humbling ourselves before God's Word brought about an openness and humility of heart. The search for His wisdom softened our hearts toward one another.

Teresa and I have made a commitment to seek the Lord's counsel through our own devotional time each day. We've experienced a deepened sense of closeness with one another and with the Lord when we've followed the same plan for our devotional readings. We reflect privately on the passage and then during the course of the day share our insights with each other. These discussions have served as an important opportunity for each of us to receive counsel and hear our spouse's insights from Scripture. We've marveled at the relevance of God's Word for each personal and family issue.

For what issue do you need to seek the Lord's counsel?
How will you involve your spouse in this search for wisdom?

You and Me, Babe

So come, therefore, and let us consult together. Nehemiah 6:7

There have been times in my marriage when I (Teresa) wanted to run to a friend for a quick fix on a problem. But God has led me to seek His Word and my husband's counsel before I seek counsel from another.

Unfortunately, it is easy for wives to fall into the trap of running to a pastor or friend first when a spiritual matter arises. Instead of asking their husbands to pray with them, they tend to call a friend. Even where the kids are concerned, women don't tend to seek their husbands' counsel.

Father, remind me to involve my spouse as a source of counsel.

Seeking counsel outside the marriage can lead to further distance between two spouses. That's because God's plan for two becoming one (see Genesis 2:24) includes the spiritual oneness of joint discernment—meaning finding the mind of God together. An atmosphere of trust and intimacy emerges when we lovingly challenge our spouses to give us their counsel and then receive and act on it.

One of the ways the evil one stole the potential and blessing of this in mine and David's marriage was to distract me into seeking counsel first from others. In an effort to build my case for presentation to David, I often collected the advice and "evidence" from many others. This would cause him to feel left out of the process and less important than those I had consulted, and conflicts followed. We came to realize that the conflicts were more about my process of seeking counsel than about the counsel itself. The Holy Spirit began to show me the depth of David's hurt, and repentance followed.

I believe God wants me to seek my husband's counsel first. When I do, God then challenges David to be the husband it is in him to be.

What steps can you take today to make sure that you turn to your spouse first for counsel?

Counsel from an Unexpected Source: Your Spouse

In the multitude of counselors there is safety. Proverbs 11:14

If the walls of ministers' and counselors' offices could talk, they would tell countless stories of people in pain and sorrow—much of it avoidable had they simply listened to the counsel of a caring spouse.

Thank You, God, for giving me a helpmate to see things I don't. Grant me the wisdom of receiving my spouse's loving counsel.

For example, Jack's financial future had been wrecked by a fraudulent business partnership. I remember his questioning plea: "Sarah tried to warn me! How could she have known?" Earlier, Jack had brushed off his wife's concerns as ridiculous, feeling that she didn't know anything about business. While Sarah didn't have X-ray vision, she could see things about the partnership Jack could not. She had a God-given sensitivity that told her "no" or at least "wait."

Here's another example of someone who should have accepted the counsel of a spouse:

Though Trudy's two-month relationship with a neighbor friend had stopped short of sexual infidelity, it had almost destroyed her marriage to Jay. "Why couldn't I see what Jay saw?" Trudy asked. "He tried to tell me that our neighbor wanted more than a neighborly friendship, but I thought he was being silly." Jay could see things about the "friendship" that Trudy could not.

The counsel within marriage is a too-often untapped source of blessing and protection. That source of blessing and protection, combined with counsel from God Himself, gives us that "multitude" of counsel we so often need. For that reason, we are to turn to God, then to our spouses, for sound counsel. He may prompt us to include others in our search for His wisdom, but He'll do so from the safety and foundation of marital oneness.

Where do you tend to turn first when you need counsel and wisdom for a marital question? Where *should* you turn?

The Counsel of a Friend

Ointment and perfume delight the heart, and the sweetness of a man's friend gives delight by hearty counsel. Proverbs 27:9

When I (David) was growing up, John Wayne was considered the archetypal American male. Strong, self-sufficient, and an independent thinker, he never admitted he needed anyone's help, least of all a woman's. In those days, these were the hallmarks of a "real man."

Well, let me put it in print for all the world to see: By John Wayne standards, I am not a real man. Why? Because I readily acknowledge that I want and need counsel from others, particularly (horror of horrors!) from my wife.

God, help me listen to my spouse's wise counsel, and help me offer him or her wise counsel in return.

I thank God for the many times Teresa has given me her views on an issue or problem I was facing. I often need my wife's counsel because she sees things from a different perspective. She sees things in ways that I don't, and on literally hundreds of occasions that has made the difference between good and bad decisions on my part.

Spouses need one another's counsel simply because each marriage partner has the advantage of differing perspectives on an issue. Listening to what our spouse tells us about a problem is often one of the wisest ways to go about solving it.

Today's Scripture reminds us that sound counsel—counsel based on the Word of God—is a gift of friendship. It is in God's design for friends to freely give and receive this kind of counsel. And there is no greater potential for that to happen than in the blessed friendship God has designed marriage to be.

So seek your spouse's counsel and offer yours. And when you receive that counsel, make good use of it. You need one another's wisdom daily.

In what areas of life could you use counsel from your spouse today?

What Should I Do?

Without counsel, plans go awry, but in the multitude of counselors they are established. Proverbs 15:22

Anyone could see that Terry had a lot of problems. She was married to a non-Christian. She and her husband had three children she stayed at home to care for, and they also had financial problems.

God, help me seek out counsel from others, including my spouse, so that my efforts to serve You succeed.

Terry asked my advice, and I (Teresa) was more than willing to make suggestions for her spiritual growth. But it often felt like my counsel had little effect. It seemed that Terry did more complaining than putting my counsel into practice. After weeks of hearing about the constant turmoil, I became concerned and frustrated by her lack of progress.

I took the situation to David for his thoughts during one of our "marriage staff meetings." After listening patiently, he said something I wasn't quite ready for: "It seems like you may be trying to fix her." He explained that Terry was like someone dying of thirst—she wanted immediate relief but had no idea how to bring lasting solutions to her problems.

I suddenly realized that my efforts to help Terry were focused more on what I wanted to offer than on what she needed. My husband's objective and kind counsel showed me that I should meet Terry's needs rather than force my agenda on her. Terry's constantly returning for more advice, which she never took, was simply a message to me that she had deeper needs that God might want to involve me in meeting. I challenged Terry about being so fear-driven and prayed with her that God's perfect love would remove the fear. Instead of constant advice giving, I reflected back to Terry the questions she was asking, along with ideas she had. She beamed with joy when I affirmed her for some great ideas.

With David's advice, Terry and I are both doing better.

What steps can you take to be certain you utilize your spouse's wisdom when you have need?

Asking for Counsel?

*By pride comes nothing but strife, but with the
well advised is wisdom.* Proverbs 13:10

Scripture says a lot about pride, and none of what it says is good. James 4:6 reminds us, "God resists the proud," and the wisdom of Proverbs tells us that strife will follow us if we are proud (28:25). We're all given to prideful independence, and God has provided for our deliverance. We're reminded that He "gives grace to the humble" (James 4:6).

But what does humility look like? What does it sound like? Our Scripture for today points out that pride brings strife but that wisdom comes to those who are humble enough to seek counsel. In short, humility often looks and sounds like the seeking out of counsel—beginning with our marriage partners.

*Lord, open my
heart to hear from
this special partner
You've given me.*

In marriage, the asking of exploratory questions can help us broaden our understanding of a particular marital issue and of one another. And just as important, it also opens us to receive counsel from a spouse because we have humbled ourselves enough to seek out answers. Here are samples of such questions you can ask your spouse:

- What is one way you would like me to grow in the next year?
- How could I pray for you in the next few months?
- What worry do you have about how our children are developing? How can I help?
- What is one of the most romantic times you can remember us having?
- What do you see as the two most important challenges we face this year?
- What strengths do you see in our relationship that you would like me to emphasize?

You will be amazed at the things you learn about yourself—and your spouse—if you have the courage to humble yourself and ask him or her these kinds of questions.

If you were seeking wisdom or counsel, what
questions would you ask of your spouse?

To Lovingly Embrace and Care For

A time to embrace. Ecclesiastes 3:5

The ancient wisdom of Solomon provides significant contemporary insight into life and relationships. In a world filled with the barrenness of busy lives, learning to stop and take time for the simple but important things is critical. Taking time to court your spouse seems so simple that you can mistakenly conclude it's insignificant.

Lord, help us show the gratitude we feel for each other in the warmth of our embrace.

To court your spouse means returning to some of those simple things. It means leaving love notes, bringing home flowers, holding hands, and calling just because you wanted to hear his or her voice. To court your spouse means doing the simple things that stoke the fires of attraction. It means to entice your spouse, gain his or her favor, and as Solomon suggests, to give an embrace.

We usually think of giving hugs as the sole definition of *embrace*, but to embrace also means to show acceptance with gladness. It means welcoming and including your spouse's differences, idiosyncrasies, and agendas. To embrace means to include your spouse's ideas and opinions in your decisions. To embrace means to incorporate his or her wishes and desires into your routine.

To physically embrace may still seem so common and simplistic, but there's often no better demonstration of intimacy than putting your arms around the one you love. To embrace—to give a hug—isn't just a polite sign of welcome. It's also an affirmation of that person's worth and a declaration that you value the relationship. A gentle touch or countless other tender expressions of "I care" separate love relationships from mere acquaintances.

Couples are often counseled to connect with physical touch as they part in the morning and again as they reunite in the evening. Don't let kids, chores, or the nightly news steal away those few moments of affirming your commitment to faithfulness and tender care.

When will you initiate the gift of a loving, tender
embrace for your spouse?

Marital Dating

I am lovesick . . . and his right hand embraces me.
Song of Solomon 2:5-6

Do you remember what it felt like to be lovesick? You know, that feeling of desperately missing the loving touch and embrace of your spouse?

Maybe you felt that way because yours was a long-distance relationship—at least for a time. Perhaps you became familiar with that ache when you and the one who would be your spouse broke up for a time, only to find that you didn't want to be apart after all. Or maybe there were times of separation brought on by work, health, or family crisis.

Lord, thank You for the opportunity to strengthen my romantic bond with my spouse by making time just for us.

Think back on these times and how much you missed your loved one. When you miss the one you love, time seems to stand still. Those few days before you were reunited with him or her seemed to drag on and on.

On the other hand, think back to the thrill of the reunion after a time away from the one you love. Remember that first embrace? Remember the closeness and deepened sense of romance you felt with that person?

I (David) believe those feelings can be rekindled in marriage. How? By bringing some romance into your relationship through dating.

Dating helps keep romance alive. I'm not talking about family time with your kids or a social time with other couples. I'm talking about two people going out alone and doing something together just for the fun of it. For example, Teresa and I enjoy Saturday brunch and a matinee movie, or an afternoon eating ice cream and watching people at the local park, or just talking over a quiet dinner.

There are countless numbers of things to do. Take turns picking what you want to do, put a smile on your face, and go!

What can you and your spouse go out and do today or
tonight to rekindle the romance in your relationship?

Come Away with Me!

Rise up, my love, my fair one, and come away.
Song of Solomon 2:10

David and I missed out on courting. We married at the ripe old age of sixteen. Then college, kids, work, and just trying to survive seemed to eat up our life together. As we've matured in our love, we have recognized how shortchanged that part of our relationship was.

Father, help me to take the initiative to "court" my spouse daily.

Over the years, as we became Christians and settled into married life, David and I subtly embraced a lie that seems commonplace today, particularly among Christian couples. The lie is that in a time of a 50 percent divorce rate, we were doing well just staying together. In buying into that lie, we gradually came to settle for much less than God desired in our relationship. We were like the frog who sits in ever-warmer water thinking he's fine, but who is soon to die.

We're grateful that God gave us a wake-up call and challenged us to move away from mediocrity and to pursue abundance. This challenge became clear to us after a trip we took to just play and relax. David really went out of his way to make the trip enjoyable for me. I loosened up and allowed him to take the lead. It was as if he was courting me for the first time.

The courting felt great, but when we got home we soon went back to our old ways: David was preoccupied with everything but me, and I was trying to control everything. Soon, we realized that we had forgotten to bring home with us what we'd found on that trip.

In the marriage context, courting is taking the time every day to say, "I love you" in many small ways. It's a way for couples to make one another feel special and loved. "Coming away" together for reconnection and romance works!

In what special ways can you begin to "court"
your spouse today?

The Pursuit of Understanding

*Then her husband arose and went after her,
to speak kindly to her.* Judges 19:3

Pursuit of one's spouse is a vital ingredient in romance, and we're not referring to chasing your spouse around the house seeking affection. Rather, we are talking about the pursuit of knowing your spouse deeply.

Pursuing your spouse reaps great marital benefits. For example, knowing your spouse's pain allows you to give effective comfort, which results in closeness. Knowing how you can meet your spouse's other needs can lead to romance.

Lord, might Your plan for our oneness be all that You desire it to be: spirit, soul, and body.

Here is one wonderful account of a husband and wife growing closer to one another through taking the time to pursue understanding of one another's ways.

Sheila and Walt had been married fifty years when they flew in to participate in one of our *Marriage Intensive* sessions. Together they had enjoyed raising their children, growing in their faith, building a business, and traveling the globe. But their marriage lacked romance and affectionate courting. Something held Sheila back, and Walt's feelings of rejection compounded his workaholic tendencies and resulted in occasional outbreaks of intense anger. Sheila's hurt and loneliness increased. Thus the cycle continued.

Two days into our workshop the couple began to find freedom and healing from decades of pent-up hurt. Sheila revealed a traumatic and abusive childhood experience she had not shared with anyone for more than sixty years, and Walt wept as he gained a new understanding of Sheila's indifference to affection. By the time of the couple's scheduled Saturday night date, both of them enjoyed affection. *Courting* had returned to their marriage!

Walt and Sheila discovered that truly understanding your spouse— which takes time and empathy—is a vital part of a romantic, courting relationship.

In what areas do you need to pursue better understanding of your spouse today?

Loving as He Loved!

Husbands, love your wives, just as Christ also loved the church. Ephesians 5:25

What a standard Christ has set for us as husbands! As today's Scripture verse points out, we are to love as He loves.

But what exactly does it mean to love my wife as "Christ also loved the church"? How can I, a mere man, love someone the way Christ loved? How can I find it in me to love someone that way?

God, help me to continue to court my spouse even though we have already walked down the aisle.

I got some answers to those questions during a year-long devotional emphasis in which I studied the Gospels, paying close attention to Christ's love and making application of what I found to my relationship with Teresa. I was convicted by numerous insights I gained in that study. Among them were:

Christ moved first. Our Lord took the initiative in caring. None of us sought after Him, but He came to seek and save us. Teresa can benefit from more of my taking the initiative in expressing love, making plans, helping at home.

Christ left His world of heaven and entered into our world. Jesus role models a challenge for me to understand Teresa's world, which is active, outdoors, and socially engaging. The Lord then prompts me with His love to leave my passive world of reading books, indoors, and being content to be alone and go love my wife in her world.

Christ gave Himself up for those He loved and kept giving all the way to the cross. The Holy Spirit seems to often quietly ask me, "David, what have you given up for Teresa recently?" The answers are sometimes embarrassing and often convicting. He seems to quietly say, "I don't believe you've out-given Me yet." Fresh ideas seem to come, providing creative expressions of my love for Teresa.

In what ways can you "leave your own world"
for your spouse today?

Flowers? For Me?

Let me see your face, let me hear your voice; for your voice is sweet, and your face is lovely. Song of Solomon 2:14

Remember how you and your spouse treated one another when you were dating? Remember those actions—small and large—that told you how special you were to each other? Courtship is a wonderful stage in a relationship, and it leaves a couple with wonderful memories.

Too many couples believe that those days of romance end after a certain amount of time in a marriage. But I (David) want you to know that you can still court, even though you're married.

God, help us to continually court each other in ways that show just how special our marriage is.

Regrettably, it was several years after we were married that I started writing love notes to Teresa again. In my first letter to her, I wrote this simple sentence: "When I realize how many ways I've let you down, I'm sure glad God has given you a forgiving heart. I love you."

I put postage on the card, mailed it, and waited anxiously over the next several days for Teresa to receive it at home. Day after day, the card didn't arrive, but finally she met me at the door with such a welcome that I knew it had come. We both reaped great rewards from that step of sending that letter. God had begun a fresh work in me as romance had been rekindled in our relationship.

An additional dimension of romance came a few weeks later when I made a simple phone call to Teresa: "I just called to see how your day is going and to let you know I love you and look forward to seeing you tonight." I could hear in her voice the touch upon her heart.

How long has it been since you sent a card to your spouse or called to say "I love you"? Do it today. The result will be worth it.

What step could you take today to rekindle the romance in your relationship?

APRIL

courting
deference
devotion
discipline
edification
encouragement

Love Map Courtship

*How beautiful and how delightful you are, my love,
with all your charms!* Song of Solomon 7:6, NASB

The Bible is complete in its instructions for life. The Song of Solomon gives us instruction in how to express our love in marriage. Solomon affirms that sexual pleasure in marriage is a gift from God, and he expresses his gratefulness for that fact.

Teresa and I have discovered that many couples find it hard to freely express their desires and preferences when it comes to sexual intimacy. So, in an effort to help couples become more comfortable in this area, we developed an exercise we call a "Love Map."

A Love Map exercise can deepen your courting of one another and bring about a special, passionate closeness. A Love Map exercise includes the following steps:

Lord, teach my spouse and me to give all of ourselves to one another—spirit, soul, and body.

Consider what a perfect sexually intimate time with your spouse would include. List at least ten preferences, including timing, location, and clothing. Be as detailed and specific as possible.

After each of you has completed your Love Maps, choose a private time and place to exchange lists.

Discuss your Love Maps in as much detail as you feel comfortable. Answer one another's questions and clarify any points as necessary.

Finally, schedule two times of intimacy. Yes, *plan* these times of closeness. The planning can create an atmosphere of anticipation.

Enjoy one another! We suggest that husbands fulfill their wives' Love Map first. Then, as they had planned, the wife fulfills her husband's Love Map.

The Love Map exercise will help you learn or relearn how to court one another. Throughout the day, spend moments anticipating the pleasures of the two of you becoming one in the physical sense.

What step can you take today to help you more freely and comfortably express your sexual desires to your spouse?

deference

Yielding to Others for Their Benefit

Submit to one another out of reverence for Christ.
Ephesians 5:21, NIV

Deferring to another means that my (David's) heart is yielded to the Holy Spirit's work. It means that I am willing to give up my agenda, my preferences, and my schedules for the benefit of someone else. Deference means that *my* needs are not always my top priority. Deferring to my spouse means that I submit myself to God and then become aware of and caring about her needs.

Father, give me the grace to yield to You and, therefore, to my spouse.

It's important to note what deference is not. Deference is never a one-way street. God doesn't appoint some to submit and some to "lord it over" others. Deference is not relinquishing all my desires and becoming a "doormat." God intends for us to give as well as receive. We need one another.

After too many years of marriage, I finally began to see the wisdom of paying deference to Teresa's impressions concerning our children's needs. Many times I was *sure* that the kids just needed a little more love or a few more fun things to do. My sweet wife, however, believed that our kids needed more structure, more routine, and more involvement with Dad. At first, I was reluctant to accept her impressions, but the Holy Spirit brought to my mind today's Scripture verse and challenged me to submit to Teresa, knowing that she too was hearing from the Lord. Our home environment changed dramatically. After I had implemented several of Teresa's suggestions and become more involved in parenting myself, our home was more calm and peaceful.

It's impossible to maintain a submissive attitude in marriage apart from the Holy Spirit's work. We can trust the Lord to bring the peace of *oneness* to two hearts as He forges a common bond of deference.

In what specific areas do you need to defer
to your spouse today?

Giving Yourself Up

*Christ Jesus . . . did not consider it robbery to be equal with God,
but made Himself of no reputation, . . . coming in the likeness of men.*
Philippians 2:5-7

I (David) am glad Christ didn't selfishly hold on to heaven. I'm glad He deferred to my world and my needs, thinking them more important than His own.

True deference always implies following Christ's example by giving up my way or my plans. It requires sacrifice. Deference means that I must ask these questions: "In light of eternity, how important is my agenda?" and "How much more important is it to love you than to have my own way?"

Lord, don't hold back Your hand from reshaping my life according to Your pleasure.

I still remember the impact Ephesians 5:25 had on me some twenty years ago. As I read, "Husbands, love your wives, just as Christ also loved the church and gave Himself for her," I was forced to ask myself, "What have I given up for Teresa?" The issue was not how hard I had worked to provide an adequate living. It was not how hard I've tried or whether I've stayed with my family, even during the tough times. Those issues were important, but the Lord seemed to be asking me what I had *sacrificed* for my wife.

I realized that the Lord wanted me to make myself of "no reputation" and humble myself and defer to my wife in many areas. God wanted me to defer to Teresa and give up my sloppiness. I needed to die to my selfishness and clean up the bathroom countertop and wipe up the coffee I spilled in the car. God wanted me to defer to Teresa and give up my procrastination. He wanted me to be more mindful of projects around the house and complete them in a specified time frame. He wanted me to die to my selfish timetable and finish cleaning out the office and finally replace the boards in the fence—like I had promised.

In what areas can you truly defer to your spouse—
sacrifice for him or her—today?

Holding Your Tongue

Even a fool is counted wise when he holds his peace; when he shuts his lips, he is considered perceptive. Proverbs 17:28

David and I went away for spring break to one of our favorite hotels. David knew exactly which kind of room he wanted. He asked for a room with a patio that had a hot tub and a view of the ocean.

Lord, help me to know those times when my spouse needs me to keep quiet and defer to him or her.

When we arrived in the hotel, we discovered there had been a mistake in the reservation. The room reserved for us had no hot tub. David was adamant that we get the room he had reserved, and after many minutes of negotiations, we were given a different room. But as we opened the door to the second room, we discovered that it had no view of the ocean. David called the hotel manager, and after some negotiations, we were assigned a room with the view and the hot tub. We moved into the "right" room the following day.

I could have made a big deal out of having to move three times in a day and a half, and to be honest, there have been many times when I would have complained. But this particular time, the Holy Spirit impressed me with these thoughts: *Teresa, this is important to David. He has looked forward to these special arrangements for a long time. Remember that part of the reason David wants this particular room is so that you can have your breakfast out on the patio. He knows that you love to do that. He's trying to give to you.* So, rather than making a tough situation worse by complaining, I kept my mouth shut.

Sometimes that's what deference looks like—keeping quiet, even when you are inconvenienced. The move from room to room took only a few minutes, but even more important was the reassurance David had of my support.

What steps can you take to make sure your spouse knows you defer to him or her?

Deference to Another's Agenda

Do nothing out of selfish ambition or vain conceit, but in humility consider others better than yourselves. **Philippians 2:3,** NIV

For years, I didn't understand that Teresa's childhood was often lonely, that as a girl she often felt that her needs and her desires were forgotten. Teresa grew up in a family of six children, and three of those brothers and sisters were deaf. Of course, the deaf kids received a great deal of attention in the household. Who gave Teresa's needs priority? Who would defer to her wishes and desires? The usual answer was, "No one."

Although Teresa understood the importance of caring for her brothers and sisters, it still hurt her to so often go unnoticed.

I didn't realize it when we first married, but God wanted me to play a "deferring role" in Teresa's life. She needed me to look out for her interests, because no one else had done that. She needed me to regard her as more important than myself.

Thank You, Father, for helping me expand my role as "provider." Help me show my spouse that I consider his or her needs more important than my own.

Deferring to Teresa meant letting her pick the restaurant or the movie or saying things to her such as, "Sweetheart, we have this Saturday free, so how would you like to spend it?" or "Teresa, I read about a celebrity event in the paper. Would you like to go?"

It took initiative on my part to take the effort—as small as it might have been—to consider what was important to Teresa. But I've loved seeing the joy in my wife's eyes as I show her that her needs matter to me. It's a blessing to see her confidence rise and security grow as she realizes how important her interests are to me.

Each time I defer to Teresa, I am struck with gratitude for having the opportunity to help heal wounds from her past.

What do you think deferring to your spouse's needs and desires should look like and sound like?

"I'll Get Up!" "No, I'll Get Up!"

Let no one seek his own, but each one the other's well-being. 1 Corinthians 10:24

Have you ever played the "Who's going to get up and take care of the baby at three in the morning" game? Let me describe it for you:

You and your spouse are dead tired from the daily rigors of life. The baby has been asleep for a few hours, and you have both nodded off.

Suddenly, that little bundle of joy decides it is time to interact with you again. You lie there pretending you are sound asleep, hoping and praying your spouse will get up to feed and diaper the baby.

Lord, I want my love to be more like that "motherly love."

Teresa and I have played that game hundreds of times. Yet, I must confess, I've probably mastered the technique of "playing asleep." There have been only a few times in the lives of our three kids when I've gotten myself out of bed to contribute. More often than not, Teresa has been the one who shakes off sleep to meet our babies' needs.

"That doesn't sound like much of a sacrifice," you might say. "Your wife stayed home with the kids; you had to work the next morning. It was only fair that she got up with the babies." Not so fast! I'm now convinced that Teresa's willingness to get up every time one of the babies cried has huge implications. It was her way of putting sacrificial love into practice.

That really is love, and it isn't easy. When you are tired, unappreciated, and have already gone the distance to take care of someone's needs, then readily give one more time—that's love. Motherly, sacrificial love lets go, gives first, and asks nothing in return.

It's a picture of love that blesses me—and challenges me, as well.

Tending to your children aside, in what ways can you put sacrificial, deferential love into action in your marriage today?

Your Way or Mine?

The wisdom that is from above is . . . willing to yield. James 3:17

I'll never forget one particular vacation David and I took together. We had nothing planned one afternoon, and I mentioned that I would really like to go shopping. But when I brought this up to David, he said something along the lines of "I'd rather die!"

David has always hated shopping. So as I made my request that day, I knew I was asking a lot. David just shrugged his shoulders, and he had a pained look on his face. He quickly suggested that I take the shuttle over to the mall that afternoon. I could shop all I wanted to by myself, and he would meet me back at the hotel for dinner.

Lord, remind me of the wisdom of yielding my heart to You and to my spouse.

Our afternoon of free time had arrived, and as I prepared to leave, I heard David call down to the bell captain of the hotel and ask for our rental car. Then, to my surprise, David announced that he would be going with me to the mall. He'd thought it over and decided that if I really wanted to go shopping, then he wanted to be with me. I was thrilled.

The second blessing arrived as we moved from store to store. Not only did David surprise me by going with me, he also went with a gracious attitude and a pleasant smile. (If you have ever gone somewhere with an unwilling spouse, you know how important attitude can be. Everyone will soon know how unhappy he or she is, and that makes the time together miserable.) I discovered that David hadn't changed his mind about shopping, but that he wanted to show me how much he cared about me by putting my desires over his.

In what areas can you and your spouse each yield
to the desires of the other?

Deferring through Sharing Your Wishes

Give preference to one another in honor. Romans 12:10, NASB

Teresa and I have discovered that it's often difficult for couples to discuss areas of needed growth in their marriage. Too often, couples are detoured by defensiveness, blame, and complaint. Bob and Sherri were one of those couples.

Thank You, Father, for the strength to look beyond myself and give to this special one You've blessed me with.

We counseled with Bob and Sherri to help them learn a few tips in how to defer to one another's wishes. First, we asked them to prepare a "list of thanks." This is a list of things they were thankful for in their marriage and in one another. After completing their respective lists, they were to share them with one another. This time of sharing helped reassure both Bob and Sherri that each was pleased with the marriage and that each saw good things in their spouse.

Next, we asked Bob and Sherri to prepare a "list of wishes." This list was to include specific, positive statements about what they might like to see changed or different in their marriage. Bob included this statement, "I'm hoping you might become more comfortable initiating affection." Sherri stated this wish, "I wish we could be cautious about criticizing one another in front of other people, especially the kids."

Bob and Sherri then shared their lists of wishes with one another. This helped them avoid the destructive cycle of having expectations of each other that they didn't share, then becoming hurt and angry when expectations weren't met. Communicating their wishes helped Bob and Sherri express specific needs to each other, not just negative generalities. It also helped them to avoid saying hurtful, negative words to one another, but instead to formulate a positive approach to communicating their wishes.

Take time to make your own "thanks and wish" lists.

What would your lists of thanks and wishes for
your marriage and spouse include?

A Firm and Dependable Foundation of Committed Care

Be kindly affectionate to one another with brotherly love. Romans 12:10

Devotion means that you can be counted on to show loving concern for your spouse. It means bringing a secure foundation to your marriage because your spouse knows that you are committed to loving him or her. Devotion means that even in the midst of marital struggles or disagreements, you are committed to telling your spouse that you care. It means that even in the midst of tough times, you share your commitment to the relationship and to the Lord.

Lord, help me to be sensitive to daily opportunities to express my devotion to my spouse.

In my (David's) own life, devotion means declaring my allegiance to our marriage. It means showing that I am zealously committed to loving my spouse. Devotion means proclaiming to my spouse my strong attachment and affection. It means expressing my earnest desire to love my spouse even in the hard times. It means "I'll keep loving you, even when things get difficult." Devotion means showing God's perfect love, a love that casts out fear (1 John 4:18).

We often see couples who have enjoyed some great times together but who have experienced rejection or disappointment. And once a spouse feels rejected or let down, she retreats. Once a spouse feels betrayed or abandoned in some way, he withdraws his love.

We've discovered that this kind of pattern often occurs in marriage because the present hurt in the relationship taps into a reservoir of unresolved hurt—from childhood or from former relationships. When this reminder of the past pain comes, one or both marriage partners may withdraw into a cover of self-protection, and when that happens, lines of communication are severed.

Counseling or mentoring with another couple can address this reservoir of unhealed pain. It's scary to look at painful issues from the past, but progress depends on daily caring devotion within the marriage.

In what ways can you openly show your devotion
and allegiance to your spouse today?

Christlike Devotion

*Jesus . . . for the joy that was set before Him
endured the cross.* Hebrews 12:2

Christ's devotion to His Father and to God's love for me kept Him on the cross. It was His unwavering commitment to His heavenly Father that prompted Him to begin His ministry by submitting Himself to baptism by John. It was Christ's devotion to His Father that motivated Him to spend forty days in the desert, alone and needy, so that He could be tempted with everything I might face—and yet remain victorious. It was because of His dedication to His Father that Christ endured the rejection, hatred, and betrayal of the very people He would die for. Christ's devoted commitment was ultimately displayed in the turning point of human history—His death on the cross.

*Lord, help me
to remember
to perform acts
of devotion for
my spouse.*

Hebrews tells us that Christ endured the cross because He looked forward to the joy of the days before Him. That means He so looked forward to a relationship with me that He was willing to die. The joy of the relationship with me is a part of what motivated Christ to put up with all the ridicule and disappointment.

We need a taste of that devotion if our marriages are to survive the tests life is sure to bring.

Couples often ask for marital help after one of life's tragedies, such as a baby lost in labor, a bankruptcy, or a rebellious teenager. None of us is exempt from life's pain, but couples seem to take two distinct paths as they recover from life's hurts. For some couples, tragedy draws them closer together. For others, tragedy seems to break the already fragile relationship.

The couples who survive life's tragedies are the ones who show devotion in the everyday things. They express commitment and devotion to one another regularly through acts of devotion, big and small.

What acts of devotion—big and small—will you perform
for your spouse today?

First Things First

To everything there is a season, a time for every purpose under heaven. Ecclesiastes 3:1

Before I started doing seminars, speaking with David, and ministering to women in our church, I was asked about the *goals* I had as a housewife. It had never occurred to me to even think about goals. All I did was change diapers and drive in the car pool. What goals could I possibly have in mind? I began to do some serious soul-searching. My searching ended with these life goals: devotion to God, to husband, to children, and finally to others.

Lord, help me to prioritize my devotion to You and then to my spouse and children.

That gave me a new perspective as a homemaker. If my goals were being devoted to God, to my husband, and to my kids, then I needed to get busy.

I started by beginning a newly scheduled devotional time with God. Before the kids got up each morning, I'd curl up on the couch and simply "hang out" with God. I learned to be still and enjoy being with God.

Secondly, I began thinking of ways that I could show David that I was devoted to him. I initiated affection with David. I verbalized my love for him more often and kissed him when he left for work and when he came home. I called him during the day, just to tell him I was thinking about him and that I loved him. Each day, I tried to show David that my love for him was consistent, ever present, and stable.

So often, I hear women complain, "I don't have a ministry." But God has given us a special ministry to our husbands and then our children. If you're at a stage of life where your husband and children require most of your time, then thank God for this season of life and get busy getting devoted.

What adjustments do you need to make in your list of priorities today to make sure your spouse and children are in their proper place?

Devoted to Me as Your Friend

No longer do I call you servants. . . . I have called you friends.
John 15:15

In the early years of our marriage, we set priorities using the "squeaky wheel" standard. That means that whoever or whatever "cried out" for attention at the moment received priority treatment. Unfortunately, our relationship didn't seem to us to be "crying out" loudly enough.

Lord, allow my spouse and me to open up to one another as friends, the same way You opened up to the disciples.

Ten years into our marriage, the barrenness of a busy life began to take its toll. The joy had left our relationship and we no longer felt like friends. We had turned into two people living in the same house but feeling very much alone. Finally, Teresa and I gave ourselves the advice we had been giving to other couples: "Schedule a weekly time to talk. Don't leave it to chance." We first met on Thursdays for lunch. If the time had to change during the week, we'd spend Sunday evening discussing our schedules.

During this time we spent together, we came to realize that the passage of John 15 held some important insights for us as a couple. This passage tells us that Jesus took His disciples into His confidence and shared the most intimate plans of the Father with them. Jesus knew His disciples, and He apparently felt it was important that they know Him and His Father.

This showed us that in order to have a deep, caring relationship, we needed to work hard to know one another. It was going to have to be a two-way street. So these "marriage staff meetings" always included a time when we shared our feelings, hurts, joys, and tender places of our hearts.

This kind of personal time together allowed us to open up to one another and to care for one another as spouses, as lovers—and as friends.

What can you do today to help establish and grow
a friendship between you and your spouse?

When I'm Sixty-Four

Let our people also learn to maintain good works. Titus 3:14

I recently caught myself humming a few bars of the old Beatles tune "When I'm Sixty-Four." One of the lines in the song asks, "Will you still need me . . . when I'm sixty-four?"

That's something most married couples think about, isn't it? Will my spouse still want to be with me when my wrinkles are set in concrete and my hair is gray? Will my spouse still love me then and want to be around? Scary question, isn't it?

God, remind us of our call to love one another like You have loved us.

In a day and age when few things seem permanent, when people change partners like they change shirts, we all wonder if love will last. Yet true intimacy is built on the commitment to love your spouse forever.

I am committed to Teresa forever, but that doesn't mean we haven't struggled. We've had our disagreements and have endured plenty of unloving moments. When I haven't felt so loving toward Teresa, I've called upon my devotion to God. I returned home to work things out with her because of the commitment I made to Him on our wedding day. When my heart and my feelings have wavered, my devotion to God has restored my path.

God has called me to love Teresa. He's called me to maintain the "good works" of our marriage. There are times when I feel as if we've been married only thirty-five *days*, and there are times when I feel every one of the thirty-five *years* we've been together. But there's no one else on the earth who has an opportunity like mine. I plan to be married to Teresa when I'm sixty-four, and she feels the same way about me. What a blessing of devotion!

In what ways can you express your lifetime commitment
to love your spouse today?

I'll Be There

Now set your heart and your soul to seek the Lord your God.
1 Chronicles 22:19

The elderly couple sat in the restaurant laughing and smiling throughout their conversation. I (Teresa) marveled at how much they were enjoying each other's company. They seemed to know one another's thoughts, but each conveyed careful interest in what the other had to say. I could see that their routines were familiar, their preferences understood. As they ate their meal, I could see the mutual fondness and genuine care.

Lord, make me completely aware of Your devotion to me. Overwhelm me with Your faithfulness.

To me, devotion means emotional investment and interest in your spouse—over a period of time. It is a sign of maturity in the relationship, and it goes much deeper than mere actions. Devotion is a matter of the heart. You can't just *act* devoted; the hardships of life will crush that out of you.

I've asked God to make devotion a part of my character. He's answered my prayer by showing me how devoted He is to me. I didn't expect it to work this way, but as I have sought the Lord and made the effort to get to know Him, He's overwhelmed me with His love. It's because of His faithfulness and dependability that I can give the same kind of devotion to David. It's because of His unwavering acceptance and unconditional grace that I can devote myself to providing the same for my husband. Devotion is dependable, foundational, and of God.

Make a commitment today to love your spouse in accordance with the vows you made on your wedding day—when you committed to being together "for better or for worse, richer or poorer, forsaking all others, till death do you part." Make a choice today to seek the Lord and bask in His devotion for you, then tell your spouse that he or she can count on you for a lifetime.

What words or actions could you use to demonstrate
your devotion to God, then to your spouse?

Devoted to Removing Marriage Lies

[Bring] every thought into captivity to the obedience of Christ.
2 Corinthians 10:5

"Why should I change?" insisted Ellen. "I thought marriage meant accepting me just the way I am." Her husband, Dale, offered his answer: "If our marriage takes this much work, maybe we're just not right for each other."

Ellen and Dale suffered from several misconceptions about marriage.

Many couples begin their lives together believing marital lies. It's never a conscious decision to believe these untruths, but believing marital lies can still be harmful, or fatal, to a relationship. In our work with Dale and Ellen, we worked to debunk the lies.

Help me, Father, to take lies captive and cast them down, replacing them with the truth.

Ellen bought into the lie that in marriage she shouldn't have to change. We explained to her the truth that while spouses must accept one another unconditionally, each needs to mature and grow in his or her faith and in the relationship. That, we explained, is what the process of becoming Christlike is all about.

Dale believed the lie that if a marriage takes hard work, then the two people must not be right for one another. We explained to him the truth that all intimate relationships take hard work and that encountering difficulties and challenges didn't mean he and his wife weren't right for one another. Rather, we pointed out, it meant they were both human.

We often suggest that married couples set aside time to talk about marital lies. Many couples find it helpful to discuss misconceptions about marriage with a counselor or mentor couple. Including a third party with an objective voice often helps expose unseen marital lies and identify the truth.

Identifying lies in your thinking process is helpful in building closeness. Set aside time this week to take turns sharing the lies you're most vulnerable to and reassure each other with the truth in each case.

What steps are involved in identifying the marital
lies you may believe to be truths?

To Reprove and Correct When Limits Are Exceeded

Do not withhold correction. Proverbs 23:13

God sets limits for me (David) because He doesn't want me to get hurt by the painful effects of my sin. God establishes boundaries for us to abide by so that we don't miss out on the blessings He has in store for us. He sets limits so that we can have a clear set of instructions on how to maintain our intimacy with Him. God doesn't want me to cross His boundaries because He doesn't want me to lose fellowship with Him.

Thank You, Father, for setting boundaries for me to live within.

Think for a moment on how the discipline of our children mirrors the heart of God when it comes to boundaries. When I tell our son, Eric, to ride his bike on the sidewalk and not on the street, I've set a boundary. I didn't set that boundary because I wanted to spoil his fun or assert my authority. I gave my son that boundary because I don't want to see him hurt. I don't want him to lose out on the blessing of riding his bike safely. I don't want to lose my relationship with him because he has been physically injured or killed.

God's heart is much the same. He didn't give us the Ten Commandments or the other rules and laws in Scripture because He wants to spoil our fun or because He wants to assert His authority. He loves us and deeply wants to protect us from harm—even from ourselves.

God sets rules and boundaries in all areas of our lives, and that includes our marriages. Scripture gives us instructions, rules, and boundaries for us to live within when it comes to marriage and family.

What marital boundaries has God set in Scripture for you and your spouse?

The Discipline of Love

As many as I love, I rebuke and chasten. Revelation 3:19

God's discipline reminds me that I (David) am part of His family. Because He cares for me, God sets limits to guide me. It is His loving correction for right living, not punishment for wrongdoing. Discipline looks to the future, while punishment focuses on the past.

Early in my Christian journey, I thought God's discipline seemed harsh at times. It was difficult not to hear my father's military voice when God's word said, for example, "Do not steal." As I have gained a little maturity in my faith, I've felt chastened just by knowing that my heavenly Father is grieved. It has broken my heart to think that I have hurt Him by my critical spirit or sharp tongue. God is hurt as a result of my sin, just like any other member of my family.

Thank You, God, for loving me enough to discipline me.

In my marriage, the wounded look on Teresa's face has been sufficient to let me know I've failed her in some way. I have seen that pained look on her face when I've given an impatient response to her loving inquiry or broken a promise for the hundredth time. Thankfully, I am now more sensitive to the times when I have sinned against my wife than in the past. It hurts me deeply to know that I've injured her. It takes fewer moments for me to clue in to the fact that I have wounded Teresa.

My gratitude for the security of God's love motivates me to change how I behave toward Him and toward my wife. I used to live in the fear of God's harsh judgment, thinking that He demanded my righteousness. I now know that it's because of His love for me that He's interested in my sanctification.

What steps can you take now to become more aware of the pain you cause God and your spouse when you sin?

Balance in Parenting

*Blows that hurt cleanse away evil, as do stripes the
inner depths of the heart.* Proverbs 20:30

Striking a balance between love and discipline can be a real test for parents. David and I have found that our parenting skills are often born out of how we were raised. My parents spanked first and asked questions later. David's parents lectured and took away privileges. So we approached discipline in our home in opposite ways. Our kids needed the security of our being one in our discipline.

*Father, help us
to prioritize one
another so that
we can give to our
family out of love,
not anger.*

We did a lot wrong in the beginning. Since we were only seventeen when Terri was born, our discipline plan was awfully sketchy. Fortunately, Terri was a very compliant child and didn't challenge our authority often. But as each child was added to our family, it became clear that we needed a discipline plan—and fast!

First, we learned to deal with each individual child differently. We learned that Robin responded to firm directions and consequences. For Eric, it was important for us to use humor and lighthearted tactics. If he sensed the slightest hint of a power struggle, you were in for a battle. We learned to make a game out of almost anything—from taking out the trash to going to bed at night.

David and I also learned that unresolved conflict between us affected how we dealt with the kids. When I felt insecure about the unity between David and me, I was unsure of how to discipline the kids. There were many times when my frustration or irritation with David would come out on the kids. As we have learned to heal our marriage hurts, we no longer use the discipline of the kids as a battleground. As we've grown together as a couple, we have learned to balance each other in discipline.

What steps do you need to take today to make sure you
are "on the same page" when it comes to parenting?

The Discipline of Natural Consequences

*Even if some do not obey the word, they, without
a word, may be won.* 1 Peter 3:1

"David, I wonder if it might be a good idea to slow down on these corners."
Teresa's tone was gentle. She wasn't very insistent, so I ignored her. I was in
a hurry to get to an important conference, and speeding seemed justified.
Since I wouldn't listen to my wife, it was time for the
discipline of natural consequences.

Around the next turn a speed trap was waiting for the husband who had just ignored his wife's
counsel. The officer wrote me the ticket, and we were
on our way. Silence filled several miles—not even an
"I told you so." I was miserable. I felt deep sorrow and
embarrassment, so I made appropriate confessions
to my wife and to the Lord. I paid the fines and took
care of the paperwork requirements of the court.
God had applied the discipline, then God reminded

*Lord, might the
quietness of my
spouse's acceptance
empower me to
listen to Your
voice.*

me of the limits He set for my behavior, which are for my safety and protection. The discipline of natural consequences had completed its work.

The Lord can greatly use the ministry of caring counsel and a quiet
spirit. In the silence of these things, the Spirit's conviction is often almost
deafening.

I'm confident that I wouldn't have heard the Holy Spirit's voice if
Teresa had continued to voice her displeasure in my driving. I'm also sure
that I would have ignored the Lord's prompting if Teresa had continued to
remind me of the consequences of my sin. Teresa wisely chose to share her
concern in a loving way, then backed off to let the Spirit do the work.

In short, Teresa didn't try to do the job that God sent His Spirit to do.

In what areas of yours and your spouse's lives might
God use the discipline of natural consequences?

Press On to the Mark

*Poverty and shame will come to him who disdains correction,
but he who regards a rebuke will be honored.* **Proverbs 13:18**

Think of some of the greatest inventions—the lightbulb, the telephone, and the airplane, for example. These things all have at least this one thing in common: It took hundreds of failed efforts before the inventors achieved final success.

God, help me to listen carefully to Your voice and heed any correction. I will make myself available to receive the same from my spouse.

We husbands and wives are inventors. We invent one of the most important "products" of all—intimacy in marriage. And just like the inventors of the items listed above, we will make many mistakes along the way as we invent this intimacy.

As I (David) make those mistakes, I must be willing to accept correction and rebuke from my spouse. When I fail, I must be willing to hear that I may need to try something else so that our marriage can be more successful. I may try and fail numerous times for every success, but each failure can be used to find a better path.

It has not always been easy to hear, "Sweetheart, I'm looking forward to the day when you are able to prioritize time for just the two of us," or "David, I would like to be able to count on you to support me when it comes to the kids." Each time I've heard those words of rebuke, they've shaken my world. But the Spirit has helped me regard them as truth. The words have been said with compassion, and the Lord has used them to change my life.

Creating intimacy in marriage is quite a challenge, and discipline is essential. Discipline includes being willing to receive correction and rebuke. After all, it's impossible to grow yourself by yourself. You and I will always need our spouses and loved ones around us to challenge us into Christ's likeness.

In what different situations in your marriage has your spouse offered loving correction through his or her words and actions?

Stop, Look, Listen

He who keeps instruction is in the way of life. Proverbs 10:17

David and I have totally different driving styles. I'm pretty laid-back, but David is a bit more aggressive. I've told him I'm concerned about the way he drives, and I've mentioned our grandchildren when I've done so. I've encouraged David to be careful with his actions in the car when they are with us. After all, they are watching, and they are impressionable.

Father, let me hear all the voices that point out the need for change.

Well, David listened, but his driving didn't change.

Then one day, our grandson Zachary was riding with us in the car as David was driving us down the freeway. He was due to catch a plane in a very short time and we were running late. David moved into the left lane of traffic, expecting it to move at the fastest rate of speed. But a huge cement truck came barreling down the middle lane and swerved into ours. David slowed abruptly, sending his suitcases flying. David was irritated and in a hurry. He said, "You dork! What are you doing in this lane anyway?"

You see it coming, don't you? Just as David finishes his outburst, our grandson chimes in from the backseat: "You dork! What ya doing?"

If you have kids, you've experienced this type of moment. It sounded fairly mild when those words came from David. But hearing those exact words coming from a three-year-old was unbearable. We both cringed.

God used that moment to further convict David to be more disciplined in handling his emotions and actions on the road. Zachary's voice helped provide some correction that day.

God uses a variety of ways to show us what changes we need to make. Our grandson's simple comment became a strong reminder to David that his driving was being noticed. It was enough to help him become more careful on the road.

What unusual sources of correction might God
use in your life?

Discipline from Common Spiritual Goals

*The word of God is living and powerful, and sharper
than any two-edged sword.* Hebrews 4:12

David and I have found that deepening our spiritual closeness is very difficult. But at the same time it is extremely rewarding.

For years our spiritual intimacy consisted of sitting on the same pew. But, gradually, we began to develop common spiritual goals. Those goals included reading through the entire New Testament during a year. We also read a Proverb each day of the month. And, at one point, we each bought a separate *One Year Bible* and read through the entire Bible together in a year.

Father, draw us together in a fresh vision for spiritual closeness.

We decided one year to memorize ten Scripture passages dealing with communication. That was an especially challenging topic for us at that point, so we memorized ten verses that helped us identify principles for talking with one another. Another year we memorized Scripture passages on gentleness and honor because we both wanted to develop those characteristics in our relationship.

Finally, David and I have worked together on topical Bible studies. We've taken turns choosing the topic and the method. One year I chose a workbook from the Christian bookstore on the book of Ephesians. We discussed how well we were doing at bringing praise and glory to God through our personal lives and through our marriage. The next year David wanted to do a word study on "grace." So we divided up the passages from the concordance and discussed what God's grace looks like and how we could create a grace-filled home.

As David and I worked toward our spiritual goals, we began to increase our intimacy with God and with one another. It's challenging to take that kind of time and effort to study God's Word, but the blessings are eternal.

What common spiritual goals can you and your spouse work on starting today? What can you do to get started?

Promoting Growth and Development

Let us pursue the things which make for peace and the things by which one may edify another. Romans 14:19

Edification means showing your excitement at being with your spouse, and it means affirming the growth you've seen in his or her life. It means removing any words of criticism or judgment and replacing them with words that build up and affirm character development. Edification means being glad to see your husband or wife. It means complimenting your spouse on a strength you see or noticing when he or she has made an effort to change. Edification means that you comment positively on progress made, thus giving further motivation for character development.

Lord, remove my "half empty" view of my marriage.

How do you respond when your spouse does something positive? For example, your spouse does something good that almost seems out of character. He asks you about your day, or she approaches you affectionately. He remembers to take out the trash, or she takes time to wash the car. How do you respond?

So often we respond to our spouse's attempts toward personal growth with sarcasm, skepticism, or suspicion. We think or say things such as, "That was nice, but not perfect," "I would have done it this other way."

Sharing edification with your spouse means looking at the positives. It means suspending the "half empty" mind-set and seeing your spouse's efforts as "half full." No, he hasn't often stopped to ask sincerely about your day, but he did today. Receive it! No, she doesn't wash the car as often as you would prefer, but she did today. Praise the effort she made this time.

I often ask couples we are working with to tell me about something positive they've noticed in their marriage since we were last together. I do that first of all because I hope to encourage the couple to develop a positive mind-set, to anticipate and look for positive interactions. I also want each partner to enjoy the edification in a spouse's good report.

Which of your spouse's efforts at change can you compliment today?

The Edifying Power of Words

Let no corrupt word proceed out of your mouth, but what is good for necessary edification. Ephesians 4:29

As our kids were growing up, they had a few favorite games we played time and again. One of those games was a strategy game called *Jenga*. In that game, players remove pieces from a tower of blocks and place them back on top of the structure. As you move the blocks, you must be careful not to cause the tower to fall. The key to winning the game is to correctly assess which blocks can be removed to actually increase the stability of the tower. Some blocks reinforce the tower, but others actually make it less stable.

Lord, station a guard at my lips to speak only words that edify.

My (Teresa's) words are a lot like the blocks in that game. Some of my words can reinforce David, while others can tear him down. My words could make our relationship stronger or they could destabilize it. It is sobering to realize the power of my words.

Research shows that it takes ten to twelve positive words or messages to build receptivity to one message of criticism. Sadly, in too many homes there are twelve words of criticism for every positive word spoken. That's obviously not what God has in mind.

Taking Ephesians 4:29 seriously has made a difference in the words that I allow to come out of my mouth. I try to filter my words through the *Jenga* test. Before I speak, I try to ask, "Will my words reinforce this person's growth, or will they undermine that growth? Will my words strengthen my husband's or children's resolve to change in a positive way, or will my words bring discouragement and doubt?"

From time to time, I still allow corruptive words to come out of my mouth, but there are significantly fewer of them. God has begun a great work in me and it still continues.

What can you do to make certain that you speak more words that build up?

Stinkin' Thinkin'

The wise woman builds her house, but the foolish pulls it down with her hands. **Proverbs 14:1**

We've all heard the saying, "If Momma ain't happy, ain't nobody happy." I've seen this to be true in our home. When I (Teresa) am critical, or when I tear other people down with my words, I can see the negative attitude in our kids. I've listened to their conversations when I'm that way, and they sound just like I do when I'm being negative or judgmental. By modeling such a critical spirit, it sometimes seems as if I'm "pulling down" all the positive work David and I have done with our kids.

Father, help me to release my hurts so I can be a positive influence on my family.

To edify the ones in my home rather than tear them down, I must change my "stinkin' thinkin'." It's hard to edify my husband when my mind is consumed with thoughts such as, *I always have to pick up after him. When will he ever grow up?* or *He'll never change. If we have to wait on him one more time . . .*

Such negative and critical thinking is usually the result of my unhealed hurts. When I've let hurts fester, the thoughts I have are going to be negative and critical. To be able to edify, I must in love share the truth of those hurts with David. That would sound like, "Sweetheart, it would mean a lot to me if you could pick up the bathroom by the time our guests arrive" or "David, I was disappointed that we weren't able to have dinner together as a family. I know you were working very hard, but we missed you."

Secondly, I must then turn loose of my anger and choose to forgive David. It's my choice of forgiveness that protects my heart from bitterness and my mind from negative thinking. Only then am I free to edify the ones I love.

What factors cause your mind to be filled with negative thoughts?

Edification Is Sometimes Silent

[Be] slow to speak. James 1:19

"Don't forget to clean up the bathroom before you leave." The more Teresa reminded me to pick up after myself, the less I did it. I know that's not the most mature way to act in a marriage, but it was true. We'd had this conflict for almost twelve years, and we'd made no progress toward resolution.

Heavenly Father, if this thing that irritates me is important to You, I'll trust You to bring the changes. I know You can do a much better job of changing my spouse than I can.

Then one Monday morning, a miracle occurred. The reminding stopped. I left my side of the bathroom a total mess and went to work, almost proud that I had outlasted Teresa. I returned that evening to my messy countertop and to a second miracle: Teresa was in a good mood and warm with affection—and she never even mentioned the mess.

She told me later that she had been focusing on my behavior instead of just accepting me. She prayed about her attitude, and God led her to ask, "Will this issue matter ten years from now? Will it matter in eternity?" The answer was a resounding "No!" Teresa also realized that God could be trusted to bring changes He thought necessary.

A few days later, a third miracle took place. I began to want to put away my mess in the bathroom. Teresa's loving silence had helped me hear God's prompting, which brought edification. The war was over, and our marriage had won.

What conflicts in your marriage is God prompting you today to give up to Him so that He can make the necessary changes?

Building Up Your Marriage

The tongue of the righteous is choice silver. Proverbs 10:20

Teresa and I recently experienced the joy and the challenges of remodeling our home. The contractors laid the foundation, framed, put up plasterboard, painted, and carpeted. We've endured the unending dust, intrusive workers, and complete inconvenience of the whole process. We enjoyed seeing the progress every few days and we love the final product, but the process was indeed painful.

God, please help me to build up my spouse with my words and actions. Help me rely on You so that I don't labor in vain.

This remodeling process has been a great illustration of how I am supposed to treat Teresa. Like each step the contractors took in remodeling our home, each word I speak or action I take should add to her life, not tear it down. And, just like our remodeling process, some days I see lots of progress, but on other days I feel as if I should scrap the whole project and begin again.

Build up, not tear down. That's easier said than done. But I've realized that my tongue is a powerful tool, and God wants me to bring that tool under His control so that my words give great value to Teresa.

I've realized that one way I can ensure that my tongue speaks words that build up is to submit myself daily to the "Ultimate Construction Manager." As I give my gripes, irritations, and complaints to the Lord instead of to Teresa, He calms my heart and mind. As I obey Him and complete my job as "joint builder" in our marriage, He allows me to see the beautiful "product" that Teresa and I are building—our marriage.

What positive words can you speak to your spouse today to build up him or her *and* your marriage?

Tolerance Isn't Enough!

*Let each of us please his neighbor for his good,
leading to edification.* Romans 15:2

David and I spent too many years of our marriage tearing one another down. It was never outright insults; we put one another down in more subtle ways. One of us might make a little joke at the other person's expense, or the other would bring up an embarrassing story. We might speak to each other in a condescending tone or shoot down the other's opinion as if he or she were an ignorant oaf.

*God, help me not
to just tolerate
my spouse, but to
lovingly uphold
him or her.*

The Lord began to convict both David and me about the way we talked to one another. Today's Scripture passage was especially convicting for me. In this passage, Paul asks the church at Rome to not merely tolerate or put up with others, but to lovingly uphold them. God wanted the church of Rome to act in a pleasing way with one another so that each neighbor would be edified.

For most of the previous years, I had thought I was achieving great maturity by the simple fact that I had learned to tolerate some of David's characteristics. I was proud that I had learned to put up with his little idiosyncrasies. But God seemed to be saying, "That's not enough."

God wanted me to look for ways to help David grow into maturity and praise him for his attempts or efforts at growth. God wanted me to get involved in David's personal growth and development by affirming strengths he displayed. It didn't mean that my job was to change David. It meant that I was to become sensitive to what God was doing in David. What a difference that has made!

Instead of tension in our home, there is harmony. Instead of pain, there is healing. Instead of fear, there is comfort.

In what ways can you look to lovingly promote
spiritual and emotional growth in your spouse?

Guidelines for Gab

*Let no corrupt communication proceed out of
your mouth.* Ephesians 4:29, KJV

Teresa and I have worked diligently over the past several years on simply how we talk to each other. We've determined to speak only words that are wholesome and that benefit one another.

First, before I speak to Teresa, I check to make sure that the purpose of my words is to build up, encourage, or esteem her. If my purpose is to hurt, attack, or defend my position, then it's not time for me to talk to her.

Heavenly Father, filter my words so that only wholesome, edifying words come out of my mouth.

Secondly, I must discern the need for my words before I speak. Today's passage in Ephesians tells us that we need to only speak words that fit the need of the moment. This is why it is important that I listen to Teresa. I must try to see things from her perspective. Is she sad? Then I'll want to show her how much I care. Is she afraid? Then I'll want to reassure her of my love and presence. Is she angry about something I've done? Then I'll want to ask the Lord to convict me of any way I might have hurt Teresa.

Third, I try to make sure the timing of my words is right. Teresa's receptivity to my words is often directly related to the timing of my speaking them. For example, I've learned that it's rarely a good idea to talk with Teresa about something important late at night. Her exhaustion in the evenings makes receptivity low, so we usually have our talks early in the morning over coffee. We've also found that bringing up important issues during our quality times of weekly talk works well. We both know that those times are dedicated to giving one another undivided attention.

What steps can you take to learn the best way to lovingly and effectively communicate with your spouse?

To Urge Forward and Positively Persuade toward a Goal

Encourage one another. 1 Thessalonians 5:11, NASB

Encouragement, one of the true blessings in a relationship, means urging another to persist and persevere toward a goal. It means to stimulate another person to show love and good deeds. Encouragement looks like calling your spouse on his or her "big day" just to say, "I love you and I'm praying for you." Encouragement sounds like, "I know you can do it! I believe in you."

Father, produce in our home an atmosphere of encouragement. Help me to see this need in my spouse and respond accordingly.

Encouragement helps keep us from growing weary in doing good. It helps us keep trying even when things are tough or when we encounter obstacles. Encouragement stimulates us to keep doing what we know is right. It means to inspire courage and determined resolve.

To give encouragement means I declare myself a cheerleader for my spouse. With sincerity and genuine praise, I tell my spouse how much I believe in him or her. By not taking over, I show him that I know he can do it. By speaking confidently about her abilities, I show her that I know she can do it.

Encouragement is not just for the hard times. It's not just something to give as a last resort. Encouragement is continued gratitude for your spouse. It means that I share words of hope about our marriage, words such as, "Sweetheart, I'm so thankful that you and I were able to resolve our differences. It gives me confidence for the days ahead." It means that I share words of excitement about the character I see in my spouse: "Honey, I'm so grateful for your enthusiasm. I know we'll still be having fun even when we're in our golden years."

Encouragement is truly one of the great blessings of married life.

In what areas of his or her life might your spouse need encouragement today? What words of encouragement can you speak?

MAY

encouragement
enjoyment
entreaty
exalting
exhortation

Encouraging Good Deeds

*Let us consider one another in order to stir up
love and good works.* Hebrews 10:24

What a joy it is to play a role in seeing Teresa flourish in positive growth by giving encouragement. And it is an extra special joy to see the seeds of encouragement spring forth into the fruits of love and good deeds.

Lord, allow my spouse and me to enjoy the closeness that mutual encouragement brings.

Encouragement can come in many forms and in many circumstances. It can come verbally or in a special written note. It can come on the heels of a personal victory or in the valley of discouragement. It might come privately during a quiet talk, or it can be proclaimed publicly.

Couples who come to our conferences wanting increased intimacy or oneness in their marriage are often surprised at how encouragement fits into the equation. Sadly, many couples lack a deep sense of intimacy because theirs are two relatively independent, self-reliant existences. They both may have careers, or one may be career focused while the other is more home focused. No matter what their circumstances, discovering the power of encouragement can help bring them together. Thus, *my* career becomes *our* career. You share *my* efforts at home through *your* encouragement and it becomes *our* family.

In God's wisdom, He knew that each of us—no matter how motivated or dedicated we may be—can benefit from another's encouragement. It's the wise couple who makes their marriage the first source of this blessing. Many a home has been wrecked and families torn apart when those outside the marriage provide what God seeks to provide within. God warned Cain that "sin is crouching at your door; it desires to have you" (Genesis 4:7, NIV). Encouraging your marriage partner helps shut the door on such attacks and stirs him or her on with deepened love.

That's what encouragement within marriage is all about.

In what specific ways can you make your marriage a
center of encouragement for your spouse today?

All for One, One for All

Say to those who are fearful-hearted, "Be strong, do not fear!"
Isaiah 35:4

Eric, our only son, was to graduate in May 1992, but first he needed to get some extra credits. One of the credits Eric needed was in English, his least-favorite subject. He had to take the English course by correspondence, and it was a major understatement to say he needed our encouragement. If Eric was going to successfully complete his required English project, he was going to need encouragement from David, from his sisters, from his grandmother, and from me.

> *Lord, may our families make consistent use of the gift of encouragement.*

We encouraged Eric in his studies, and when it was time to take his final test, we all encouraged him just to do his best. He completed the test and mailed it in, and we all anxiously waited and watched the mail because we all wanted to know whether he had received a passing grade. After what seemed like an eternity, we received his test results. Eric passed!

Our family will always have fond memories of working toward the common goal of Eric's graduation, largely because it was something of a team effort. We were careful to make sure Eric was the one who did the work, but at the same time no one in the family announced, "It's your problem, Eric, so you solve it." We offered him all the help we could, but more than that we offered him encouragement. We all felt that when a Ferguson needs help, we're ready as a family to pitch in.

Encouraging one another—whether it's in English, work projects, child raising, or spiritual growth—helps remind families of eternal priorities. English papers, work accomplishments, and children's toys assembled at Christmas in and of themselves will all eventually fade away. But the encouragement offered in these things continues. Encouragement helps seal in our hearts the joy of others' care and the specialness of their love.

In what specific areas do members of your family need encouragement today?

Encouraging Sexual Intimacy

Behold, you are fair, my love! Behold, you are fair!
Song of Solomon 4:1

Janice and her husband, Steve, often found themselves in conflict over sex. They had compared the frequency of intimacy with the "averages" they had heard about. They had tried to bargain their way to a solution by, for example, trading one more sexual encounter for a dinner date or for cleaning out the garage. It had not worked for them, and Steve had often become angry over Janice's lack of sexual desire.

Father, with Your perfect love, empower me to take the initiative to love my spouse in the physical sense.

How tragic it is that some couples reduce the God-designed plan for two becoming one flesh (Genesis 2:24) to mere numbers. Sadly, questions such as, "How long has it been?" or "How often should we have sex?" are common among couples we encounter.

Sexual union is surely envisioned in Scripture when it speaks about a married couple "becoming one." But there's much more to God's plan. It's often true that conflicts in this area of sexual intimacy have their resolution in deepened friendship and even spiritual closeness.

When times of dating and dreaming are forgotten, sexual closeness goes. Failing to draw together spiritually through shared faith experience allows the coldness of life to quench the warmth of love—including sexual love.

During individual time with Janice, Steve talked about his emotional need to be found sexually desirable. Janice agreed to try an experiment that week. As Steve left for work, Janice sent him off with tenderness and touch and said to him, "I'd sure like to be together with you tonight. Can we plan on it?" Steve later reported that he was shocked but excited.

Janice's initiative encouraged Steve. It began to answer his inner longing to know that his wife found him sexually desirable. His pressuring of Janice subsided, and the frequency struggles diminished.

What steps can you and your spouse take to make the two of you becoming one a more fulfilling part of your marriage?

It Will Be Fine!

But exhort one another daily, while it is called "Today," lest any of you be hardened through the deceitfulness of sin. Hebrews 3:13

David and I recently finished remodeling our home. There are a million decisions to make when you are remodeling, and none of them seems very easy. And if you are perfectionistic like I can be, each decision has to be absolutely right.

On more than a few occasions something wasn't done quite to my liking, and I found myself getting upset. You know, kind of a "this is the end of the world" reaction to something like a light fixture not being hung perfectly. Dozens of times David said, "It will be fine" when I was in one of those overreactive moods. Those words were just what the doctor ordered, and I often found myself handling my feelings better because of his encouragement.

God, help me be encouraging to my spouse, especially when times are stressful.

Such experiences give insight into why our marriage partners are often so different from us. Intense versus laid-back, reflective versus social, thinker versus doer, wait versus react—the list of differences seems endless, and we often miss their purposes.

Could it be that some of my spouse's differences are intended to be encouragements to me when I become extreme in my emotions? More than once, David's laid-back nature has tempered my extreme perfectionism. His tendencies to wait, reflect, and think have encouraged me at times when I was prepared to "Ready! Aim! Fire!" Because of that, I've grown and matured in curbing my inclination to react first and pick up the pieces later.

I appreciate David's calming influence when I am feeling troubled or upset. It means a lot to me to have his perspective and soothing words during those emotional storms I sometimes create. Those storms often calm because of what he does to help, and I am able to see things more clearly.

Encouragement—what a critically important need in marriage! Offer some to your spouse today.

In what ways can you encourage your spouse
by easing his or her stress?

Goaded to Action

Comfort each other and edify one another. 1 Thessalonians 5:11

How ironic that I (David) would resist encouragement rather than receive it gladly—resent it, in fact, rather than joyfully accept it. A classic example of this weakness has been my resistance to Teresa's encouragement concerning my driving speed. For years she tried every imaginable approach—some of them more Christlike than others. None had a positive effect on my driving, and most, in fact, resulted in relational conflict.

God, help me to encourage my spouse and, more importantly, accept encouragement.

When Teresa "encouraged" me to slow down, I would rationalize my reactions with countless justifications such as, "I don't need someone telling me how to drive," or "If I get a ticket, I've earned the money to pay for it," or "If our insurance rates go up, that's how I've chosen to spend our money." In retrospect, these answers sound a lot like speaking and thinking as a child (1 Corinthians 13:11).

God often gets my attention through His Word. I love studying Scripture—obviously much more than obeying it! Over the years I've sensed God guiding my life through the Word, sometimes in a humorous fashion. I still remember teaching a class about the book of Acts when I encountered the passage where the Lord said to Saul, "It is hard for you to kick against the goads"(Acts 26:14, NASB).

Amidst considerable research on the text, which used an illustration from the training of farm animals (a goad is a stick used to urge on an ox or other beast of burden), the Lord spoke to me of something more relevant to my own life: "I've given you Teresa's encouragement about your driving—for your good. Why do you kick against it?"

I then recognized Teresa's role in my life as a "goad of the Lord." Changes were underway in my life, particularly that part of my life behind the wheel.

In what areas has your spouse attempted to "encourage" you, only to have you make excuses?

Encouragement from Marriage and Family Goal Setting

Where there is no vision, the people are unrestrained.
Proverbs 29:18, NASB

After ten or so years of marriage, Teresa and I began to observe a degree of aimlessness in our relationship. Routine and boredom had set in. We were very busy with activity, but we had little real joy. Around that time, we came to find that King Solomon, the writer of Proverbs, was indeed wise when he wrote of the importance of vision. We needed vision, a fresh sense of direction and destiny.

Encourage me, Father, with a vision for my marriage, and then make me an encourager as we seek the vision together.

We began to use exploratory questions to help identify our specific goals. Then we focused on working together and encouraging each other to accomplish them.

During our sharing times we used questions such as: In what two key ways would you like to see me grow personally in the next year? What is an important item you'd like to see included in our romance? What improvements or changes would you most like to see around our home? As we together explored some of our wishes and dreams, many of them became common goals.

Over the years, our goals each year have varied from the great to the small. They have ranged from exotic trips to bathroom wallpaper, from retirement accounts to making new friends. A noticeable change has taken place in where we find our joy and excitement. First was the joy of accomplishment, the excitement of attaining the goal. Over time that has shifted to the excitement that "we did it"—the joy coming more from the journey together.

As Amos 3:3 wisely reminds us, "Can two walk together, unless they are agreed?"—agreed on where they are going, we would say! There is joy in the vision for where we're going and there's joy in the walking together.

What steps can you and your spouse take together
this day to establish vision for your marriage?

Fulfillment in Another's Company

Trust . . . in the living God who gives us richly all things to enjoy.
1 Timothy 6:17

God is "pro-enjoyment"! Remember His conversation with Adam in Genesis 2? God said it was not good for the man to be alone. Adam needed a helpmate, a companion to enjoy God's creation with him.

Thanks, Father, for the joy of companionship.

It's important to remember that God thought up the "helpmate" plan. It wasn't man's idea or society's invention. God wanted Adam to experience the deep joy of a relationship. Enjoying another person, in God's design, isn't determined so much by what we're doing but simply by being together.

To enjoy another person means looking for ways to delight in him or her and to find out things that make that person special to you. To enjoy another person means taking pleasure in his or her company, discussing ideas, or just being quiet together.

Teresa and I have learned to enjoy one another. It wasn't automatic. At first we thought that our common interests had to become more and more entertaining so that we didn't get bored. Age, maturity, and possibly deepened companionship have brought us to a joy coming more from just being together. We enjoy the deep joy of relationship when we sit outside on the patio and have breakfast together. We enjoy one another while we watch the grandkids play. Teresa and I enjoy being with one another when we go to the movies or as we sit quietly and talk. We enjoy one another's company and share the experience of togetherness.

Teresa and I have been grateful for the results of making a concerted effort to be with one another. The sweetness of our relationship returns as we spend time with one another. And the sweetness of our relationship with God is deepened as we reflect on His generosity. He has richly blessed us with the gift of one another.

What could you and your spouse do together that would help you focus on being with one another? How might you initiate this idea?

God Did Good

He did good . . . filling our hearts with food and gladness.
Acts 14:17

God did good! He did good because that is His nature. He's not a celestial killjoy but a caring Father who desires every good thing for us. He longs for us to come to enjoy everything pertaining to life and godliness. Enjoying another person is a special part of God's plan for marriage. God "did good" when He created your spouse just for you.

Decades of married life have challenged not only our spiritual walk but also our concept of God. If He's distant and disengaged, then His personal and specific care can be questioned. If He's on a perfectionist inspection tour—hiding at every turn ready

Thanks, heavenly Father, for being a good God!

to jump out at us with judgment—then we can question His motives for creating us. But if His heart's longing is for our good, then the wonder of God reshapes our lives and helps us to see every aspect of our lives and our relationships differently. Seeing Him differently, for who He really is, leads to seeing our spouses differently. This leads to seeing our spouses as good gifts from Him.

Many couples come to our conferences thinking that marriage is to be tolerated at best. Coping is the most they hope for. But into this attitude of mediocrity and complacency comes a God who desires to give life and give it abundantly. This doesn't mean special protection from problems, but it means joy, peace, and liberty in the midst of them. Part of His plan for such abundance is the divine relationships through which He works—marriage, the family, and the church.

We can be grateful for His goodness in giving us those relationships, and we can start by thanking Him for our spouses.

For what specifically about your spouse can you give
thanks to God today?

Relax a Little

*Live joyfully with the wife whom you love all the days
of your vain life.* Ecclesiastes 9:9

I just love it when David takes a Monday or Friday off so that we can both relax and just enjoy one another's company. These days feel like holidays to me. We don't have to plan our day. We don't need any kind of agenda. We don't need to do anything but enjoy being with each other.

Lord, help me to stay out of the world's trap of the tyranny of urgency and remember to take time to relax with my spouse.

The world tries to convince us that we constantly need to be "doing" something. Consequently, we can fall into the trap of an overly busy life. When we stop enjoying just being in each other's presence, it's usually a sign we've given over more of ourselves than is healthy to keeping ourselves "busy." How can we feel romantic or get to know one another on a deeper emotional level unless we make time to enjoy each other—alone, without the kids or anyone else around, and without "doing" something?

It's this rebuke of anxious "busyness" that we hear in Christ's words to His friend when He says, "Martha, Martha, you are worried and troubled about many things" (Luke 10:41). Activity was hindering Martha's relationship with Christ, and that is never good. Activities are to serve relationships through shared joy and common experience, but never to supplant them.

Mary, Martha's sister, was affirmed in her focus on relationship as Christ said, "Mary has chosen what is better" (Luke 10:42, NIV). It seems insightful that Christ specifically refers to Mary "choosing" to give priority to relationship. This demonstrates to us that we don't simply *slip* into intimate fellowship and close friendship—we have to *choose*.

We should all follow Mary's example and focus on relationship first—with our God first, then with our spouses.

What steps can you take to be certain you have time with your spouse—alone, uninterrupted, and with nothing planned to "do"?

Seizing and Enjoying the Moment

Therefore, as we have opportunity, let us do good to all. Galatians 6:10

Teresa and I have often found the "joy of now" being stolen by past disappointments or future anxieties. It is amazing how difficult it sometimes is just to deal with the present. But great joy began to come as we have learned to "seize the moment" and make the most of every opportunity to do good.

Intimacy develops and deepens as couples seize the daily experiences that draw them together. Intimacy doesn't *just happen* without effort, but neither can it be *programmed* to happen. Couples grow in closeness, for example, as they encounter one another spiritually, emotionally, or physically. Such encounters can include ecstatic moments of common joy, tearful sharing of genuine apology, or an affectionate embrace. It is during these intimate encounters that couples learn to deepen their marital closeness. Those things are far more likely to happen as a couple learns to live in freedom from hurts from the past and fears over the future.

Father, might we seize today's opportunities to enjoy You and each other. Help us to put aside the pain of yesterday and the fears over tomorrow.

Christ is our example of living every day in the freedom of the present. Jesus was not hindered by any failures from yesterday or fears of tomorrow. Unlike Him, we experience failures. But with confession, forgiveness, and comfort, the Great Physician frees us to enjoy today's goodness (see Matthew 5:4, James 5:16, and 1 John 1:9). Unlike Him, we experience fears of the future. But with the reassurance of His perfect love, our fears are "cast out" and give way to present joy (see 1 John 4:18-19).

Imagine the abundance, intimacy, and joy of a husband and wife—unencumbered by past pain or future fears—seizing His goodness together.

What past pains or future fears do you and your spouse need
to release today so that you can enjoy "now" together?

The Joy of Enjoying

We have great joy and consolation in your love. Philemon 1:7

God's love leads to joy and joy abundant. Joy doesn't come easy to a "half-empty" person like me (Teresa). I seem to be wired to see only what's not right, not done, can't work, or won't happen. Each of these is a painful joy killer. But God has sent His love into my life so that I can have joy. A big part of God's "joy plan" for me is my marriage to David.

God, help us as a couple to really enjoy life together.

David is the eternal optimist, seeing the good in everything and everybody. He also knows about joy and seems to find it everywhere. God involves my husband often to help me find the "silver linings." For example, several years ago David had me join him in making a long list of things I might enjoy—like lunch with friends, quiet reading times, shopping trips, trips with grandkids, and so forth. He kept after me until I had more than fifty possibilities, and then he set out to support me in scheduling each one. The plan was to help me better understand myself and to learn to experience joy. As we carried out our plan, I learned a great deal about myself and about real joy.

Another significant change began to happen as a result of David encouraging me to experience joy. I began to see more of God's blessings in my life. I began to have greater joy in my relationship with my heavenly Father because I was able to see demonstrations of His care for me. I became more at peace with myself and the world around me because I could rest in His love.

I was amazed to discover that life wasn't half-empty after all!

Thanks, David, for showing me how to more fully enjoy the blessings God brings.

What activity could you plan for you and your spouse
to enjoy together?

You're Fun to Be With

The Lord takes pleasure in His people. Psalm 149:4, NASB

"Taking pleasure in someone" speaks of enjoying his or her presence. In today's verse, the psalmist references the wonder that the Creator takes pleasure in the created. The Lord longs to enjoy my presence. This truth fills me (Teresa) with gratitude and draws me to Him.

Abraham was referred to as a friend of God, and it raises the possibility that others can become His friends as well. Possibly me? It's this same possibility of friendship that God has built into His establishment of marriage.

Dear God, help me to focus on my spouse and the special joy we feel when we are together.

David has meant a lot of different things to me, and high on the list would have to be that he's *my* best friend. We laugh at the same things and cry at the same things. We enjoy trying new restaurants, watching movies, and playing on the floor with the grandkids. We both enjoy talking to one another about interesting books we've read. We especially enjoy vacations together. Whether it's with the whole family or just David and me going, we love to explore new places and see the sights. I also really enjoy the seminars that we give together. We enjoy discussing afterward how we saw God work, who was there, and any suggestions for follow-up.

I take pleasure in being with David. As I've reflected on how much I enjoy being with him, it's helped me understand how God might in much the same way enjoy being with me. Having such a fond affection for David and cherishing his friendship has helped me believe that God might have that same affection for me. I've realized that He, too, cherishes His relationship with me.

He takes pleasure in me, just like I take pleasure in my husband.

How will you take pleasure in your spouse today?
How will you cultivate your special friendship?

Enjoying Each Other's Company

My times are in Your hand. Psalm 31:15

Time has only three tenses: past, present, and future. Intimacy is experienced only in the present. Living in the present is difficult, but it's essential for experiencing intimacy and abundance. In reality, the present is all we really have to enjoy.

Teach us, Father, to seize the enjoyment of today.

Christ's earthly ministry gave us a great example of life in the present. Regardless of the external stressors, He continued lovingly meeting the needs of those around Him. As crowds pushed in around Him, Christ stopped on His journey with the disciples to ask, "Who touched My clothes?" (Mark 5:30). Likewise, the Holy Spirit, unhindered by yesterday's concerns or tomorrow's uncertainties, desires to express His care and love—right now.

We often give couples several suggestions for enjoying each other in the present. Our first suggestion is, talk about common interests. Second, we encourage couples to communicate their enjoyment of one another with words such as, "I'm not sure I've ever told you, but your friendship is extremely important to me. I enjoy you so much." Third, we encourage them to discuss their friendship and ways they can deepen that friendship.

We've also found it helpful to encourage couples to return to some "first loves." We tell them to recall some of the particularly meaningful activities they enjoyed during courtship and then to surprise one another by returning to some of them. We tell them to review their hobbies and pastimes—things such as hunting, golfing, fishing, shopping, tennis, and walking—to make sure they don't exclude one another. We encourage them to plan times to sit and talk, to go for walks, to go out on a date, or to get away for an overnight trip.

More than anything, we remind them that a true friend takes time for a true friend.

What kind of friendship-enhancing activities can you and your spouse take part in today?

To Beseech Another with Exhortation, Comfort, and Care

I, therefore, . . . beseech you to walk worthy of the calling with which you were called. Ephesians 4:1

Caring entreaty helps give purpose and passion to life. It's easy to fall into the barrenness of a busy life, thus faithfully addressing the tyranny of the urgent while the truly significant goes unnoticed. Caring entreaty brings me back to eternal reality. Life is short, but people are eternal, and I (David) can make a difference in their lives.

Christ often gave testimony of being "entreated" by His Father: "Truly, truly, I say to you, the Son can do nothing of Himself, unless it is something He sees the Father doing, for whatever the Father does, these things the Son also does" (John 5:19, NASB).

Father, keep me approachable and easy to entreat.

Maybe such times of entreaty reminded the Son of His first day of ministry, when at the river Jordan He heard His Father say, "This is My beloved Son, in whom I am well pleased" (Matthew 3:17). In many ways, His earthly ministry can be seen in terms of a relationship between the Son and His Father. It's this priority of relationship that seemed to guard Christ from being caught up in temporal things, allowing Him to remain free to reach out in love.

Christ's example encourages my openness to entreaty. Teresa seems to have a special sense about the children's needs for time and attention. As the tyranny of busy schedules begins to take its toll on family closeness, she seems to sense the need to reconnect. Her loving entreaty maintains our family priority. "Honey, I think it might be important to plan some relaxing family time," she will tell me. "Everyone seems to be needing it."

I've just been reminded—entreated—in a loving way about what really matters.

What would you and your spouse put at the top of your list of priorities today?

A Cry for Help

I exhort first of all that supplications [and] prayers . . .
be made for all. 1 Timothy 2:1

There's an urgency about entreaty. It takes place when one or both partners in a marriage relationship recognize the needs of the other.

A partner in a marriage might share entreaty during an evening of quiet reflection or during a private time over dinner. Entreaty might be made after seeing a partner miss out on achieving treasured goals. It might be made over the burden of a child missing special time with Mom or Dad. Entreaty says, "I care about you and about priorities that I know are important to you. I care too much to let you miss out on these important priorities."

Lord, keep me open and sensitive to my loved ones' cries for help.

Entreaty is founded on mutual understanding and the vulnerability it takes to share the truth in love. It is the result of true marital intimacy.

The Bible's encouragements for prayer and supplications are reminders that we've been created "needy" of God and of others. Prayer reminds us of our dependence on the divine. Our vulnerability with one another reminds us that we can really benefit from our spouse's perspective. Our spouse's vulnerability in sharing their needs reminds us of our commitment to think more highly of others than we do of ourselves.

"Sweetheart, I'm overwhelmed this morning by all that's in front of me. Could we pray together before you go to work?" Such an entreaty is Teresa's loving way to remind me that she needs me. She needs me to appreciate her struggles and support her with prayer and attention. Her loving entreaty touches within me a "need to be needed"—a beautiful win-win situation.

We all need to keep an eye open for opportunities to entreat our spouses, and we need to be ready when they entreat us.

In what situations is your spouse most prone to entreating you?
How can you meet his or her needs in those situations?

I Need You!

He received his entreaty [and] heard his supplication.
2 Chronicles 33:13

I had been feeling lonely for several days due to David's coming home later and later. After he made it home I knew how tired he was, so I pretty much left him alone. The lack of intimacy, the loneliness, and the feeling that I was in second place to him were taking their toll on me. But I knew that if I had approached David with "I'm sick and tired of your being late!" or "Why can't you ever come home on time?" it wouldn't produce a desire to change. In fact, it would have made things worse.

Father, thank You for knowing my needs, and thank You for a spouse who hears You.

One Thursday evening when we were in bed, I felt the need to bring up my feelings to David. I reached over and touched my husband, looked at him, and said, "I've been really feeling lonely lately. I'll be glad when we can spend some quality time together." He responded in just the way I had hoped he would.

I had directed the focus at my need rather than at his behavior, so he didn't feel defensive. He realized how busy he'd been, and he wanted to make some adjustments in his schedule. He took that Monday off to spend time with me.

You see, my vulnerability in sharing my need with David was the tool God used to convict David of the need to change his schedule to make time for our relationship.

Hearing the Lord's quiet voice through our spouse's vulnerability can be challenging, but the certainty and security it brings into the marriage relationship are very fulfilling. God uses loving vulnerability in marriage to heighten our sensitivities to His voice. Our spouse is blessed by divine encouragements, and God is blessed that we've sought Him in the matter.

What needs do you need to bring to your spouse's attention today? Have you brought them to God first?

Marital Entreaty

We do not know what to do, but our eyes are upon you.
2 Chronicles 20:12, NIV

"I think we should save more money for our children's education."
"I think we should pay off our debts."
"I don't like the church we are attending."
"I love our church."
"I can't go on like this!"
"Things aren't nearly that bad!"

Father, unite our hearts in entreaty for Your wisdom and direction. We know not what to do!

Marital oneness is tested as marriage decisions abound. Sadly, sometimes marital intimacy is lost during these tests.

Married life is a series of daily, fork-in-the-road decisions that bring the potential for harmony or for discord. A good place to begin making these decisions is to acknowledge our need for divine intervention and entreat the Lord together.

Teresa and I struggled for years with typical marriage discord. But just as troubling as the discord was the pain we felt over not being able to experience oneness in all areas of our marriage. We knew this oneness was a critical part of God's plan for marriage, but it seemed so elusive. We mistakenly thought that if we could only resolve these conflicts, then we'd find oneness. God had another plan in mind.

Notice the oneness among the people in this Scripture passage. "We know not what to do" means "We're united in not having the answers." That's the start of oneness. "But our eyes are upon you" means "We're united in looking to God for wisdom and direction." Then, oneness can proceed. Together we trust a good God to grant a "peace that passes all understanding."

Where or to whom do you turn first when you have
marital discord?

I Urge You to Consider This

Now we exhort you, brethren. 1 Thessalonians 5:14

Have you ever known someone so concerned about an issue that he or she strongly urged you to do something about it? To that person, the issue was so critically important that just asking you or mildly pleading with you wasn't enough, so he or she urged youstongly to take action.

God, help us to know when to urge our spouse about something.

There are issues like that in marriage. For example, when I was going through some tough emotional struggles in church ministry, Teresa urged me to get some wise counsel from a church elder. I was losing sleep, seldom eating, and becoming very moody. Teresa was so concerned about my pain that she urged me to get another's perspective. Unfortunately, I felt a sense of threat about going. After all, the way I saw it, those in full-time ministry are supposed to have it all together.

I'm glad to report that I went and sought counsel and that the added perspective helped me a lot. But I trace it back to my wife caring enough to urge me to go.

In today's Scripture verse, Paul exhorts readers with passion and urgency. As we read the letter of 1 Thessalonians, we find his exhortation is not about minor or insignificant issues but major ones. Issues of right believing and faithful living are at stake. Saving strong exhortation for the "big" things is a great lesson to take from this passage.

When a situation in marriage is serious enough to require much more than a simple "please" or "I hope you will," we need to urge our spouse to take a course of action. When someone is urging you about something, make sure you listen to what he or she says. The fact that the person is urging you about it means he or she sees it with utmost seriousness.

What steps can you take today to know if you and your spouse need to strongly urge each other to take action?

Don't Miss Out

Warn those who are unruly, comfort the fainthearted, uphold all the weak, be patient with all. 1 Thessalonians 5:14

"Daddy, will you play with me?" The question was fine. It was Bill's response lately that concerned Janet.

"No, honey, I'm too busy. Maybe later."

Father, help me to love my spouse enough to speak out when I see something wrong.

But of course "later" never came. And day after precious day was lost without Bill's spending time with his kids. Janet wondered if her husband couldn't see the pattern he was getting into, and she felt compelled to bring it to his attention. "Honey," she said, "I'm really concerned about the kids' missing time with you. They seem to be taking a backseat to other things. What do you think?"

Next came the moment of decision. Would Bill respond with attentive concern or react in defensiveness? In this case, the foundation of trusting love made all the difference. Bill had come to trust that Janet's exhortations were not attacks or criticisms but statements of genuine concern for Bill. Janet didn't want Bill to miss out on what she knew were his true priorities, and thinking highly of her husband, she risked being vulnerable with her concern.

"I think you're right," Bill replied. "I feel as if I'm just filling my time with more things I need to get done. I want to get back on the right track with my family. Any suggestions?"

"Why don't you plan on spending thirty minutes to an hour each night playing with the kids?" Janet replied. "You could do different things each night—reading, playing outside, or crafts. Maybe you could set aside one night a month as special for each child."

Janet didn't want her husband to look back at his life with regret, but she realized Bill could do more with their children. So she lovingly pointed out that those relationships bring joy and satisfaction.

How do you think you should approach your spouse when you see something amiss at home?

Entreaty from Shared Reading and Reflection

He began to entreat Him earnestly. Mark 5:10, NASB

Entreating your spouse can be scary. We recommend shared reading as a neutral setting to promote vulnerable exchanges—another term we use for entreaty.

Teresa and I have benefited from reading together books on communication, parenting, goal setting, and sexual intimacy. As we share ideas, insights, hopes, and fears about a topic, our closeness deepens.

Lord, make me open to the ideas, feelings, and opinions of this special person in my life.

As today's Scripture passage points out, entreaty is based upon a personal trust that the entreaty will be made with all earnestness and honesty. The key to this in our marriage relationships is the vulnerability we risk when we approach our spouses with that kind of earnestness. That implies trust in our spouse—a trust that he or she will want to hear what is on our heart and mind.

Many of the couples we work with have benefited from shared reading followed by a time of reflection. Books or other writings often serve as a neutral third-party source of ideas to help stimulate discussion and interaction. We might encourage couples to take turns picking reading material. For example, this month he may pick a popular Christian book or a world events magazine. Each spouse then reads the selected material, particularly noting items of keen interest. Maybe they take turns reading one chapter at a time, or perhaps they read aloud to each other. The couple then schedules times of reflection to comment on the reading and share particular items of personal or practical interest. This setting gives couples an opportunity to be more vulnerable about their ideas, desires, and wishes.

This plan opens the doors for entreaty between the two, and that helps them cultivate closeness and intimacy in their marriage.

What special materials can you read that might help promote openness and honest entreaty between you and your spouse?

Lifting Up Your Spouse as a Person of Great Worth

He who humbles himself will be exalted. Luke 14:11

It feels great to have someone—a friend, a business associate, or a family member—view you as a person of great worth. To have such a promise of exaltation from the Lord is tremendous. But to be valued as important by one's spouse may be the highest exaltation one can receive from another human. Others in work, church, or community may lift you up, but there's no comparison with the impact of "I'm proud of you" from your spouse.

Lord, let my words and actions exalt the great worth of my spouse today and every day of our marriage.

That—being exalted by your spouse and exalting him or her in return—is one of the truly great benefits of marriage.

Our Scripture passage encourages us not to pursue exaltation, but humility instead—this with the confidence that the Lord will "lift you up" in His time and in His way. Important in such an encouragement and promise is the idea that He intends that sometimes the exaltation of my spouse come through me. It's a tremendous privilege to be involved in God's plan of the exaltation of others, beginning with the one closest to me: my spouse.

This exaltation might come from a private compliment or public praise. It might come in declining to commit to one of your children's requests until you discuss it with your spouse. It might come in a tender moment of reflection and with words such as, "I'm sure glad you are my wife, and I love you."

In whatever form it comes, lifting up your spouse as a special person is essential for an intimate marriage. It's also a tremendous privilege reserved for two people who share the love and intimacy reserved for marriage.

What words could you speak and what actions could
you take part in to exalt your spouse today?

Mary's Exaltation

My soul magnifies the Lord. Luke 1:46

We can experience in our souls emotions such as gratitude, thankfulness, and wonder. Wonder and awe must have been at least part of what Mary felt when she made her joyful declaration to God, as recorded in today's Scripture verse.

Mary's exaltation and gratitude were not about possessions or position, but about relationship. As the most blessed of all women, her blessing came through a divinely provided relationship. Her exaltation and worship were responses to such favor from the Father.

Lord, let me never forget the blessing You have sent me in the person of my spouse.

In a similar way, we who are married have been divinely favored with the spouse God has uniquely provided us. The apostle James reminds us that every good and perfect gift comes down from the Father above (James 1:17). The same God who blessed Mary with His announcement of the Christ child has sent me Teresa as one of His most special gifts.

The mysteries of God's workings are a joyous wonder, and that includes the spouse He has given me. His blessings are endless, and many of them come through this life partner.

More and more frequently in these passing years of marriage, I've recognized a touching sense of deep gratitude for my life partner. She's a partner who has seen my "darker side" and still accepts me, a partner whose strengths lovingly balance my weaknesses, and a partner who thinks of me, gives to me, cares about me. She's the partner my God has given me.

Because of this, my soul magnifies the Lord.

In what specific areas is your spouse a blessing to you daily? How do you bless him or her?

Build Up Your Spouse

Edify one another. 1 Thessalonians 5:11

I didn't realize how often I'd undermined David's authority in the home until the evening we went out with some friends and I saw myself in another wife.

God, help me to be a good example to those around me.

The husband had grounded their son and had already given him instructions on what he was and wasn't allowed to do. The mother started to add to the father's instructions with the father standing right there. In doing that, she conveyed the message, "Your father's instructions weren't sufficient, so here are the ones you're to abide by."

I was forced to look at the many times that I had interrupted David as he showed the kids how to set the table for dinner or how to help in the yard. I always seemed to need to put in my two cents, just sure that my husband didn't know how things really needed to be done. I had to face the stark reality that I had neglected opportunities to exalt my husband but found plenty of things to criticize or complain about. I realized that David needed me to build him up and support his role as father rather than communicate disrespect.

This has meant biting my tongue rather than "correcting" something minor in David's actions. It has meant giving David the freedom to do things differently than me and giving up some of my own perfectionism. It's often been important to ask the Lord to give His wisdom to separate little things from big things. I have a tendency to make everything *big*, and my complaints and criticism don't edify.

Building one another up is one of the important opportunities we have as married couples. Sometimes it's words of gratitude and appreciation. Sometimes it's love notes and special gifts of thanks. More often than not, it's the little things that go the longest way in edifying.

How will you edify, support, and exalt your partner today?

Exaltation through Priority Time

There is an appointed time for everything. Ecclesiastes 3:1, NASB

Teresa and I have found if you don't plan time for your marriage, the "tyranny of every other thing" will destroy it. For more than ten years, we have met for lunch once a week. We each made the time a priority, avoiding conflicts and distractions as much as possible. Each week we did our family "calendaring" together for the next week, including social engagements, kids' activities, and nights for working late. We noticed an immediate benefit just from both of us knowing ahead of time what our plans were. Namely, we were less irritated and had less conflict.

Lord, might there be an exaltation of my spouse through the priority of my time.

After getting a grip on the urgent things in our schedule, we used our weekly times to begin eliminating activities of a lesser priority and adding items we saw as more important, items such as a weekly date together and periodic getaways. One guideline for using our time commitments was that neither of us would commit to an activity that would affect us both until we discussed it together. With our schedules better under control and more fun activities on our calendar, we began to use our time to talk more about goal setting and dreams for the future. The benefits were self-evident: Appreciative reflections and caring words between us came more frequently.

We changed our meeting time from Thursday to Saturday some time back, but the benefits are so great that our meetings are here to stay!

Time is one of our precious resources, and how we "invest" it represents an important aspect of our life priorities. The priorities are: time with God, time with one another, time for family, then time for other things.

How will you set your priorities where your use
of time is concerned?

Happy Birthday!

*In Your hand is power and might; in Your hand it is to make
great and to give strength to all.* 1 Chronicles 29:12

My "Big Five-Oh" birthday was nearing, and I (Teresa) wasn't particularly pleased about it. I felt old, and I did a pretty good job of letting anyone within earshot know. David did his best to counter my complaints, but it didn't help. I was determined to have a pity party about the unfairness of getting older.

*God, help me to
join You in making
my spouse feel
exalted.*

I assumed David and I would just go out for dinner together to celebrate. As we headed toward our table, I looked up and saw eight of our closest friends sitting there. David had secretly asked them to come celebrate my birthday with us.

That really lifted my spirits. David had gone to a lot of trouble to let me know that I was a person of great value. He turned what I was bent on making an unpleasant birthday into one of the best I've ever had. I felt exalted that day—like a queen.

It's really the Lord who "makes great," but He may often want to involve me in His plans for my spouse. David's time and effort made me feel great, and I have the same kind of opportunities to exalt my husband. It is within my power to make my spouse feel special. In my hands lies the power to praise my husband, lift him up, and treat him with honor and respect.

Since that birthday evening, I have begun to look for ways to make David feel great—like a king. I've looked for opportunities to praise him in front of our kids and grandkids. I've made sure our home (and my heart) is ready to provide him with much-needed rest and tranquillity at the end of the day.

What a blessing it is to colabor with the Creator in making your spouse feel great!

How will you use the power that is yours to make
your spouse feel "great"?

I'm Walking on Air

An excellent wife is the crown of her husband. **Proverbs 12:4**

Have you ever overheard your spouse bragging to someone about you? That happened to me (Teresa) the other day.

David was on the phone with a friend. I had just finished cleaning up the kitchen, and I walked into the bedroom where he was. His back was to me. I heard him say my name, so naturally my ears pricked up. He was telling his friend what a great attitude I'd had over the delay in remodeling our house. We were remodeling our house, and for various reasons it had gone over completion time by several months. He went on to say how appreciative he was that I hadn't spent my time complaining, but had sought instead to make the best out of current living arrangements. He talked about what a help that had been to his peace of mind.

Lord, help me to lift up my spouse as valuable and to share my thankfulness for my spouse with others.

That compliment meant so much to me because I knew it was from his heart. David was lifting me up to his friend as a wife of great value. And believe me, because of hearing what I did, I'm especially careful to continue being a good sport about the house. I'd hate for David to have to change his mind.

Public praise is one of the most powerful ways you can build up your spouse. We've never had a husband or wife come to us complaining about being embarrassed by his or her spouse's praise.

A great place to begin in this area is to voice your appreciation of your spouse in front of your children and family members, then expand it to friends, church members, and those in the workplace.

Praise for your spouse can be contagious!

For what can you publicly praise your spouse today?
To whom will you voice those praises?

Speaking Words of Exaltation

*Speak and so do as those who will be judged
by the law of liberty.* James 2:12

Sandy and Rod desired enrichment in their marriage, but there was a bit of a communication problem. Each of them cared deeply for the other, but they rarely expressed it. They were both extremely reserved people. In addition to having trouble verbalizing their feelings, they also made poor eye contact and exhibited very closed body language when they talked to one another.

Lord, open my mouth that I might speak words that exalt and edify this special person.

After taking some time with them to address some unresolved hurt within their relationship, we tackled their lack of expressiveness. We started by giving them each a list of twenty things they could say to exalt each other: You're incredible! You're fantastic! You're beautiful! You're unique! You're precious! You're important! You're sensational! You're exciting! You're good for me! You're a good friend! You're a delight to live with! You mean a lot to me! You make me happy! You make me laugh! You brighten my day! You mean the world to me! You're a joy! You're wonderful! You're the best! You're a blessing from God!

We asked Rod and Sandy to each pick one of the exaltations that expressed their inner feelings, then hold hands, look each other in the eye, and verbalize it. It was difficult for them at first, but as Rod softly said, "You mean a lot to me" and Sandy replied, "You're special to me," tears flowed and they were closer to their goal of enrichment in their marriage.

Today's Scripture verse reminds us that the law of liberty, Christ's law of love, will impact our speech. It's an important truth that words carry with them the power to tear down as well as the power to build up.

May we always purposely speak words that build up our spouses.

What words of exaltation can you speak
to your spouse today?

Urging toward Positive Conduct and Decision Making

*Be ready in season and out of season; . . . exhort, with
great patience and instruction.* 2 Timothy 4:2, NASB

Teresa and I learned early in marriage how *not* to live married life. One of
these fateful lessons came from my trying to "preach" at Teresa. I took what
I thought was the role of exhorter, quoting Bible verses and telling her how
she ought to live. Of course, it didn't work.

I became a Christian at twenty-one, several
years before Teresa. I wanted her to come to the same
point in her relationship with God that I was at. But
my pressure for her to hurry along in her spiritual
journey did everything but help. I realized that God
had His timing for her as well as His lessons for me.

*Father, keep me
patient in my
confidence that
You produce
Christlikeness,
not me!*

I learned about true exhortation with patience
by looking at the Spirit's work in my own life. I realized that He prompts me toward Christlikeness, but
always with patience. He doesn't expect me to get it
perfect the first time, and He doesn't try to motivate me through the fear of
His rejection.

This realization of God's patience for me changed how I approached
Teresa with spiritual matters. Instead of preaching to my wife, I talked with
her about what the Lord was doing in my life. Instead of quoting Bible verses
to prompt change in Teresa, I only quoted verses that God was using to produce change in me.

Teresa and I began to grow together and became more unified. As
she began to sense my patience and acceptance, we began to read Scripture
together. When we discussed a passage, I talked about what God might be
saying to me. Each step along the way, I learned that my role of exhorter
was really to share my enthusiasm for God's work in my life and wait
patiently for His work in Teresa's.

How might you show patience with your spouse and his
or her spiritual growth?

By What Authority?

Speak these things, exhort, and rebuke with all authority.
Titus 2:15

True exhortation is grounded in God's authority—the Scriptures. Pushing my (David's) opinions or advice on my spouse may be giving advice or even nagging, but it is not exhortation. "Exhortation with all authority," as it is stated in today's Scripture verse, implies spending time in the Scriptures becoming familiar with the authority of God. "These things," which were to be the content of Titus's urgings, were the things the Holy Spirit had inspired Paul to write.

Thanks, Father, for the unshakable foundation of Your Word.

The best exhortation from Scripture is the living letter of my own life. Without this example of a life truly changed by the power of God's Word, my exhortative words are shallow and have little impact. Over the years of our marriage, more exhortation has come through example than through preaching. When words of exhortation have come, their true impact has come through the confirmation of a changed life.

Each relationship and each home looks to some authority for its direction and standards. Homes are built upon sinking sand or upon the solid rock of God's everlasting Word: "The grass withers, the flower fades, but the word of our God stands forever" (Isaiah 40:8).

Scripture is our firm and eternal foundation. During many a time of confusion I've needed direction or answers for my family. What a joy it is to have a scriptural insight or principle come to mind at just the right time— during drive times, during time alone, or during moments of prayer—and what a blessed joy to share these things with my wife.

That's what real exhortation looks like!

What steps can you begin taking today to make sure the words of exhortation you speak are backed up by the Word of God and by a life changed by that Word?

Gentle Words

Which do you choose? Should I come with punishment and scolding, or should I come with quiet love and gentleness? 1 Corinthians 4:21, NLT

Weight control is a constant battle for me (Teresa). Often, I can become so wrapped up in trying to get my weight where I think it needs to be that I can lose balance in my thinking. It is during those times that I can become compulsive, short-tempered, or overly perfectionistic. I say and do things that I later regret. I'm ashamed to say that I sometimes make life miserable for everyone around me.

It would be easy for my family to be impatient with me and to scold me for my attitudes and actions. But deep down they know that won't work.

They know what the apostle Paul knew. Scolding is hard and abrupt, but Christlike exhortation and correction, done in love and gentleness, is very effective.

Father, thank You for gently correcting me through my spouse. Help me to offer that same loving direction to others.

When David sees me going over the edge in my compulsiveness or perfectionism, he gently exhorts me to rethink what I am doing and how I am behaving. It is a release and a comfort to know I can talk to David about my feelings, even—maybe especially—when they aren't very pretty. He listens to me and often prays with me. His exhortation always comes with patience and gentleness. I've never felt put down or belittled, and I know David would never use my weakness to tease or hurt me in any way.

When he treats me that way, I know that he is allowing God to work through him. Receiving loving and gentle correction from my husband often sets me on a new direction, freeing me to have a better perspective.

How do you correct your spouse? Do you scold or ridicule? Do you use sarcasm or sharp words?

In what specific ways can you correct
with loving gentleness?

Exhortation in the Bedroom

*On my bed night after night I sought him whom
my soul loves.* Song of Solomon 3:1, NASB

Amy and Greg fought constantly over sexual intimacy in their marriage. According to Amy, every night after the kids were in bed, Greg would begin to "exhort"—nag was more like it—her about her lack of sexual desire. The result? The situation grew worse, as Amy's desire diminished even more.

Lord, allow our physical intimacy to be a testimony of Your plan for abundant marriage.

God's plan for "two becoming one" includes sexual intimacy. He thought it up. Part of that sexual intimacy is communication, which was meant to guard homes and marriages and to give couples the opportunity to give to one another freely. But God's will always has content, method, and timing. We can have all the best content when we approach a problem, but if our timing and method are not right, things don't get better. In fact, they often get worse.

With that in mind, we suggested that Amy and Greg move their "exhortations" concerning sexual intimacy out of the bedroom and to a place where they could talk in a quiet, relaxed setting. When they did this, they were able to discuss their sexual relationship in a positive, proactive manner rather than in a reactive way.

Amy and Greg made great progress with this approach. Previously, their mistake was that they never "planned" times to have sexual intimacy. This kept one of them looking forward to sex all day long, only to find that there was no mutual desire at the end of the day.

They learned to part in the morning with tender touches and expressions such as, "I'd sure like to be together with you tonight. Let's plan on it." They even began to set aside a night alone without kids, friends, or other distractions for some unhurried lovemaking.

All of this because they learned to communicate with one another in a loving, tender way.

What steps can you take today to establish or improve
communication between you and your spouse in the area of sex?

JUNE

exhortation
forgiveness
freedom
gentleness
grace

First Things First

And let us consider one another in order to stir up love and good works. Hebrews 10:24

A few years ago, I (Teresa) was going through what I thought was significant growth in my spiritual journey. My quiet times with the Lord were a daily blessing, and my Scripture memorization was renewing my mind. I was feeling particularly "spiritual," so I took it upon myself to try to exhort David.

God, remind me to give thorough consideration to the needs of others.

At first, I noticed that David's quiet time seemed different from mine. He would read passages of Scripture and then often go for a walk outside or sit in his lounge chair and meditate on what he had read. He even had a different way of memorizing. He would simply read the verses over and over again, then meditate on them.

Seeing those differences between his quiet time and mine, I was certain that David needed my exhortation in order to increase his spiritual intimacy with the Lord. What was my exhortation? I told him he needed to write something down! You see, my style of personal devotion included filling in devotional guides, writing in a journal, and writing out my memory verses on handy index cards. I mistakenly concluded that if David wanted to have a really good quiet time, then he needed to do it the same way I did.

As I tried to convince David of the truth in my exhortation, the Holy Spirit prompted me with today's Scripture verse. The first few words jumped off the page: "Let us consider one another." The Spirit reminded me that before I could exhort David, or "stir him up," I need to first "consider him." That means asking questions about him. What are his preferences? How does he learn and relate? I realized that I am ready to truly exhort David only after I have considered him and who he is apart from me.

How will you give thorough consideration to your spouse today?

Truth or Consequences

For God did not call us to uncleanness, but in holiness. 1 Thessalonians 4:7

Jim dominated every conversation he was in, no matter who he was talking to or what the discussion was about. It got to the point where people at church dreaded seeing him coming their way. Patty, his wife, could see it in their eyes. Once she even saw a couple turn right around in midstep and walk the other way. It was heartbreaking to watch, but she just couldn't bring herself to tell him the truth.

God, please help me to be able to be lovingly honest with my spouse.

One day, Patty read in the Bible that sharing the truth with others was a sign of true love. So she prayed that God would provide just the right opportunity to talk with Jim about her concerns. Out of the blue, her husband started telling her about his frustrations with beginning a men's Bible study because he couldn't get anyone interested.

Patty drew a deep breath, squared her shoulders, and said, "Jim, I want to tell you something that may be hard for you to hear. I think one of the reasons you're having trouble recruiting people may be that you tend to dominate conversations."

Jim looked at her in stunned silence, and then tears began to roll down his cheeks. In muffled tones, he replied, "I know I talk a lot. Patty, no one has ever had the courage to tell me to my face. It hurts, but I know you're right. In fact, the Lord has begun to show me that I've needed attention from other people, but that I've been selfishly trying to meet that need. He wants my holiness instead of my selfishness."

It wasn't easy for Patty to talk to her husband about her concerns. But when she did, it was a catalyst for change in his life.

What approach do you take when you need to tell your spouse something that may be difficult for him or her to hear?

Common Exhortations

And when [Paul] had gone through those districts and had given them much exhortation, he came to Greece. Acts 20:2, NASB

Today's Scripture verse reminds us that from time to time Paul felt it necessary to give exhortation to his fellow believers. Teresa and I have found it necessary to play that same role with couples who come to our conferences and retreats. It's often our role to exhort couples to face issues they've been reluctant to face, in order to heal the pains of the past and enjoy the present.

God, help me to receive Your exhortations and respond with a teachable heart.

One exhortation we often give couples is, "Heal hurts quickly." We know that occasional misunderstandings, irritations, and impatient words are inevitable in close relationships. It is critical to heal the hurts from those things through gentle and immediate apology and forgiveness. It is a good goal to not go to bed without resolving hurts that occurred that day.

A second exhortation we often share is, "Time doesn't heal all wounds, but God's comfort does." I (David) often hear couples say, "Why should we look at hurts from our childhood? We can't change the past." My response usually sounds like this: "You're right. We can't change the past, but we must look at it and heal it, because it definitely affects the present."

I tell them about my mother's controlling tendencies and how disrespected I often felt as a child. I recount a few instances when I became enraged when Teresa innocently questioned my plans. I also recount my sinful response to my wife: "I've had women tell me what to do all my life and I'm sick of it!"

I encourage couples to take a serious look at how their own growing up has affected their marriage and then to mourn those hurts with their spouse. I often say to couples, "If you don't think your childhood is affecting your marriage, just ask your partner."

How would you respond if your spouse confronted you about a past hurt that may be affecting your marriage?

Canceling Out Wrongs Committed

*Be kind . . . , forgiving one another, just as God
in Christ forgave you.* Ephesians 4:32

Forgiveness means canceling out a debt. It carries with it a reference to accounting—to be forgiven means it is paid in full. Forgiveness is not the same as forgetting. Forgiveness is something I choose to do, while forgetting is something I do not control. Forgiveness means choosing to let go of my anger and hurt. It means turning the offense loose and letting the other person off the hook.

Father, thank You for the unspeakable glory of Your forgiveness.

God demonstrated His forgiveness at Calvary. Through His Son's death, God the Father stamped "Paid in Full" across every sin ledger. Christ paid the debt for all of my selfishness and pride. He paid the price for my eternal life. Now I can ask God's forgiveness for my sin, confident that Jesus has paid the price. God grants His forgiveness because of the Savior's payment on my behalf! Hallelujah!

If each married person would receive this free gift of forgiveness and then freely share it with his or her spouse, all marriages would be transformed. Were this to happen, families could become units of soothing refuge—for both spouses and their children.

We often speak of the stewardship of forgiveness. By this we mean that we first receive forgiveness from God and then share it with others. In this sense, forgiveness is a divine gift to be shared. It is up to me to keep God's forgiveness in circulation. He has an abundant supply and gives from it generously. I must be a good steward of His forgiveness and give as He has given to me.

When I do that, my life, including my marriage, will be transformed.

What steps can you take in order to be a true steward
of God's forgiveness—to your friends, coworkers,
children, and most importantly, your spouse?

Forgiveness: A Divine Reality

Through this Man is preached to you the forgiveness of sins.
Acts 13:38

Proclamation of the Good News of God's forgiveness is what my Christian testimony is all about. That includes forgiveness within my marriage. There is great testimony of God's power when I forgive Teresa as He has forgiven me.

Nothing about myself wants to forgive. It is only through the work of the Holy Spirit that I am able to forgive. Forgiveness is a divine reality that I must first receive from my Creator. Only then can the Spirit prompt me to share that forgiveness with others.

Father, thank You for your gift of unconditional forgiveness.

I remember when God humbled me with this truth through the words from Isaiah 53:4-6. Christ took on my sickness of selfishness and pride and carried my pain to the cross. Jesus was pierced for my harsh words and snippy attitudes with my wife. He was crushed for my "white lies" and subtle dishonesty. The Savior took on the punishment for my years of neglecting my wife and forgetting my kids.

Isaiah had good news for me as well. By Christ's wounds I am healed, and because of His death I can have peace. That day the Lord impressed me with these words: "David, before you were even born I knew all of the ways that you would sin against Me. And yet I chose to die just for you. I chose forgiveness even before you asked."

Because of Christ's forgiveness, Teresa and I can proclaim that it is possible to live in harmony with one another. We are grateful to be able to proclaim God's work in our marriage, to be able to demonstrate to those around us that we don't go to sleep with unforgiveness or bitterness in our hearts. This testimony has only been possible through the divine provision of His forgiveness.

In what ways can you openly proclaim forgiveness
for your spouse today?

Finished Business

Today you will be with me in paradise. Luke 23:43, NIV

One of the most dramatic stories of forgiveness in history is recorded in the Gospels. It occurs at the climax of human history, as the Savior of the world hangs on a cross with His arms outstretched, a picture of unspeakable love and horrific agony.

On either side of Him hangs a thief. We don't know what these two men stole or how much. We just know they were criminals. One of those criminals hears remarkable, forgiving words from the Savior.

Father, thank You that I, too, can look into Your eyes and find forgiveness.

As if it wasn't enough to need forgiveness for thievery, the men who were crucified with Christ that day would need an additional measure of God's mercy. Matthew tells us that the crowds mocked the Savior as He hung against the Jerusalem sky. But Matthew also tells us that the two thieves joined in the verbal assaults. It's hard to conceive of men who were about to die an unspeakable death insulting Jesus, but the robbers also heaped insults on Him.

At some point in all the chaos of the scene, one of the thieves begins to watch the Savior. He hears the people shout insults, but he notices that this One does not retaliate. He hears the jeers and sees the hatred in their eyes, but this Man makes no threats. Instead, he hears the Savior cry out for mercy—and not for mercy for Himself, but for those who curse Him.

This one outlaw looks toward the man beside him and says, "Remember me . . . " As the thief peers into the tender eyes of the Savior, he doesn't see hatred, condemnation, or judgment. He sees only one thing: forgiveness.

Christ forgave this criminal who only moments before had shouted insults at Him. And He offers you and me the same forgiveness today.

In what ways can you and your spouse celebrate the forgiveness of Christ today?

The Freedom of Forgiveness

[Forgive] one another, just as God in Christ also forgave you.
Ephesians 4:32

David has always said I (Teresa) am a person who could easily forgive. I have always believed that to be true, but I didn't realize that I didn't complete the process of forgiveness.

Father, help me to completely release my pain and forgive my offenders.

In the Greek, the word for forgiveness means "to release." Before, when I forgave I released the person and the action, but I failed to release my pain. I forgave, but I still felt hurt later. I wasn't dealing with the pain associated with the hurt. Forgiveness means dealing with the person, the action, *and* the emotion behind the action.

It's been difficult, but I've discovered that I need to share my pain with the Lord. It's not enough just to "gut it out" and forgive my offender. The Lord wants to heal the hurt that I've endured, and that requires that I share it with Him. He wants me to tell Him about my disappointment and let Him comfort me. He wants me to talk with Him about my rejection so that He can remind me that His own received Him not, so He understands how deeply I hurt.

Once I have taken my hurts to Jesus and let Him comfort me, it's often time to take my pain to David. If David has hurt me, I must carefully communicate to him the hurt. My only responsibility is to lovingly share my hurt with the one who hurt me. Then it's the Holy Spirit's work to prompt confession or change.

If David has not been a part of my hurt, it's still crucial that I take my hurts to him. There is unique healing that comes when I share my hurt and allow David to comfort me. It is his caring words, prompted by the God of comfort, that allow me to truly forgive.

What steps should you take to bring about healing
and restoration when you have been hurt?

Looking Back, Looking Forward

Even as Christ forgave you, so you also must do. Colossians 3:13

The month of January is named after the Roman god Janus. He had two faces, one looking back and one looking forward. The beginning of the year is when we take time both to take a look back to learn from the previous year, and to take a look forward for ways to make things better.

Building marital intimacy can also involve both looking back and looking forward. Sadly, many couples look back in order to unearth painful events with which to punish one another. Spouses who do that will look to the future with bitterness and hopelessness.

God, please help us to forgive hurts from the past so that we can have a more enjoyable, blessed future.

We encourage couples to look back and learn from the past. We encourage them to first look back at conflicts and struggles from the past and identify any ways they have caused pain in one another's lives. Having done that, each spouse then takes those issues to Christ to ask for His forgiveness. When they have developed a compassionate heart toward their spouse's hurt, they are ready to confess to one another and change their ways.

Secondly, we encourage couples to look back and forgive the past. As hard as it is to do, couples need to forgive one another for wrongs committed so that they don't carry anger and resentment into each day.

Even if your spouse hasn't confessed his or her wrong, even if he or she seems to have little remorse for pain inflicted, take your hurts to the Lord. Ask God to show you ways He experienced the same kind of hurt, rejection, abandonment, sorrow, disappointment, or grief. As you allow God to pour His compassion out on you, you can, out of gratefulness for His love, forgive your spouse for wrongs committed.

Then you will be ready to look forward!

What sins or shortcomings might keep you and your spouse
from looking forward to an enjoyable life together?

A New Beginning

If you have anything against anyone, forgive him, that your Father in heaven may also forgive you your trespasses. Mark 11:25

I (David) was looking forward to a vacation with Teresa. We were finally getting away from kids, ministry, church, work, and the stresses of life.

As we arrived at the bed-and-breakfast, we checked in at the front desk. I could sense that something was wrong with Teresa, but I waited until we got to our room to ask what was bothering her. Teresa talked about feeling uncomfortable with the facilities. The hotel I had chosen was somewhat rustic, and Teresa doesn't "do rustic." We discussed our options and decided to go ahead and stay for the weekend.

God, please help me forgive my spouse, so that I am free to enjoy my relationship with You and with him or her.

Several upgraded rooms later, we were finally settled and had a few minutes to relax before dinner. I began to reflect on several of our past trips together and began to get increasingly angry. *I work hard so we can go on these trips!* I thought. *Boy, a little appreciation would be nice! She hasn't said "thank you" for any of this. All she's done is complain.*

I never said anything to Teresa that weekend, and I had certainly not worked through the process of forgiving her. I have since realized what a mistake that was. I spent my whole weekend fuming and sulking. I never talked with the Lord about my feelings that weekend. I wasn't able to enjoy my relationship with Him. My getaway vacation was spoiled because of the unforgiveness I harbored in my heart.

Teresa and I have since worked through the issues of that weekend. I just wish I'd done it sooner.

God wants us to restore our relationships with one another as soon as possible because He doesn't want us to be robbed of the joy of a forgiving marriage.

How do you usually respond when your spouse does something to offend or hurt you? How *should* you respond?

Healing Marital Hurts

Let all bitterness, wrath, anger, clamor, and evil speaking be put away from you, . . . forgiving one another. Ephesians 4:31-32

As I (David) have worked through the forgiveness process in my relationship with Teresa, I have discovered several significant issues.

First, hurting Teresa also hurts God. God calls it sin when I say disrespectful or demeaning words to Teresa. When I display an unloving attitude or am impatient with Teresa, God says I have sinned against Him and need His forgiveness. It is sobering to realize that my sinful words and behavior toward Teresa are part of why Christ died for me.

Lord, lead us to seek Your forgiveness, then one another's forgiveness.

Secondly, hurting Teresa saddens God. God feels deep sadness when His precious child feels abandoned because I have failed to make her my top earthly priority. He feels compassion when He sees her disappointment over my broken promises.

As I have reflected on what my sin does to God's heart, it has produced in me a measure of godly sorrow. It's that godly sorrow that produces change within me.

I've discovered that saying "I was wrong" is much better than saying "I am sorry." Saying the word *wrong* conveys more personal responsibility, remorse, and repentance. The word *confess* means "to agree with God," and God says my disrespect and impatience are wrong.

Next, I must ask the question, "Will you forgive me?" This brings closure to the issue. The vulnerability it takes for me to ask this question demonstrates my humility, and it also challenges Teresa with her decision to forgive.

Lastly, Teresa and I have found that forgiveness is a choice, not a feeling. We are commanded to choose to put away anger, wrath, and bitterness, and forgive each other. Verbalizing our forgiveness by saying, "I forgive you" helps us seal the choice. This choice to forgive is what enables us to put away anger toward one another.

What is your course of action when you realize you have hurt your spouse through your words and actions?

freedom

Liberty from Fear and Obligation

Live as free men . . . live as servants of God. 1 Peter 2:16 NIV

Giving freedom in marriage means I (David) allow my spouse to be different from me, to be unique. Freedom means not dwelling on past hurts. It means not being fearful about the future, but being committed to living in the present. Freedom means learning to relax and enjoy life with one another. It means not fearing rejection or a withdrawal of love. Freedom means living in liberty in all that we share—physically, emotionally, and spiritually.

Lord, help me to seize those opportunities to enjoy my wife and my family. I want to live as a free man, not bound to work or ministry. I want to be free from anger, guilt, and fear. I want to be free to love my wife and give myself freely to her.

Living as a free man in my marriage and as a servant of God means freely submitting myself to God and to my spouse yet living life to the fullest. It means seizing the opportunities to enjoy my wife and my family.

True freedom means that I can live and love liberally and yet I am constrained by the love of Christ. What an awesome thought: Christianity isn't about what I can't do, but about all God has provided. God has given me a tremendous gift in my wife, Teresa. It's up to me to focus on enjoying God's gift.

A free man is under no obligation and is not motivated by fear. Such is the Christian's heritage. God's grace frees me from the bondage of performance, and security in Christ frees me from the fear of His judgment or rejection. Because of the gift of such love, I now have something to share with others, beginning with my spouse. I can share grace and acceptance, not fear and rejection.

How will knowing you are a free man or woman in Christ motivate you to love your spouse and freely give to him or her?

Set Free!

Stand fast . . . in the liberty by which Christ has made us free.
Galatians 5:1

God's plan in freeing me (David) from the penalty of my sin was that I might enjoy still more freedom. There will be a future freedom from pain and sin, but just as certain is the promise of present freedom.

Christ died so that I could be free today from fleshly control and selfish preoccupation. Christ died so that I could have the power today to love my wife like Christ loved the church. I have the power today to forgive when offended, to give grace liberally, and to accept unconditionally. It's only because of His death and resurrection that I can stand fast in the certainty that I can give abundantly to my wife as He gave abundantly to me. There's great freedom in that.

Thanks, Father, for filling our marriage with freedom. Help me to capture Your power to live life abundantly with my spouse.

Another part of God's abundance for the "here and now" is the freedom to enjoy marriage and celebrate being with one another. Teresa and I find great freedom in learning to allow each other to relax. There are times one of us has a schedule so hectic that relaxing doesn't seem like an option. At those times we have the unique opportunity to give one another permission to relax and enjoy our lives together.

I have often said, "Sweetheart, I know the kids have been especially difficult this week and you've been at the church every night. Why don't I take the kids out for a long breakfast Saturday morning? You sleep in and enjoy the quiet." This has helped Teresa recharge and refuel. There have been times when Teresa has lovingly said to me, "David, I've noticed how hard you've been working lately. I think we would enjoy some quiet time just for us." She helps reorient my priorities and ministers freedom to me.

In what specific ways can you and your spouse
enjoy freedom today?

Our Three Kids

I want you to be free from concern. 1 Corinthians 7:32, NASB

The biggest challenge I (Teresa) faced in raising our children was trusting David's decisions. I thought I knew the most about child rearing because I'd been doing most of it (David was frequently away for business).

Lord, teach me to trust You and my spouse with our children.

I was hesitant when David suggested that the kids get a pet hamster. I wasn't sure they were responsible enough, but he wanted to use the experience with the hamster to help foster responsibility. I also wasn't confident when David let Eric help with the gardening or when he gave Robin permission to go to sleepovers.

In time, God showed me that I had to release my children and my husband to Him. The Lord had to bring unity in our marriage so that we could have the freedom to raise our kids with the oneness God desires.

God wanted to free me from some of the concerns I had about our kids. One of the ways He wanted to free me from concern was to prompt David to be more involved in parenting. The more involved David was with our kids, the less alone I felt in parenting. But it wasn't easy. I had to learn to trust God and David.

I have to say my concerns about the kids were unfounded. The hamster did indeed foster responsibility. We even went on to purchase a second hamster. "Snoopy 1" and "Snoopy 2" were fantastic pets. Also, Eric learned a lot about gardening that spring. We had a few carrots pulled too early and a few tomatoes stepped on, but the time David and Eric spent together was worth every little mishap. Robin's experiences with sleepovers produced some of her most special friendships.

God removed my fears and concerns about my children because I trusted in their heavenly Father *and* in their earthly one.

In what specific areas of parenting do you need
to free yourself to trust your spouse?

Freedom to Accept Me Spiritually

Where the Spirit of the Lord is, there is liberty. 2 Corinthians 3:17

Teresa and I met with a couple after one of our conferences. Russell and Ann expressed embarrassment and frustration over how little they shared spiritually. Their spiritual oneness consisted of weekly church attendance, sitting in the same pew, and singing from the same hymnal. They had come from different religious traditions and rather than risk controversy or rejection, they avoided discussing anything "spiritual."

I suggested a simple homework assignment. Russell and Ann were to visit quietly for a few minutes before going to sleep each night that week. After visiting, they were to hold hands and pray silently together for a minute or two. Then, as they each felt

Lord, might Your Spirit be ever present in our marriage.

more comfortable, they could say a few sentence prayers about the concerns that were on their heart. Russell and Ann were then to squeeze hands affectionately and go to sleep. The couple agreed to try it.

The next time we saw Russell and Ann, they reported a special closeness. They said they wanted to continue the "talk-prayer" times as a part of their evening routine. They seemed especially enthused about how much less concerned they were about controversy or conflict. They told us how great peace had come from uniting together in the name of the Lord.

It seemed that calling upon God together, humbling themselves before their Creator, produced in Russell and Ann a sense of freedom and liberty. Teresa and I knew that Russell and Ann's testimony thrilled the heart of the Father. After all, He promised to be with us whenever two or three of us gather in His name.

Spiritual intimacy in marriage doesn't happen without effort, but neither can it be "programmed." Why not try this talk-prayer exercise with your spouse?

In what specific ways will you initiate opportunities for spiritual oneness in your relationship with your spouse?

Freedom to Be Different

Christ has made us free. Galatians 5:1

I like coffee black; Teresa won't drink it without Sweet'n Low. I prefer the indoors; Teresa would rather be outside any time. I prefer to stay up late; Teresa is an early riser.

God, help me support my spouse's freedom to be who he or she is.

Isn't it amazing how different we can be from our spouses? Sadly, though, instead of accepting these differences, we often try to force "our style" on spouses as the correct way to do or be.

One of the toughest challenges in marriage is to accept and support our spouses' freedom to be different from us. I'm no exception. It's inconvenient at times to ask a waiter for Sweet'n Low. I'm tempted to say, "Teresa, if you'd just learn to drink it like I do . . ." I also don't like it when I've stayed up late and Teresa gets up at six o'clock to clean house. I often want to say, "If you'd stay up with me, you wouldn't be awake at the crack of dawn!"

But I've come to realize that God made my wife different from me and granted her the freedom to be who she is. Who am I to try to take that freedom away or dismiss His carefully formed uniqueness?

When I see Teresa through the eyes of her Creator, I am less inclined to want her to change. God's handiwork gave Teresa her knack for fashion and ability to "work a crowd." God designed her preference for high activity and bent toward frequent change. Those characteristics are who Teresa is: God's one-of-a-kind masterpiece.

I've reflected often on how many of Teresa's characteristics are different from mine, and I've realized that those differences are reminders of the multifaceted talents of our Creator. He has made Teresa, and He has made her free indeed. And He just wants me to support His agenda.

What steps can you begin taking today to begin accepting the differences between your spouse and you?

Free to Be You and Me

Freely you have received, freely give. Matthew 10:8

I (Teresa) know *exactly* how much I have in my checking account; David knows *approximately* how much money we have in the bank. I love to exercise and work hard and eat right; David never exercises or watches his diet and yet passes physical exams with flying colors. I'm outgoing; he's an introvert. I'm a feeler; he's a thinker.

Do you have a marriage like this? Those differences probably attracted you to each other at first, but later they can help drive you apart. I believe God brings people who are different together for a purpose. It stretches us as human beings and forces us to call upon His strength to share freedom with one another.

Lord, as I have freely received from You, let me give to my spouse.

In Christ, we have incredible freedom. God gives us limits about behavior and principles to live by, but for every loving limit, God provides unbounded freedom.

Just think: God didn't tell us what to eat and what not to eat; He gave us abundant provision and said, "Enjoy." He gives us freedom in our choices. God doesn't dictate that we pray to Him ten times a day or attend church fifty-two times in a year. He just wants us to have a relationship with Him—personally and corporately. He honors our preferences.

As we have received freedom from God, we must also freely give to our spouse. As I have received freedom from God about many of my choices, I must grant the same for David. As God honors my preferences in how I relate to Him, I must honor David's unique preferences as well.

God wants us to grow and uses our differences in marriage to help us accomplish that. Strange as it may sound, we can thank God for how different we are as spouses.

In what specific areas do you need to give your
spouse freedom to be different from you?

Freedom in the Bedroom

May he kiss me with the kisses of his mouth! For your love is better than wine. Song of Solomon 1:2, NASB

Couples often ask us about sexual difficulties in marriage. We are asked questions such as, "Why is there so little interest?" or "Why do I not look forward to being together sexually?"

Thank You, Father, for Your plan for our abundant intimacy.

Physical oneness is an important part of the marital relationship. God wants us to be free to enjoy His design for a man and wife. Here are some ways to make that part of your relationship more fulfilling:

During one of your times alone, discuss typical hindrances to a fulfilling sexual relationship. Heal emotional hurts that come between you, because resentment and romance don't go together. Increase your nonsexual touching, as touching only when it leads to sex develops resentment rather than mutual affection. Discuss sexual preferences or changes you'd like to make during private conversations outside the bedroom. Wait until you are relaxed and unhurried, then share with one another.

Freedom in the bedroom can be stolen by the sexual guessing game. Assuming your spouse knows how to sexually stimulate you and then becoming angry when he or she doesn't is a common trap. Break this cycle by switching roles. Make love to your spouse exactly the way you'd most enjoy having him or her make love to you. Show your spouse how and where you would like to be touched. Then reverse the process. Remove boredom in the bedroom by changing routines. Bring variety into the location, time of day, dress, and positions in your times of intimacy. Make changes in who initiates and how lovemaking begins. Talk more to each other during your sexual times together. Share feelings, desires, and excitement.

Which of the steps listed above can you take today to enhance physical intimacy between you and your spouse?

Kind, Good-Natured Caring

Be completely humble and gentle. Ephesians 4:2, NIV

Gentleness in marriage means treating my (David's) spouse according to her inherent worth as declared by our Savior. It means talking in a way that is free from rudeness or abruptness. Gentleness means being considerate of my spouse's feelings and preferences. It means being free from roughness or harshness. It means giving a caring response to my spouse's hurts, questions, or needs. Gentleness means guarding my tongue and keeping it from speaking sharp words or sarcastic remarks. It means treating my spouse the way I would want to be treated.

Lord, allow me to demonstrate Your gentle spirit to my spouse.

Jesus modeled gentleness as He interacted with children. In one particular Gospel account, Jesus was teaching in a house in Perea, and some parents had brought their children to see the Lord. The disciples dismissed these "unimportant ones," claiming to be too busy doing "kingdom business." Jesus rebuked the disciples for keeping the children away from Him. Then, the Scriptures tell us, "He took the children in His arms, put his hands on them and blessed them" (Mark 10:16, NIV).

Jesus didn't treat the children according to how well they behaved or how much they could contribute to conversation. Christ cared for the children according to their worth to the Father. Jesus saw beyond what the children could do and responded to them according to their value, which the Creator demonstrated when He sent His Son to die for them.

This same heart response applies to marriage. My spouse's inherent worth and value, as declared by our Savior, prompts my gentle and caring responses. If I am truly mindful of my wife's declared worth, I will treat her with the most tender care. If I see Teresa's value to the Lord, my actions will be kind and my manner gentle.

How can you begin to demonstrate true gentleness
to your spouse today?

A Gentle Savior

Take My yoke upon you . . . , for I am gentle and
humble in heart. Matthew 11:29, NIV

The Gospel writers used various words and phrases to describe the Messiah: filled with grace, compassionate, loving are but a few examples. But Christ described Himself using the words *gentle* and *humble*. He must have wanted to underscore this characteristic about Himself. I (David) wonder if He would underscore this characteristic in me as well.

Christ demonstrates the truth of His description of Himself time and again.

Lord, thank You for Your gentleness toward me. Thank You for always being tender and kind in Your relationship with me.

He addresses Martha with tenderness and affection, yet He gently reminds her that fellowship with Him is a matter of priorities: "Martha, Martha, you are worried and troubled about many things. But only one thing is needed" (Luke 10:41-42).

Christ weeps over Jerusalem as He looks into the future and sees her inevitable pain. "O Jerusalem, Jerusalem . . . , how often I have longed to gather your children together, as a hen gathers her chicks under her wings" (Luke 13:34, NIV).

Jesus calls the woman with the disease of blood "Daughter" as He heals her body and gives back her lifelong dreams (Mark 5:25-34).

And finally, Christ gently prepares Peter for his fall with, "Simon, Simon, Satan has asked to sift you as wheat. But I have prayed for you, Simon, that your faith may not fail" (Luke 22:31-32, NIV).

Gentleness is not often valued in our fast-paced, go-for-it society. Getting our own way and asserting our own rights seem to be more in vogue. But to be like Christ, I must convey tenderness and warmth. I must not call attention to myself or demand from others.

The Savior of the universe, the King of kings, and the Lion of Judah described Himself as gentle and humble of heart. It is only fitting that I, a sinner saved by grace, pursue the same for myself.

How can you demonstrate Christ's gentleness
to your spouse today?

Rude and Crude

Be completely humble and gentle; be patient, bearing with one another in love. Ephesians 4:2, NIV

Speaking with gentleness hasn't always been one of my (Teresa's) strong points. I could be gentle in how I touched, but not always in my words. Many times, my abruptness hurt David and the kids. David even called me "rude and crude" during our early years of marriage. I laughed it off at the time, thinking, *That description fits. It shows people I'm strong.*

Lord, as You show me what I need to change, help me to receive it.

My words often wounded my kids when I corrected them harshly. I used to be almost proud of those harsh words, thinking that I was parenting successfully just because they stopped the misbehavior. As our kids got older, they would tease me about how I "cut to the chase" or "got to the bottom line." That was their way of saying Mom's words were often cutting.

I was motivated to change when I began to see myself through my family's eyes and to see the hurt I had caused. My husband shared his hurt and anger about the times he needed my compassion and instead received insensitive comments and harsh responses. I saw how my kids shut me out in anger and were reluctant to share their hearts with me. I know now that they feared my coldness and recoiled in self-protection.

I felt God's gentle voice prompt my heart to make changes in how I talked. He has always been such a gentleman with me, and I asked Him to make not just changes, but drastic changes.

I now take careful assessment—not only of my words, but of my tone of voice, my facial expressions, my eye contact, and my emotional openness. I often ask the Lord to soften my heart and make that softness apparent in my communication with my family.

How can you soften your communication
with your spouse today?

gentleness
JUNE 21

Miracles from a Gentle Answer

A gentle answer turns away wrath. **Proverbs 15:1,** NIV

Fourteen hours after leaving for the office at daybreak, I (David) drove home for the night. I was angry. I was angry about people's incompetence and about how they had unnecessarily prolonged my day. "If only everyone else was like me, we wouldn't have such mix-ups," I fumed to myself.

Lord, remind me to respond with divinely empowered gentleness when I am faced with another's anger. Also help me to see beyond the fiery words of others to see the needs of their hearts.

It was well after dark when I thundered into the house, my feelings of martyrdom running high. Teresa was still awake. She had graciously reheated my dinner and greeted me warmly. "Honey, you look like you had a really hard day," she said. "I'm so sorry."

"Yeah, well you'd look bad too if you'd gone through what I've gone through today!" I blurted back. The wound was struck. Teresa stood there, hurt and shocked at my insensitive, angry response.

My wife stood silent for about ten seconds—ten seconds that seemed to last forever. Then she spoke with divinely empowered gentleness: "I can really see that you've had a hard day, and I'd like to visit about it if you would like. But it feels like you're taking it out on me, and that hurts."

When I heard her gentle answer, the Holy Spirit convicted me. There was only one response the Lord would allow: "You're right," I said. "It was wrong of me to hurt you with my anger. Will you forgive me?"

My wife's response was such a beautiful example of offering a gentle answer when she was attacked. She could have responded defensively, but instead she answered with godly gentleness.

How do you usually respond when you are faced with your spouse's anger or frustration? What steps can you take to make sure your response is a loving and gentle one?

Strength in Gentleness

Let your gentleness be known to all. Philippians 4:5

I've heard it said that words hurt like punches. When I (David) first heard that said, I felt regret because I realized how many "punches" I have hit Teresa with over the years when I spoke mean or insensitive words. I have thrown many a sarcastic remark or underhanded insult her way. The words I spoke weren't true, and I didn't mean them, but they were like punches nevertheless.

God, remind me that gentleness is a trait of the One who displayed ultimate courage. Let me be known for that kind of gentleness.

I don't want to be known for mistreating my wife. I don't want to be known for venting my anger at Teresa or for hurting her with my angry words. I want to be known for my integrity, giftedness, character, and achievements. I want to be known for gentleness.

It's difficult to be known for gentleness in today's world, as I often feel the pressure to be aggressive in order to succeed. I often sense society's message that I need to be tough, hard-nosed, and never let "them" see my weakness. And I know that many today see gentleness as a sign of weakness.

What a contrast that is to what the Word of God says! Christ Himself was described as gentle, yet I can think of no mightier man in history. Jesus told us that He was "humble in spirit," yet I can think of no one with more strength. The apostle Paul appealed to the church in Corinth "by the meekness and gentleness of Christ" (2 Corinthians 10:1), yet he was well known for his boldness and strength for the cause of Jesus. Second Timothy 2:24-25 tells us that church leaders ought to exhibit gentleness and Christlike consideration for others.

Obviously, in God's kingdom real power comes in displaying gentleness of heart.

What steps can you take today to replace an attitude
of "toughness" with a heart of true gentleness?

Inner Beauty

We were gentle among you, just as a . . . mother cherishes her own children. 1 Thessalonians 2:7

I (Teresa) recently helped out a friend of mine. Her husband was having minor surgery, but he was pretty apprehensive about it. She arranged for me to look after their young son so she could give her husband her full attention and energy. I went to the hospital to help care for the infant, and I learned a great lesson that day.

Lord, help me be gentle toward my spouse in my attempt to meet his or her needs day by day.

I could see my friend's gentleness in her gestures, in her speech—in her whole demeanor. She never showed irritation at her husband's complaints of pain or put him down for his anxiety. My friend kissed her husband and gently stroked his cheek as he went in for the surgery. She was at his side immediately after the operation, attending to his every need.

My friend inspired me to be more gentle toward David. I was motivated by her example, but also by how much her gentleness meant to the person on the receiving end.

In times past, I had little tolerance for David's physical complaints or emotional lows. There was a part of me that thought, *He's a big boy! I shouldn't have to baby him.* I've realized that although my husband is an adult, he still needs the same gentleness I've shown our kids. So I've begun to check my tone of voice and facial expression when David tells me about his backache. I've begun to carefully choose my words when I sense that David is stressed from a long day.

These acts of gentleness have meant a lot to him. I see David's pains ease a bit when I tenderly respond to him. His shoulders relax and his face softens when I show consideration for his needs at the end of a long day.

What action can you take today to show your spouse gentleness and tenderness?

Involving All Five Senses

My beloved extended his hand . . . and my feelings were aroused for him. Song of Solomon 5:4, NASB

Christine and Larry came to us for help in dealing with sexual intimacy. Christine characterized Larry's foreplay as "mauling" and sex as intolerably rough. The roots of Larry's behavior were common: He often felt sexually inadequate, and when he wasn't sure what to do, his anxiety came out in increased roughness.

We first worked with Larry and Christine on emotional oneness. We encouraged Christine to share her desires with Larry—gently and without criticism—and to reaffirm her desire to share intimate times with him and to celebrate their love. We encouraged Larry to hear Christine's desires so that he could get to know her even more intimately. We cautioned him against assuming he knew Christine's desires and against trying to read her mind.

Lord, thank You for Your divine purposes in sexual intimacy.

In talking with Christine and Larry, we sought to add more gentleness to their sexual intimacy by informing them that sexual closeness is often enhanced as more of the five senses are involved.

We encouraged Larry and Christine to involve their sense of sight through soft lighting, intimate sleepwear, and through undressing each other. We encouraged them to increase touch through body massage, bubble baths, sleepwear fabrics, and satin sheets. We let them know that they could be creative with the sense of taste with soft kisses, fruit drinks, and body lotions. We suggested they stimulate hearing with pleasant music, sound tracks of nature sounds, and soft whispers to each other. Finally, we encouraged Larry and Christine to enhance their sense of smell with scented candles, perfumed bath oils and powders, colognes, and perfume.

This couple also found it helpful to take turns initiating and leading in their times of physical intimacy—each experimenting with involving all five senses.

What can you do with your spouse to increase or enhance your expression of gentleness during times of sexual intimacy?

Favor Freely Bestowed on a Valued Person

This is My beloved Son, in whom I am well pleased. Matthew 3:17

In order to define what kind of environment the Lord wants for our marriages, we need to look at the environment the heavenly Father created for His Son.

God, thank You that You first loved, accepted, and gave great value to me apart from my behavior.

We read in Scriptures that as Christ came up out of the baptismal waters, the heavens opened up and the Spirit of God descended on Him like a dove. A voice then began to say, "This is My beloved Son, in whom I am well pleased."

It's important to note that this Fatherly expression of acceptance, approval, and grace came on the very first day of Jesus' public ministry. He hadn't yet done anything "messianic." He hadn't preached one sermon, performed one miracle, or cast out even one demon. Jesus' Father was saying, "I love You, and You don't have to do anything to earn or deserve my love. I just love You!"

That, friends, is the definition of grace.

We can infer from the account of Jesus' baptism that God felt such love and joy for His Son that He blessed Him publicly. The Father wanted His Son to be reassured of His love and grace before He began His public ministry, before He began to do the work of the Father.

Intimate relationships are founded upon first being accepted, loved, and valued—the way the Father accepted, loved, and valued His Son at the baptism. And once the assurance of this acceptance and love is in place, the object of that grace desires to "do" the work necessary within the relationship.

To give grace to my spouse will mean bestowing favor upon him or her without expectations of behavior or performance.

What can you do today to demonstrate grace—
that is, love and acceptance bestowed apart from
performance or behavior—on your spouse?

Receive Grace, Then Share It

*From the fullness of his grace we have all received
one blessing after another.* John 1:16, NIV

Grace can't be earned or deserved. It can't be demanded or claimed as a right. It is a gift, freely given by a Giver who has an endless supply.

Gratitude is one telltale sign of a recipient of grace, followed by stewardship and giving. Receiving grace from God makes giving grace to others possible. In fact, God calls me to give from His boundless supply.

We base our approach to helping couples upon the principle that we first need to receive grace from God so that we will have something to give to others, particularly our spouses. For example, we might encourage couples who struggle with forgiving one another to explore the forgiveness that God gives them. Also, we might challenge couples who deal with rejection to explore God's unconditional acceptance of every believer.

God, help me to remember the grace You've poured out on me and to share that grace with my spouse.

Giving God's grace means that I (David) give undeserved favor, unearned love, and unmerited kindness. I am empowered to love my spouse this way only when I develop gratitude for God's grace toward me.

I remember when I first understood that God had shown me undeserved favor. I remember the absolute disbelief I felt when I realized that God—in spite of all I had done, in spite of my open rebellion to any kind of authority, including His—could love me and save me from eternal separation from Him. I remember the incredible gratitude I felt when I came to an understanding of God's love, which He demonstrated to me even though I had done nothing to earn it or deserve it.

When I consider God's grace, I can do nothing less than pass that same kind of grace along to Teresa.

What unmerited acts of love and acceptance can you do
for your spouse today?

Our Inheritance

It is by grace you have been saved. Ephesians 2:5, NIV

Have you ever wished for an inheritance? Boy, I (David) have! But the closest Teresa and I have ever come to an inheritance was when we received some money from an unexpected source.

Father, thank You for so freely giving Your love to me and for me.

Each year our local newspaper runs the names of individuals who are entitled to collect money. I always check to see if our names are listed. One year, our son's name made the list. We were so excited! But how much was it? Where did it come from? It turned out his grandmother had started a savings account for him when he was born, and we'd forgotten about it. We were excited to collect our free, unearned, and undeserved twenty-eight dollars.

God gives to us in many ways, but His primary gift of grace is His Son. Even though we did nothing to deserve it, God demonstrated His love to us by sending His Son to die in our place. God loves us and wants a special relationship with us, but He can't have that relationship without payment for the sin in our lives. In fact, because of our sin, we deserve eternal separation from God. We deserve hell!

The only way we can have a relationship with God and avoid hell is by accepting the work of His Son, Jesus Christ. Jesus came to earth, lived a sinless life, died on a cross, and rose from the dead. That death and resurrection pays the penalty for our sin. God considers Christ's death a substitute for our sin. God's free gift of eternal life in heaven is now possible through Christ.

This free gift is a perfect picture of God's grace. We did nothing to deserve it, and there is nothing we can do to earn it. It is a gift freely given by God. That's grace! That's our inheritance! All we have to do is, by faith, collect it.

In what ways can you and your spouse celebrate
God's grace in your lives?

Liberty or Bondage?

My thoughts are not your thoughts. Isaiah 55:8

In the early years of our marriage, it seemed as if Teresa and I were constantly trying to "whip one another into shape." After all, we seemed to believe, if we didn't keep the pressure on, the other one might never change. How wrong we were!

God has a better way. His thoughts are very different from ours. He told us, "Accept one another unconditionally and give one another grace. I will prompt and empower you to make needed changes!"

Father, please remove my tendency to want to change my spouse. Rather, make me one who demonstrates true grace.

Couples in performance-oriented marriages focus on what each person does. Behavior dictates how much acceptance and approval each person gives. What each person *does* dictates his or her worth. This kind of environment produces bondage, fear, conditional love, and a focus on "works."

In grace-filled marriages, however, couples give unconditional acceptance, approval, and worth to one another. When they do that, each of them is more likely to become motivated to "do" or to change. This kind of relationship leads to freedom, truth, and unconditional love.

It is clear what God wants for a husband and wife. He intends for our marriages to be refuges of grace.

At times I have wanted to whip my wife into shape. For example, I have wanted to change her tendency to see things as only black and white, and I have wanted to withhold my love and affection when I've been the recipient of her harsh words. But when I've been tempted to withhold grace from Teresa, the Lord has prompted me with this question: "Should one for whom Christ freely died have to earn your acceptance and grace?"

Teresa doesn't have to earn God's love and acceptance, and neither should she have to earn mine.

What can you do today to make your marriage a grace-filled relationship and not a performance-oriented one?

Grace Liberates Us to Give

Do not turn your freedom into an opportunity for the flesh,
but through love serve one another. Galatians 5:13, NASB

For the four years of their marriage, Anthony and Cecelia had fought over the most bizarre issues. She boiled the tea too long and let the bath water run too long before entering the tub. He bounced the baby too high on his knee and didn't secure the diapers well enough.

God, show me today ways that I might unconditionally serve my spouse.

As we began to explore the underlying issues prompting such criticisms, it became clear that Anthony and Cecelia were "hiders," meaning they were afraid to communicate their longings. Anthony hungered for the verbal affirmation and appreciation he had missed from his dad. Cecelia yearned just to sit and talk, to be listened to, and to feel the investment of time in her life—all things she had missed during her childhood. Instead of communicating these needs to one another, they waged petty wars.

As our work with Anthony and Cecelia progressed, they slowly began offering grace to one another. Each began giving without requiring the other to change. Each began serving the other without expectation.

Anthony sat and listened to Cecelia. He listened to her hopes and dreams for the baby. He gave her his undivided attention as she shared her apprehension about being a mom. Cecelia verbally expressed her appreciation for Anthony. She thanked him for being so involved with their daughter and working so hard to provide for them.

Before they knew it, Cecelia wanted to change the way she made tea because she knew it would better serve Anthony. Anthony wanted to be more careful with the diapers because he knew how important that was to Cecelia. They both realized that they had been waiting impatiently to receive, when God really wanted them to look for opportunities to serve one another.

This was a radical change in thought, and it produced radical changes in their marriage.

In what specific ways can you unconditionally
serve your spouse today?

Golden Grace

It is good for our hearts to be strengthened by grace.
Hebrews 13:9, NIV

One of my (David's) favorite movies is *On Golden Pond*, a wonderful story about love and commitment between an elderly couple, Norman and Ethel Thayer.

Norman is a crotchety man with a fairly cynical attitude. He tends to look on the negative side of things and is pretty bad at emotional intimacy. His stubborn pride keeps him from having an intimate relationship with his daughter, and his prideful self-reliance causes pain for the entire family. Ethel is sensitive, loving, and a great encourager. She is full of grace. It is Ethel's grace-filled manner that strengthens the marriage with Norman.

God, help me to be gracious toward my spouse no matter how he or she acts. Remind me often of Your grace so that I may contribute to the strength of our marriage.

Watching them interact in the movie is often funny, sometimes painful. Norman's crusty persona is often a source of frustration for Ethel, but she keeps hanging in there with him. He tests her commitment frequently, yet Ethel never fails to meet the test.

I want to make sure that I am an "Ethel" in our marriage. I want to initiate. I want to go first to give grace to Teresa. I want to be sensitive and loving with my spouse. I want to hang in there even when Teresa is less than becoming. I want to confirm my commitment to Teresa frequently, even when she tests me.

I definitely don't want to be the "Norman" in our marriage. I don't want to be negative and crotchety. I also don't want my prideful self-reliance to keep me distant from the ones I love.

After all, God resists the proud and gives grace to the humble—and that includes my wife's husband.

What can you do daily to strengthen your marriage, even if your spouse is the "Norman" in the relationship?

JULY

grace
happiness
harmony
honor
hospitality
instruction

A Place of Grace

Be strong in the grace that is in Christ Jesus. 2 Timothy 2:1

My friend Lucy is a stay-at-home mom. Money is tight, so she baby-sits another child and does occasional part-time work. Even then, Lucy and her husband, Larry, can barely pay their bills, especially when an unexpected expense comes along. When a car breaks down or a child gets sick, the family finances are especially tight. Movies and eating out are out of the question. At times it gets discouraging for Lucy.

A friend of Lucy's called to invite her down for a weekend visit, but she told her Lucy would need to pay for her own transportation. Lucy told her friend it wasn't a good time and that maybe they could do it later. Sadly, she hung up the phone.

Lord, help me to do all I can to meet my spouse's needs and let him or her know how much he or she means to me (and to You).

Larry saw how Lucy's eyes lit up when she received her friend's invitation. He let her know he wanted her to go. He knew they could work out the money. He pointed out to her that there were five weeks in that month, so he'd have an extra paycheck. Lucy was ecstatic! It was just the right thing to lift her spirits and encourage her.

Larry's willingness to sacrifice for Lucy helped her exchange her sadness for joy. He showed her what grace in action looks like, and it strengthened her.

Lucy's story and Larry's sacrifice helped motivate me (Teresa) to demonstrate more grace toward David. I now look for opportunities to bestow favor on him when he least expects it. After all, marriage is supposed to be a place of grace.

In what specific ways can you strengthen your
spouse's heart today?

A Triangle of Grace

As each one has received a gift, minister it to one another, as good stewards of the manifold grace of God. 1 Peter 4:10

Marriage is one of God's gifts—an extension of His divine grace. In marriage, God has designed a three-dimensional relationship where two people share friendship, fellowship, and passion. We often encourage couples to draw a triangle, representing these three dimensions, as a tool for reflection and communication.

Father, enlarge our capacity to enjoy intimacy.

Friendship helps guard us from the barrenness of a busy life. Psalm 127:2 speaks of the vanity of rising early, retiring late—and missing out on what is most important in life.

Fellowship in marriage gives life a sense of divine mystery. The aging apostle John speaks of sharing what he had seen and heard so that others might have fellowship (1 John 1:3).

Passion in marriage provides opportunity for one spouse to "know" and "be known" in ways that are not possible in any other human relationship. The privilege of selfless giving offers a private place of fulfillment, refuge, and protection.

Leslie and Jimmy drew their perceived triangles as they answered questions in three important dimensions of their relationship. First, they drew the base of the triangle, which represented their perception of friendship. It dealt with mutual enjoyment, common interests, and emotional support.

Next, they drew a side of the triangle to represent their fellowship. This side dealt with security, spiritual closeness, and common eternal goals.

Finally, they drew a side of the triangle that represented their passion. It dealt with comfort in areas such as touching and kissing, and dealt with the importance of this area of marriage to each spouse.

As Leslie and Jimmy shared their drawings with one another, they were prompted to be open and honest. Jimmy even apologized as he commented on how short the base of his triangle was, as that represented his realization of how Leslie was hurting over their lack of friendship.

In what ways can you strengthen the three areas of your marriage as listed above?

Enjoying Cheer and Joy with Someone Who Cares

Be of good cheer, I have overcome the world. John 16:33

Joy, cheer, and courage have their origin in one ultimate victory, and that is Christ's victory over hell and the grave. The Old Testament saints looked forward to it, and the New Testament church looks back upon it. True happiness rests in the certainty that God cares—not just a little, but a lot; not with a small sacrifice on our behalf, but with the ultimate sacrifice.

Remind me, Father, of the joy in giving that others might be blessed.

When it comes to my marriage, it's always good for me (David) to remain mindful of this type of sacrifice. You see, Teresa seems to enjoy our time together most when it involves a sacrifice on my part. Giving her my "leftover" time doesn't make her feel special.

Only recently have I come to enjoy more of God's intended blessing that comes from sacrificial giving. This happened when I spent time just walking with Teresa. Now, walking will never appear on my list of the top one hundred things to do for enjoyment. The sentence "I enjoy walking" will never leave my mouth. Those occasional times when I gave in to Teresa's pressure and went walking with her brought me lots of perspiration but no joy.

Gradually, however, the Lord impressed me with this simple truth about walks with Teresa: "This is not about walking. It's about Teresa's longing not to be alone and to share this part of her life with you."

Little by little, the Spirit's work within me turned my reluctant participation in the walks into joyful, sacrificial giving. The perspiration is still there, but now there is true joy to go with it. I can still truthfully say, "I don't enjoy walking." But now I can just as truthfully say, "I enjoy walking with Teresa."

In what way can you begin sacrificially giving
to your spouse today?

Taking a Praise Break

Is anyone cheerful? Let him sing psalms. James 5:13

Praise is a logical extension of true happiness, the kind of happiness that comes to those who know the one true God—that God doesn't withhold any good thing from His children, the God from whom all blessings flow.

Lord, remind me to praise You often for the blessings You pour on me.

Praise flows from a grateful heart, and this gratitude motivates us to give to others, including our spouses. Scripture warns us not to "grow weary while doing good" (Galatians 6:9). When I (David) find myself growing weary in doing good in my marriage, then I know it's time for a *praise break*. That means taking the time to name His benefits one by one, which always fills my heart with praise.

In much the same way auto makers have installed warning lights in a car's dashboard, God has installed "warning lights" in our marriages to let us know that it's time to pull over for a "praise break." When daily care for my spouse becomes duty, I know it's time to "go vertical" with God. When giving to my wife becomes an obligation, then it's time for refreshment from above. Ignoring these warnings means heading toward dryness, distance, distractions, and worse.

The closeness and complexities of marriage require us to regularly undergo fresh infusions of divine grace. During times of weariness in our relationships, the God who longs to relate to us on an intimate level invites us to turn aside and take time to be with Him.

I often use my driving-home time for my praise breaks. I praise God for the joy of my relationship with Him and for the joy of the love and acceptance of my wife and kids. As I meditate on such blessings, gratitude builds within me. When I arrive home, my grateful heart paves the way for an enjoyable evening.

What specifically about your family can you take time
to praise God for today?

A Matter of Focus

By a sad countenance the heart is made better. Ecclesiastes 7:3

I (Teresa) am convinced that my happiness is purely a state of mind—a matter of where I put my focus. If I focus on what I don't have or what isn't happening in my life, then I will be unhappy. On the other hand, if I focus on what I do have and what is happening, then I will be happy.

Many women have confessed to me that they're just not happy in their marriages. When they do, I ask them if their focus has been on the things God would have it be on. The apostle Paul put it this way: "Finally, brethren, whatever things are true, whatever things are noble, whatever things are just, whatever things are pure, whatever things are lovely, whatever things are of good report, if there is any virtue and if there is anything praiseworthy—meditate on these things" (Philippians 4:8).

Father, help us to take our thoughts captive and think only on things that will build up.

When I feel the need to refocus on the positives of my marriage, I look at the truth of Romans 8:32: "He who did not spare His own Son, . . . how shall He not with Him also freely give us all things?"

Meditating on this truth helps me to guard my heart from negative attitudes toward David. Since God freely gave me His Son and promises to freely give me all things, I can rest in the assurance that He has given me a husband who is everything He knows I need.

As I think on these things, my heart is filled with gratitude for David and for the God who sent him to me. I am then free to see David for all the wonderful things he is and not worry about what he isn't.

What things in your spouse can you begin focusing on
in order to make yourself happier in your marriage?

Happiness in the Here and Now

*Trust . . . in the living God, who gives us richly
all things to enjoy.* 1 Timothy 6:17

A common pattern in many marriages is the seeming inability to live in the present. It's great to have special memories and to make big plans, but we need to remember that happiness takes place in the present, not in the past and not in the future.

*Father, remind my
spouse and me to
see each day, each
moment, as a gift
from You for us
to enjoy.*

When Jesus promised His believers abundant life (John 10:10), He was referring to this present life. Teresa and I have enjoyed Christ's abundance in the past, and we have the promise of abundant life in the future. But we've learned that the key to abundant happiness in our marriage is to live in the present.

In that same verse, Christ warned His followers that "the thief comes only to steal, and kill, and destroy" (NASB). How does the thief do that in our marriages? By keeping us in bondage to the past through hurt, anger, and guilt, or by keeping us in bondage to the future through fear, anxiety, and worry.

For too many years in our marriage, the thief robbed us of God's abundance. Gradually, however, through our times of confession and forgiveness, the Lord did a healing work in our relationship. As time went on, fewer and fewer of our conversations focused on questions concerning what we did or didn't do in the past. Likewise, less and less of our conversation concerned what each of us needed to do in the future.

Commonly we challenge couples to go out for a time to talk, with this ground rule: No talking about anything in the past or in the future, only about the present. We tell them to talk about sunsets and stars, about their love and appreciation for one another. Mostly, we encourage them to learn to live in and enjoy "now."

What about each day and each moment can you and your
spouse focus on and enjoy?

Happy Together

A merry heart makes a cheerful countenance. Proverbs 15:13

A musical group called the Turtles had a lot of hits in the late sixties and early seventies, and one of my (David's) favorites was titled *Happy Together.* The lyrics talk about being completely happy with the one you love and how the world is "so very fine" when romantic love is in full bloom.

For me, that song captures some of what we all hope for our marriages: blue skies all around, wanting to be with your spouse the rest of your life, and the anticipation of being together again.

God, help my spouse and me to mature in our love for each other and to hang on to that "happy together" feeling.

I know the lyrics sound overly romantic, but I like the song anyway. Even though romantic love gives way to a more mature, sacrificial love, it doesn't hurt to remember the "happy together" feeling that we had when our love first bloomed.

The apostle John rebuked the Ephesian Christians because they had left their "first love" (Revelations 2:4), and he encouraged them to rekindle their love for Christ. Similarly, marriages can often benefit from times of stirring up their first love, which can be quenched through the seriousness of routines, daily obligations, and schedules.

It's often helpful and fun to prioritize time for first-love reflections. For example, we can remember:

- Music we shared, particularly "our songs"
- Sacrifices or silly things we did just to be together
- Ways we "made up" after arguments and breakups
- Diaries we kept, notes and cards we shared
- Special gifts and keepsakes
- Endearing nicknames we coined
- Places we went just to be alone

These reflections help renew our first love and challenge us with the simplicity of keeping romantic love alive.

What can you do today to rekindle that "first love" between you and your spouse?

"Forced" to Enjoy One Another

A cheerful heart has a continual feast. Proverbs 15:15, NASB

We recently completed what many thought could never be done: a nine-month-long home remodeling, *with us living in the house.* The contractor encouraged us to move out of the house, but we decided to stick it out and hide away in one of the rooms not affected by the remodeling.

Lord, help my spouse and me to create an atmosphere of joy and cheer.

Others had told us to expect this situation to bring the worst out in both of us. But the remodeling was a happy time because we concentrated on our relationship. Most of our belongings were in storage and not available to us, including our modes of "escape"—such as television, radio, books, and computer. It simplified our life, but it also made us concentrate on one another.

We spent lots of the remodeling time renewing common interests, having quiet talks, and enjoying breakfast out. We committed ourselves to time together, to avoiding being sucked under by overscheduling. I planned my workload around spending a morning a week with Teresa, just having fun. We also planned a date night out every couple of weeks, along with movies together and frequent bed-and-breakfast getaways.

Teresa and I learned numerous lessons from this journey. We found out that we can converse better than we had thought. Teresa didn't get bored talking to me, and I survived having my library of books packed away. We enjoyed socializing with other couples more, which Teresa loves, and I grew to like being with people as much as being with my books. The frequent bed-and-breakfast getaways didn't turn me into a sex maniac, as Teresa had feared, and I actually came to enjoy being outside with her.

Living with your spouse in joy and cheer usually doesn't just happen. It demands time and energy, and sometimes it also takes some kind of catalyst to make it happen.

What could you do today to more deeply enjoy
your spouse's company?

"Dates," Common Interests, and Other Good Times

*I have called you friends, for all things that I heard from
My Father I have made known to you. John 15:15*

Friendship requires a commitment to spend time together, enjoying one another's company and finding common interests. Without that commitment, the friendship will never develop any real depth.

Very late in Christ's earthly ministry, He reminds the disciples of the things they've shared together. The multitudes would have missed most of what the Father revealed, but Christ had shared it with these close friends.

Lord, help me to give today toward a strong friendship in my marriage.

This demonstrates that the key to true friendship is sharing life together. Here are the ways Christ and the disciples developed friendship:

- They "did life" together—work, fun, ministry, etc.
- "Their" time together came first, then came time with the multitudes.
- They got away together to guard themselves from weariness.
- No subject was off-limits, which made their relationships special.
- He gave to them and encouraged them to give to others.

Likewise, we develop closeness in marriage as we enjoy memorable, fun times. This encourages us to increase our "giving" to our spouses in many important ways.

You can do this by "dating" again, by returning to some little things you enjoyed during your courtship—sitting together, holding hands, wearing favorite perfumes or colognes, playing "your" song, or going to that special restaurant. Develop common interests and take turns picking fun things to do. Share thirty-second phone calls that might sound like this: "Hi, honey, I was thinking of you and wanted to call to remind you that I love you and look forward to seeing you tonight."

Initiate! Initiate! Initiate! Verbalize your love. Enjoy hugs, touch, appreciation, love notes, and sexual sharing. Communicate how glad you are to be with one another.

What specific things can you do today to cultivate close
friendship with your spouse?

Acceptance and Secure Love

And He put all things under His feet. Ephesians 1:22

"It is finished!" The battle is over. From Calvary and the empty grave come the keys to peace and harmony between God and humanity. The God-man Christ has spanned the gap caused by my (David's) sin, and in Him I can find rest from the pain of guilt and from the struggle to perform. Just as God labored six days and then rested, so now also I can enter into His rest through Christ (see Hebrews 4:4-5). Harmony with my Creator floods my soul, and I am prompted to share peaceful love with those for whom I care.

Father, help me to share the inner harmony I have in knowing You.

Too often, though, my inner stress and turmoil spill out on Teresa and the kids. I become impatient, withdrawn, unavailable. At these times, I need divine intervention. I need time alone to cast my cares upon Him, time for His peace. Then harmony at home is possible.

It quiets my soul and eases my anxious mind when I meditate on Christ's love and sacrifice at Calvary. From the cross, we hear amidst His agony the shocking words: "Father, forgive them" (Luke 23:24). How startling it must have been to those who tormented and mocked Him—those whose futures would be filled with memories of this supposed "King of the Jews"—to hear His words of care and concern. Imagine the shock as the thief hanging next to Him hears the words, "Today you will be with Me in paradise" (Luke 23:43). And then we hear the Messiah's care for Mary, His mother: "Woman, behold your son! . . . Behold your mother!" (John 19:26-27). From that day forward, Mary lived in the house of the apostle John.

Here hangs the Christ—crucified and caring for all those around Him.

Such care reassures my own anxious heart.

What can you do daily to share with your spouse the inner harmony and peace you have in knowing Jesus Christ?

Harmony at Home

All of you be of one mind . . . be tenderhearted, be courteous.
1 Peter 3:8

Harmony attracts, just as conflict repels. Create a harmonious home, and marriage partners will want to be there. Create a harmonious family, and children—even teenagers—will want to be there.

My (David's) workaholic tendencies have often caused conflict between Teresa and me. After a decade or so of marriage, we noticed a connection between the harmony we enjoyed at home and the number of hours I worked. We found that the more marital harmony we had, the less I worked late. I found myself wanting to hurry home.

Father, thank You for bringing harmony to our home.

The journey from conflict to harmony has been a long one for us. Teresa saw my workaholic tendencies as my making a priority of my plans, my goals, my dreams, and my agenda. But all the while the Spirit was working through my striving to challenge me to actually do as Philippians 2:3 told me: Think more highly of another [Teresa, Terri, Robin, Eric] than I do of myself.

Teresa had her challenges also. Rather than saying angry things such as, "You've worked late every night this week and I'm sick of it," she embraced the Spirit's work of tenderheartedness and began to embrace the instructions in Ephesians 4:15 to speak the truth in love. Instead of harsh attacks, I heard her tender words: "You've been working hard this week, but I've really missed you. Could we plan some time just for us?"

God was powerfully working to bring harmony to our home.

Harmony comes from an atmosphere where husbands and wives can safely share their feelings with one another. Harmony is related to the connectedness we feel as we learn to "rejoice with those who rejoice, and weep with those who weep" (Romans 12:15).

When that happens, the husband and wife have become one flesh.

How do you believe God would have you bring more harmony to your marriage and family today?

An Environment of Pleasantness

*Better a dry crust with peace and quiet than a house
full of feasting, with strife.* Proverbs 17:1, NIV

I (Teresa) know there will be harmony in the Ferguson home when I don't compete with David for the role of leader. David says I have the gift of taking over, and when I'm in that mode, I "whip and drive." Believe me, that's no compliment!

*God, help us to
remember that
when we seek You,
we'll have peace
and harmony in
our home.*

I fall into the whip-and-drive mode when I'm feeling insecure over any number of issues—over finances, over what's happening with the kids, or over what David's not doing. When I fall in that mode, there will be disharmony in our home. That disharmony always filters down from the parents to the children. It affects how we adults perform in our jobs and how the kids perform in school.

When instead of falling into that whip-and-drive mode I talk to David about my fears, he helps me with those fears, and we maintain the harmony in our home. But the seemingly simple challenge of communicating my fears brings me face-to-face with an even greater obstacle: my self-reliance.

My self-reliance started in my growing-up years, when being open about my needs was not an option. David and I struggled to break my pattern of self-reliance. It wasn't easy, though. In the early years of our marriage, my husband was really no more "available" than others in my life had been. It took years for me to learn to "[speak] the truth in love" (Ephesians 4:15) concerning my needs and fears rather than criticize or complain.

It's been a long journey from self-reliance to vulnerable humility, but the harmony we enjoy in our home has been worth every step.

What tendencies do you and your spouse have to overcome
in order to have harmony in your marriage?

The Power of Harmony

For to me, to live is Christ, and to die is gain. Philippians 1:21

Doug and Pam fought constantly over how to raise their children. There were many issues: Should the kids be made to say their nightly prayers? What TV programs should they be allowed to view? Their list of parenting conflicts was endless, and they presented them for me (David) to referee.

My response to their questions shocked them: "The main issue isn't how you deal with these issues. The main issue is your harmony about the answer." Having two adult parents in oneness on an issue is more important to a child than the "perfect" answer about bedtime, TV, diet, or teeth brushing, as it brings them freedom from anxiety over parental conflict.

Lord, help us to walk in harmony with You that we might walk in harmony with one another.

Over several decades of marriage and family life, we have learned this truth: What we often think is the issue is *not* the issue. We have learned that the Lord may often use these "surface" conflicts in order to address deeper issues—namely, our own harmony with God.

Romans 8:28-29 reminds us that as believers we've been "predestined to be conformed to the image of His Son." When God works within me to bring forth the selfless and gentle love of Christ—that is, when He moves me to put "self" to death—my heart and mind become His heart and mind. And when He does a similar work in Teresa, His heart and His mind prevail, and we have harmony with God and with one another.

God doesn't argue with Himself. And the testimony of two becoming one—true harmony—is evidence of the mystery of Christ's love for His church (see Ephesians 5:1-2). When we have this harmony with God, we can have true harmony with one another.

What steps can you and your spouse take to be in harmony with God and with one another?

Don't Sweat the Small Stuff

Be of the same mind toward one another. Romans 12:16

Your spouse leaves the dishes in the sink after promising to clean them up, and there is nothing clean to eat on when dinnertime rolls around. Your spouse is supposed to pick up the dry cleaning and doesn't, leaving you without an article of clothing you needed for an important engagement.

God, through Your love help me to let molehills be molehills in my marriage.

Do these kinds of conflicts sound familiar? Small things, really. They don't rank with losing a job, a serious illness, or the death of a loved one. Yet they can seem huge, particularly when you are in a bad mood or have had a rough day.

We often "make mountains out of molehills" in marriage. But marriage requires seeing events in their proper size. Letting molehills be molehills and mountains be mountains is part of building true intimacy in marriage.

Scripture's reminder that "love will cover a multitude of sins" (1 Peter 4:8) helps us keep things in perspective in this area. The overwhelming and boundless love with which God loves us covers the multitude of our shortcomings. So we should ask ourselves, What if God were as quick to constantly point out every act of disobedience or every un-Christlike attitude in my life? We'd never get a break, would we?

The Holy Spirit, because of His loving grace, brings attention first to the "mountains" of needed sanctification in my life, leaving the "molehills" to be looked after as needed. His love is like that! Since He has my best interests in mind, the patience of His *agape* love brings gentle and gracious covering to the molehills in my life.

Freely I receive such love. Freely I can give it!

What small imperfections or flaws in your spouse do
you need to see as molehills?

Keeping the Peace

Fulfill my joy by being like-minded, having the same love, being of one accord, of one mind. Philippians 2:2

Carrie really wanted a dining-room table and chairs. For a year, Tom, her husband, had promised her she could have them. She grew angrier by the day as the table and chairs didn't come. To motivate Tom—and perhaps to get even—she frequently brought up in front of others how he was not taking very good care of them. Tom knew if he wanted peace in the house he'd have to give in, but when he did, the peace didn't last long.

Lord, help me to work with my spouse to create an atmosphere of harmony in our home.

Do you know at least one couple who functions like this? One spouse wants something—a bigger house or a better car—and treats the other spouse unkindly until he or she gets it. Even then, the harmony lasts only until the spouse wants something else. This is what we call "marriage bartering."

The worst part of marriage bartering is that even if we get what we think we want, it won't satisfy. God seems to have "wired" relationships in such a way that we're never fulfilled if we have to "take" things from our spouse. For example, when we have to badger our spouse for his or her attention, it is very unfulfilling for us when finally they reluctantly and begrudgingly share it.

God's plan for marriage harmony is that two spouses, each of them abundantly blessed with God's love, freely give their love, affection, and devotion to one another—with nobody *just* taking!

Nothing gives us the kind of security that being loved and cared for gives—not material possessions and not the affection and attention that we "bartered" for. These things weren't intended to give us security. The need for real love is met within the framework of marriage harmony.

What step(s) can you take starting today to make sure your marriage is free of the disharmony "taking" is sure to bring?

Harmony through Budgeting Time

Unless the Lord builds the house, they labor in vain who build it.
Psalm 127:1

Many couples are like Jenice and Mark, who fought often over prioritizing family time with the kids. Jenice would complain, and Mark would promise to do better. Jenice would then get her hopes up, but Mark would let her down because of other pressing issues.

Lord, help my spouse and me to budget our time as You would want us to.

Time for the family is a little like money for the family budget—there never seems to be enough to go around. Time is also like money in that it is important that we budget it. Most families budget by committing money first for living expenses, transportation, health care, and so forth. If there is any money left, they use it for the "frills." Family time budgeting can work the same way. Couples can start this time budgeting by committing time to worship, to "marriage staff meetings" for one another, to "family nights" for the entire family, to work and school, then to other areas of life.

We encouraged Jenice and Mark to review their time commitments and consider scheduling a family night each week. We suggested that a family night include each family member's committing to be on time for dinner together—with the children's homework completed, with no friends over, with no phone calls or TV, and with no interruptions of any kind. It might include a dinnertime filled with positive and appreciative conversation (no rules, criticism, or conflicts), followed by spending the next one-and-a-half hours having fun.

In Jenice and Mark's case, family nights proved to be a hit with the kids. They also reduced conflict in one major area. Jenice looked forward to making the night special with fun desserts for dinner and new game ideas. Mark enjoyed being able to set aside time in his schedule for these family times.

What would your priorities be if you were to "budget"
your time today?

To Treat as Precious and Valuable

Marriage is honorable among all. Hebrews 13:4

God is a jealous God who jealously guards His testimonies. He protected the ark of the covenant, bringing judgment upon those who would defile it. In 1 Kings 8 we read the testimony of glory filling the temple in such an awesome way that no one could stand. His presence was a testimony to Him and thus to be honored. Today, the ark is nowhere to be found and the temple is in ruins, but a powerful testimony remains.

Marriage is a testimony to God and it is to be honored. Paul speaks of this testimony as he encourages us to become one, making reference to the example of Christ's loving the church (Ephesians 5:25). It's almost as if Paul were saying, "If you want to see the reality of Christ's love, spend some time with David and Teresa and:

Lord, remind my spouse and me daily that You intend to honor Yourself through our marriage.

See how they live out a divine acceptance of one another in spite of their being so different from one another (see Romans 15:7);

Learn how deeply they've hurt and betrayed one another, and then observe a forgiveness that can only be divine (see Ephesians 4:31-32); and

Notice their tenderhearted care and comfort for one another and remember that it only comes from the God of all comfort (see 2 Corinthians 1:2-4)."

God has chosen many ways to honor Himself on this earth, and one of the ways He chose is my (David's) marriage.

Teresa and I had been married several years before I began to *honor* our marriage with divine importance. Too many other priorities had crowded it out, but after God's gentle intervention in our lives, my priorities began to change.

In what specific ways can you and your spouse honor God through your marriage?

Honored by the Gift of God's Son

*You were not redeemed with corruptible things, like silver or gold,
. . . but with the precious blood of Christ.* 1 Peter 1:18-19

The power of words is one of those mysteries only heaven will reveal. Our words have the power to bless and to curse. Only humans, created in His image, have been entrusted with such power and privilege.

Thank You, Father, for prompting me to speak words that honor my spouse.

No doubt, each of us carries or has carried the scars of words that wound—words that criticize, names that ridicule. These are "unwholesome words" that tear down rather than build up (see Ephesians 4:29). But might God be willing to use the hurtful words spoken to us to make our hearts sensitive to words that edify and our mouths more willing to speak those words?

Imagine the privilege and opportunity to speak words of affirmation and approval, words that reflect on the divine and remind hearers of the unexplainable worth God has placed on us.

Our Creator has "honored" us by the precious gift of His Son. Through that gift, He has declared our worth and value. Knowing that, how can I (David) devalue through my words what God has honored? How can I speak words that demean, neglect, or ridicule my spouse, knowing that to do so is to trample on the blood of Christ? On the contrary, this truth encourages my lips to speak only words that edify my wife.

Many couples find it startling when Teresa and I remind them that they don't have to say every critical or negative thing they think. We tell them that because we know that hurtful words can't be taken back after they've wounded their "target." We remind husbands and wives to always speak words that reflect the great value God has placed on each of them.

What encouraging, uplifting words can you speak
to your spouse today?

Being a Ready Listener

[There is] a time to keep silence, and a time to speak.
Ecclesiastes 3:7

I (Teresa) used to fear hearing about David's thoughts and plans. I feared that because I knew there were so many of them and because I knew they'd affect my life in some way. David has more ideas and plans than most people could have in ten lifetimes. When he talked to me about an idea or dream of his, I'd often sit there thinking up all the reasons why he couldn't or shouldn't do what he was talking about.

God, help me honor my spouse by listening with my heart and not my fear.

Several years ago, David and I saw a marriage and ministry nearly destroyed when a wife, out of her own fear, failed to be a source of comfort to her husband. The husband, a pastor, had returned home from a troubling elders' meeting where words of rejection had been spoken and where friends he had poured his life out for had betrayed him. In deep sorrow, he began to share his hurt with his wife. He needed comfort, but out of her own fear she spoke these words: "Whatever you do, don't quit." This man's wife gave him no comfort, but worse than that, her fearful words caused him to withdraw from her. Sin awaited him, seeking to devour him (Genesis 4:7), and the husband soon found himself in the arms of another church member. His choices were sinful and painfully wrong, but so were his wife's fearful and self-focused words.

One day David told me he felt that I was treating his thoughts and dreams as if I were skeet shooting. He'd throw out a thought, but out of my fear I'd shoot it down. Now, I want to hear David's dreams and ideas. I want him to continue to feel safe sharing his thoughts with me, but I know this can only happen when I honor him by being a good listener.

What steps can you take now to make yourself a better listener?

Wives, Honor Your "Little Boy"

An excellent wife is the crown of her husband, but she who causes shame is like the rottenness in his bones. Proverbs 12:4

Tom brought his wife, Andrea, to see us so that we could "fix" her. He reported that she tried to be his mother by always correcting him and competing with him over every decision. Andrea conceded that what Tom was saying was often true and that she was ashamed of her behavior. But she struggled with the fact that she saw him as a know-it-all tough guy who had all the answers. She merely wanted to remind him that he wasn't perfect.

God, help me to encourage the child in my spouse.

We challenged Andrea to trust God with her husband and be confident that God would bring to Tom's attention whatever changes He wanted to bring about. As she came to trust God to do this work, she was able to focus on better understanding her husband, including his tough-guy exterior. Andrea was amazed to find that underneath Tom's self-reliant exterior was an insecure, frightened little boy trying desperately to cover up his feelings of inadequacy. Once she understood this, she was able to let go of her mothering behavior and try to take care of the little boy in more appropriate ways.

There is a child in all of us. Some childlike qualities—laughter, simple fun, vulnerability, and compassion—can have a positive effect on a marriage. However, childish insecurities, inadequacies, and fears can prove to be painful.

Teresa and I have found both the good and the bad childlike qualities in each other. We struggle sometimes with insecurities and inadequacies, but the struggles have provided opportunities for growth. When we can lovingly reassure and accept each other, we experience many tender moments and deepened intimacy.

Happy is the husband who has a wife and not a second mother. A helpmate and not another boss. A "completer" and not a "competer."

How will you resist parenting your spouse and comfort the insecure child?

Not-So-Great Expectations

Give preference to one another in honor. Romans 12:10, NASB

"I *expect* you to love me!"

"I *expect* you to listen to me when I'm speaking."

Nasty word, *expect*. Have you ever stopped for a minute to examine what it implies?

When we say "I expect . . . ," we are basically saying that we are owed a specific kind of treatment and that it had better be coming. That way of thinking has permeated our society today. Our world is filled with messages of entitlement, and these messages do great harm to our marriages.

God, help me to honor my spouse by humbly presenting my needs.

Intimacy and expectations are mutually exclusive concepts. By that I (David) mean that when we get what we expect, we end up not appreciating it. After all, why should we appreciate what we believe is due us? On the other hand, when our spouse doesn't do what we expect, we get angry and try to make him or her pay.

Let me suggest an alternative to expectations: communicating your needs. When you talk to your spouse, talk about what you need and not what you expect. That will go a long way toward getting your spouse to meet your needs. After all, "Honey, I *need* some quality time with you" is a lot easier to hear than "I *expect* you to be home more."

Matthew 10:8 reminds us of God's way: "Freely you have received, freely give." This grace—the unmerited, unearned favor from God—we have received motivates us to give to our spouses without feeling *entitled* to anything in return. Abundance in marriage hinges on our never getting over the wonder that we've received unbounded grace and limitless love, which prompts grateful giving to the needs of another.

We dishonor our spouses when we present expectations to them, but we honor them by humbly presenting to them our needs.

What expectations of your spouse do you need
to let go of today?

Keeping the Main Things the Main Things

The wise shall inherit glory. Proverbs 3:35

Teresa and I recently remodeled our home. It was a special time as we drew up plans and then—step-by-step—watched our "dream house" become reality. As we went through this process, we found that each of us occasionally likes to have the final say-so. The decisions of what to add, what to remove, or what color to paint something was great fun, as long as we agreed. When we didn't agree, there was friction.

God, thank You for Your gift of my spouse. Help me to honor my spouse second only to You.

Things such as house remodeling can bring out the selfishness in you and your spouse. If things aren't settled quickly, your whole relationship can be contaminated. In our situation, I sometimes had to sit back, take a deep breath, and ask myself, "What or who is more important—Teresa or some house?"

It's been helpful for me during such times to consider the "main things." It can be so easy to get sidetracked from honoring one another by honoring the wrong things—in our case, the wallpaper or the color of paint we chose.

The apostle Paul wrote to the Corinthians about being "led astray from the simplicity and purity of devotion to Christ" (2 Corinthians 11:3, NASB). Being "led astray" is a painful but appropriate description of how I don't always keep the main things the main things. One question I've found helpful in this area is, "How much priority will I give today to eternal things like God, His Word, and the people around me?" This question reminds me that God, His Word, and the people I love all have eternal significance. In other words, they are the main things.

I've learned that renovations to a house are never more significant than the people who will call that house a home.

What do you think should be the "main things" in your and your spouse's lives?

Honoring Your Spouse's Strengths

Let marriage be held in honor. Hebrews 13:4, NASB

Over the years I've come to appreciate Teresa's character qualities—those strengths within her that bless me and others. For example, she is very supportive and loyal to me. She is convictingly diligent about getting her tasks completed. She is discerning and insightful, truthful and hospitable. Those are just a few of her many qualities.

Lord, help me to see the unique strengths within my spouse.

Honoring your spouse's character strengths is an important aspect of genuinely knowing him or her. Honoring your spouse this way has its focus more on who the person is than on what the person does.

We often ask couples to reflect on selected character qualities. We encourage them to identify qualities that exemplify their spouse. We have them ask questions such as, "Is my spouse a content, creative, forgiving, or generous person?" and "Do I appreciate his or her gratefulness, patience, resourcefulness, or self-control?"

Identifying our spouse's strengths is often challenging, particularly if we've grown accustomed to focusing on complaints and criticisms. It challenges us to look beyond behaviors and actions and seek to more deeply know our spouse. Here are two great ways to begin looking for partner strengths in your spouse:

Identify some of your own limitations and see if God hasn't blessed you with a partner who has compensating strengths.

Remember some of what originally attracted you to your spouse—qualities such as being outgoing, sensitive, easygoing, fun loving, etc.

After you identify positive character strengths in your spouse, then speak words of praise when the two of you are alone together. Then find other ways to praise one another. For example, send an appreciative note to the home or office or slip a special note into a suitcase or lunch box. Finally, share public praise. In the presence of others, voice your appreciation for your spouse's character qualities.

What specific strengths and qualities can you privately and publicly praise your spouse for today?

hospitality

Open Reception of Another with a Loving Heart

Be hospitable to one another without grumbling. 1 Peter 4:9

Hospitality comes from a grateful heart. It never comes from a sense of obligation, for that would lead to complaint, or from a sense of duty, for that would lead to pride. True hospitality comes from a heart that is grateful that the King of kings swung open the gates of heaven and declared me a beloved saint and a joint heir with Christ. Because of His grace, God has attended to my every need. He initiated His daily acts of loving-kindness without my even asking. It's this divine hospitality that enables and encourages me (Teresa) to share hospitality with others—particularly my spouse.

Thanks, Father, for the hospitality my spouse and I can show one another daily.

In an effort to encourage hospitality within marriage relationships, we often encourage couples to more often address each other with words of endearment such as "sweetheart" or "dear." That's because we believe that such simple words, when they are lovingly shared from a grateful heart, can bring a more inviting atmosphere to a relationship.

Hospitality is not something we show just to visitors or at special holiday occasions with extended family. Hospitality in marriage helps make our home a place of refuge and rest. The warmth of affirming words and tender care welcomes a spouse home. Preserving harmony with kindness and selfless giving draws us together for reflections on each day.

Considering together the exciting, fun things that happened each day allows us to "rejoice with those who rejoice," while considering together the disappointing or sad things that happened during each day allows us to "mourn with those who mourn" (Romans 12:15). This keeps us connected in the good things as well as the painful things.

That is a beautiful picture of hospitality within a marriage.

In what specific ways can you demonstrate hospitality to your spouse today?

Jesus, a Gentleman

Behold, I stand at the door and knock. Revelation 3:20

Jesus enters only into those places where He is welcomed. Only a stable welcomed His birth, so there He was born. Only sinners and the lowly welcomed His earthly ministry, so with them He cast His lot. Two discouraged disciples on the Emmaus road gave a testimony of the hospitable heart when they said, "Did not our heart burn within us while He . . . opened the Scriptures to us?" (Luke 24:32).

Father, thank You for bringing hospitality into our home.

The Emmaus disciples give insight into a key ingredient of hospitality. Their hearts were warmed as Christ opened the Scriptures to them, and then they shared tenderly and fondly with Him and with one another.

Early in our marriage, home was the last place Teresa and I wanted to be. Teresa was stuck at home with kids all day, so she still remembers the fun of walking to the store just to be around "big people." Fearing marital conflict, I often escaped into my own activities. Our healing journey into intimacy has made a difference. Home is now a refuge—a place that is warm, inviting, and secure—and each of us longs to be there.

Teresa and I have come to find that Christ's opening the Scriptures to each of us prepares us for hospitality. For years, we accomplished this by each of us reading the same chapter of Proverbs according to the day of the month, then prayerfully seeking insight, direction, and fellowship with the One who breathed the words. Thanksgiving touched us on many days; conviction touched us on others. Then over coffee or lunch we shared with one another the "warmth" in our hearts.

Gradually, as we welcomed one another in a spirit of true hospitality, our house became a home.

What steps can you take today to ensure that you and your spouse "welcome" one another into your home?

Welcome Home

Be hospitable to one another without grumbling. 1 Peter 4:9

David came home exceptionally late from work on a retreat Wednesday night. Thursday morning he told me that he was just about to burn out, that going and giving too much was taking its toll.

Father, give me ways to make my home a place of Your kind of hospitality.

I knew he'd be home by seven o'clock that Thursday night, and I decided to make his evening one he would really enjoy. I wanted David to feel special. I wanted to share hospitality, to go out of my way to make him feel welcome in our home.

I planned a big meal—grilled fish, baked potatoes, salad, and ice cream with blueberries—for dinner that night. I knew that David loves to sit on our deck, so I planned for us to spend some time out there that evening. I planned to fire up the hot tub after that, so he could totally relax before bed.

"Going out of my way"—doing a little extra, foregoing my convenience out of love for another—is often what hospitality is all about. Selfishness, or thinking more highly of my own agenda than that of another, can be a major obstacle to this kind of hospitality.

On the other hand, reflecting on the selfless giving of the Son encourages hospitality. We see Him "going out of His way" as He left heaven to humble Himself to the point of death (see Philippians 2:8). Throughout the pages of the Gospels, we see Christ choosing to give caring priority to others. His example is encouraging and convicting.

I want my home to reflect Christ's kind of hospitality. I want those who visit to feel that hospitality, but more important than that, I want those who live there to dwell in it daily.

In what specific ways can you "go out of your way"
to make your home a place of hospitality?

Make Yourself at Home

Practice hospitality. Romans 12:13, NIV

A church in Ohio once arranged for me (David) to stay in the home of a couple who were members. I don't like to do that because I feel I'm disrupting the normal flow of my hosts' lives. But the arrangements were made, so I agreed to stay with them.

This couple could not have been more gracious. Whatever they could do to make me feel at home and comfortable, they did. They left nothing out. They showed me true hospitality in action.

God, help me open up my life to my spouse and share the best I have with him or her.

My time with this couple reminds me of the hospitality I am to show Teresa on a daily basis. The message I want to send my spouse is, "Make yourself at home here in my life. You are welcome here. Whatever I have is yours." I want to let my spouse know that she is valued and joyfully invited into my thoughts and feelings, hopes and dreams.

Teresa and I first began to enjoy the benefits of true marital hospitality when we started scheduling our weekly "marriage staff meetings." These two-hour times of weekly talking and sharing helped us voice our intent to connect on a deeper level as husband and wife and as parents.

First, we saw the benefits of comparing calendars and scheduling periodic "dates," getaways, and social times. Later, as we grew more comfortable actually being together for an extended time, our sharing became more personal and vulnerable as we "welcomed" one another into challenges and disappointments, wishes and dreams. Our friendship deepened as our hospitality increased.

Teresa and I have been blessed as we have learned to show one another hospitality, and we encourage any couple to try the same in their marriage.

How can you begin today to communicate with your spouse that he or she is welcome in any and all parts of your life?

Come On In! The Door Is Open!

*Distributing to the need of the saints, [be]
given to hospitality.* Romans 12:13

Jody was a minister's daughter. People watched her every move and remembered her every word. In order to protect herself, Jody hid whatever she felt on the inside. The good of the family depended on her playing a role, so she became an actor playing a part on a stage. The real Jody—her likes, dislikes, weaknesses, and gifts—got lost in the shuffle.

*Dear God, make
our marriage a
haven of security
where we are free
to be ourselves.*

The one word Jody used to describe her life then was "fear." Jody couldn't say that anyone truly "knew" her. In fact, no one had ever really pursued her with a caring desire to get to know her. That all began to change as God brought Bob into her life.

First attracted to Jody by her quiet gentleness, Bob gradually felt a deepened sense of compassion for this quiet lady who he sensed was at times very alone. Bob sensed that Jody had built protective walls around her, but that motivated him to care more deeply. God gave him supernatural patience as the protective walls slowly began to come down.

Jody's unpredictable outbursts of rejection were difficult for Bob to handle, but God's gracious love prevailed. When Bob got too close, Jody, in her fear, pushed him away, hoping deep down all the while that Bob wouldn't stay away. He learned not to take the rejection personally, but instead to see it as Jody unintentionally testing him. Little by little, God's perfect and accepting love, which "casts out fear" (1 John 4:18), began to take down Jody's walls of protection.

What a demonstration of true loving hospitality! Bob, knowing he was risking rejection and hurt from this young woman, gave of himself anyway. This is a picture of the kind of love each of us should have for our spouses.

What can you do daily to make your spouse
secure in your love?

A Hospitable Home: A Child Will Lead You

A little child will lead them. Isaiah 11:6, NIV

Ann and Scott brought their three-year-old daughter, Amy, to one of our family conferences. Scott was frustrated over the lack of peace in his home, over his not feeling Ann's warmth and hospitality at the end of his long day. Ann complained of Scott's daily white-glove inspections of her housework. She had desperately tried to please him with her looks, her cooking, and her parenting. Eventually, she finally gave up and burst forth in fits of rage, sometimes throwing things.

Lord, help my spouse and me to share Your acceptance of one another and with our children.

After an evening session, we all went back to our room and discussed Ann's periodic rages. As we talked, Amy explored the new surroundings, touching everything she could reach, playing with the phone, and throwing pillows off the couch. After no more than five minutes together, Scott had told Amy at least twenty times, "No!" "Stop!" "Quit!" and "Put that down!" Finally, in a fit of anger, Amy hit her dad with the phone.

We could see that both Ann and Amy had grown tired of seeking Scott's approval and were retaliating. As Scott learned, doing things for the approval, acceptance, and love of others reaps a hollow victory and robs a home of warmth and openness.

Teresa quietly began to entertain Amy with an imaginary "peep-eye" game. She then reached down to welcome Amy into her lap and began to whisper secrets to her. Amy settled down and was soon fast asleep in Teresa's arms. Scott was amazed when his daughter's bad behavior had subsided.

The lessons from Amy that evening were just what Ann and Scott needed. They saw a demonstration of what Christ's love looks like. Jesus looked beyond our faults and saw our needs, and that is what our marriages, families, and homes are meant to do.

How can you begin today to see beyond your
family's faults and see their needs?

Show Hospitality to "Your" Saint

Be hospitable to one another. 1 Peter 4:9

Wayne and Julie had come to take each other for granted. Neither focused on the positive things about the other. They described their home atmosphere as one of distance and boredom, particularly now that their two children were away at college.

Father, help us make our home one that reflects divine hospitality.

Marriage is filled with challenges that make ever-increasing hospitality vital. We often tell couples that after children enter the picture, they will need intentional times of reconnecting with one another. We also often warn parents to prepare their marriage as their children approach their teen years. These can be times of "divide and conquer" if Mom and Dad don't guard their relational oneness.

Wayne and Julie, on the other hand, were being challenged with the "empty nest" stage, and they needed an increasing sense of warmth that comes through hospitality. We worked with this couple on restoring an inviting, open relationship, taking the following three steps:

Keeping a journal of gratefulness. We encouraged Wayne and Julie to take one month and keep a written record of how God blessed them through one another. We instructed them to enter the date, how they were blessed, and how they showed appreciation. This focus on blessings was to help them overcome critical attitudes, which helped them show appreciation for one another.

Expressing private praise. We asked Wayne and Julie to focus on one another's character strengths. During quiet reflective times, they were to move toward one another with touch and eye contact, then verbalize their appreciation and love to one another.

Asking about needs. We encouraged this couple to ask one another lovingly how they could be better helpmates to one another.

Wayne and Julie took these challenges seriously and are now actively involved in helping other couples. Do the same as you take these steps.

What steps can you take today to reestablish
marital hospitality in your relationship?

Equipping for Life through Words and Examples

The purpose of the commandment is love from a pure heart. 1 Timothy 1:5

Teresa and I had been married almost ten years and had two children. I was reading and studying everything I could find on the Christian life. I tried every way imaginable to get my family as excited as I was. Then I heard a conference speaker adapt a familiar saying to the Christian home: "Your wife and kids don't care how much you know until they know how much you care." I slowed down on trying to "know" everything and focused more on caring.

Thanks, Father, for the instructions that You give through Your Word.

That seems to be a part of what the apostle Paul is reminding Timothy in this verse. Paul reminds us, too, that the whole reason for the truth of the gospel is to point others toward a love relationship with God. The purpose of the Word is to promote God's love among His people.

With the background of 1 Timothy, as I try to meet my wife's need for instruction I must first examine my own heart. Are my words of instruction for her benefit or for mine? Are my words of instruction going to point her toward a more loving relationship with God or one of His people? Are my words of instruction coming from a pure heart, with a good conscience and a sincere faith?

Keeping this kind of standard has helped me hold my tongue on many occasions. But keeping this standard has allowed me to avoid hurting my wife and has brought her instead to a stronger love for me and our Lord. As we have truly applied the guidelines of the apostle Paul, Teresa and I have helped equip one another for life with our words and our example.

Have you thoroughly examined your heart before giving instructions to your spouse? Have you looked at God's instructions and looked closely for evidence of His loving heart toward you?

AUGUST

instruction
intimacy
kindness
leadership
love

Instruction Says, "Follow Me!"

As You sent Me into the world, I also have sent them. John 17:18

Paul's parents referred him to me (David) after he had repeatedly sneaked out of his bedroom to join his friends for a night of mischief and pranks. Of most concern to his parents was that Paul refused to accept responsibility for his actions. "We want him to see the wrong of his actions and apologize for the worry and sleepless nights he's caused us," they insisted. But Paul wouldn't budge. He only regretted that he had gotten caught.

Father, keep me mindful of the example I set for others.

In one family session, I asked Paul, "When is the last time someone apologized in your family?" The silence was telling. His parents squirmed on the couch. Finally Paul responded, "The adults don't ever have to apologize, only the kids. I've never even heard Mom or Dad apologize to each other." We were all reminded that day that example is the best teacher.

Christ did not say, "Do as I say, not as I do." His instruction was first and foremost through His life and His example. This is a part of the meaning behind Jesus' prayer in John 17. He prayed out loud so the disciples could hear His interactions with the Father. He wanted them to know that just as God had sent Him into the world, He was sending them out. Christ confirmed His life as an example to the disciples and then encouraged them to follow that example.

In our marriages one of the most effective tools for instruction is example. As I live to please and honor our heavenly Father and concentrate on the changes He wants to make in me, I communicate this positive message to my spouse: "Follow me in this area because God is doing a great work."

In what areas do you need to give better instruction by being a better example to your spouse and to your children?

A Bad Attitude

Let this mind be in you which was also in Christ Jesus.
Philippians 2:5

Sometimes I (Teresa) only half listen to David when he tries to instruct me. My attitude is often that I know more than he does about a particular topic, so I mentally turn him off, nod my head, and let the words go in one ear and out the other. At other times I interrupt him in the middle of his sentence to correct him or tell him my opinion on the matter. Or if we're in the middle of a project that has its own instructions, I may pick them up to see if he's doing the project "right."

Lord, develop in me an attitude that willingly receives instruction.

At times, I have hurt David with this know-it-all approach and driven a wedge between us. I have also hurt the Savior with my bad attitude. I know this is definitely not the mind of Christ.

The Savior's position was very different from mine because He definitely "knew it all." His *attitude* was also radically different from mine. Jesus didn't tune out the woman at the well when she asked Him about living water. He didn't interrupt Nicodemus when he asked Him about eternal life. Even though Christ knew all there was to know about these topics, He humbled Himself and lovingly responded to each situation.

I've learned that as I give up my know-it-all attitude and allow David to instruct me, he ends up asking questions to see what I already know. When he senses my teachable heart, he wants to give me respect and consideration. When I trust his judgment and allow him to give me feedback and input, he is more likely to offer assistance. It's my *attitude* that greatly affects our closeness.

In what specific areas can you really use your spouse's instruction, and what steps do you need to take to learn to accept that instruction?

Listen When He Says "No"

Let the little children come to me . . . for the kingdom of heaven belongs to such as these. Matthew 19:14, NIV

On several occasions throughout Scripture, Christ calls us to become like little children. In fact, in this passage in Matthew, He tells us that our ability to enter the kingdom of heaven depends upon our childlike trust in God.

I (Teresa) have realized that it's important for me to have the faith of a child, but not all of the "childlike" characteristics. You see, when it comes to receiving instruction, I've sometimes behaved like a toddler. When our son, Eric, was about two years old, he would absolutely lose control if you told him "no." It didn't matter if you were pulling him out of a dangerous situation or setting a limit on the amount of candy he ate—Eric hated to be told he couldn't do something.

Thank You, Father, for Your willingness to tell me "no" when it is for Your benefit or for mine.

I know there have been times when I've acted much the same way Eric acted as a toddler. When God told me it wasn't the right time to leave a very unhealthy church situation, I became enraged and was angry with God for a long time. When David hasn't agreed with my preferences on spending money or with my timing for big purchases, I've become irritated.

If I carefully consider why God tells me "no," I will respond with much more gratitude. God has shown me that if He tells me "no" or "not now," it's because He loves me and wants the best for me. When I had to pull Eric out of dangerous situations or limit his candy consumption, I did it because I loved him and didn't want to see him hurt. God's love is just like that.

For that reason, I need to listen when He says "no."

In what situations might God be telling you "no" right now? How does He use your spouse to communicate His "no" answer?

That Which Hurts, Instructs

He who heeds the word wisely will find good. Proverbs 16:20

It has been said that there are three rings in marriage: the engagement *ring*, the wedding *ring*, and the suffe*ring*. Many of us become disillusioned when we encounter the difficulties and problems inherent in married life. When we hurt, many of us tend to believe that something is horribly wrong with our marriage.

God, help me to face my marital difficulties and accept them as tools You use to teach me.

Let me (David) argue just the opposite. By its very nature marriage is difficult, and facing those difficulties is often painful. Yet we can learn from the pain if we allow ourselves to.

Teresa and I have had difficulties in many areas of our marriage. One of those areas is my selfishness. Over the years I have hurt Teresa many times through my lack of attention to her needs. The Lord began to get my attention about my selfishness. Through His Word, He impressed me that I was to do nothing out of selfishness, but to consider Teresa more important than myself.

One morning when I was fixing a cup of coffee for myself, the Lord prompted me with a thought I'd never had before: *David, why don't you take Teresa a cup of coffee too?* It had never dawned on me that I could make Teresa a cup of coffee in the morning.

I'll never forget the look on Teresa's face that morning. She was thankful but shocked. The teary mist in her eyes told me that God had helped me meet an important need in my wife's life. That motivated me to try it again.

Teresa and I still struggle over my selfishness, but as I have paid attention to and obeyed God's Word, my selfishness has decreased. That has only happened as I've accepted difficulties as one of God's ways of teaching me.

What difficulties in your marriage might God be using
to teach you right now?

I Can't Be Out of Money Yet!

Listen to counsel and receive instruction. Proverbs 19:20

Handling finances is a difficult area for most couples, and David and I are no exception. We've discovered that we can both benefit from instruction from one another in the area of finances.

God has blessed me with a good organizational mind. I can keep track of the checkbook and our household bills without a glitch. David, on the other hand, has difficulty *finding* his checkbook, much less keeping it balanced. We've discovered that by allowing me to handle the monthly bills and household expenses, our family finances run smoothly. I am able to give David instruction about the status of our monthly progress and keep track of all the regular payments.

God, help me to be open to my spouse's instruction so that we can grow together in wisdom.

God has blessed me with a husband who enjoys handling the other finances for our family. I have little understanding—and sometimes little interest—in how the stock market works or in how our retirement plans are structured. But because of David's work on our "big" finances, we are now in the best shape we can be in.

In recent years David has taken more of an interest in showing me the financial ins and outs of our life. He cares enough about me and our family to teach me the things I need to know as his spouse. I don't worry about the future as much because I know the structure of our finances.

God wants us to lovingly instruct our spouses in the things we have learned so that we can mature individually and as a couple. Receiving instruction from one another is one way we grow in wisdom.

In what specific areas does your spouse have more expertise than you? What steps can you take to begin receiving instruction from him or her in those areas?

Instructive Encounters

All Scripture is God-breathed and is useful for teaching, rebuking, correcting and training in righteousness, so that the man of God may be thoroughly equipped for every good work. 2 Timothy 3:16-17, NIV

Amy and Paul came to one of our conferences frustrated by their lack of spiritual oneness. They had only recently made individual commitments to the Lord and become active in a local church. Neither came from a spiritual background, so they were hungry to make up for lost time. We began by encouraging them to read God's Word.

Instruct us, Father, in Your Word.

During a review of Scripture, Amy and Paul noted that believers have the opportunity to hear the Word from others. The book of Colossians tells us that when we read and study the Word for ourselves, we can become Christ's messengers (3:16). The book of Revelation says the ones who read the Word and take it to heart are blessed (1:3), and the book of Acts affirms a certain group of believers for examining the Scriptures every day (17:11).

Finally, Amy and Paul noted that we are given the chance to memorize and meditate on God's Word. Psalms tells us that living out and memorizing God's Word can keep our way pure (119:9-11). The book of Joshua says if we are careful to meditate on God's Word and then live it out, we will be prosperous and successful (1:8).

Paul and Amy were astounded at the promises associated with spending time in God's Word. Each was challenged to review their weekly schedule and look for places to insert encounters with God's Word. Amy decided to plan a short time of meditation before bed. Paul chose to allot a weekly time for intense personal study of the Bible. They committed to meet weekly to share their experiences in God's Word with one another.

Paul and Amy developed such a heart for the Bible that they later went on to seminary and then the mission field.

What steps can you and your spouse take to daily spend
time in God's Word?

Deep Sharing and Communion

Thou . . . art intimately acquainted with all my ways.
Psalm 139:3, NASB

The Scriptures give us three key dimensions of intimate relationships. These three dimensions are important for our relationships with God and with other people.

First, Jeremiah 1:5 tells us that before God formed us in our mother's womb, He *knew* us. The Hebrew word for this kind of "knowing" is *yada,* which is defined as a deep, personal awareness and understanding. This passage tells us that God created each one of us and knows us individually. The word *yada* tells us that God has made an investment to know us and a choice to understand us.

Father, deepen my longing for intimacy with You and prompt my heart as I develop more intimacy with my spouse.

The second Hebrew word associated with intimacy is *sod,* which means to reveal or to disclose. Proverbs 3:32 tells us that God is *intimate* with the upright, that He reveals Himself to those who are in right standing with Him.

The third Hebrew word for intimacy is *sakan,* which means a beneficial or caring involvement. The psalmist reflects on God's heart when he writes, "Thou . . . art intimately acquainted with all my ways" (Psalm 139:3, NASB). He's saying that God knows him so that He can care about him in tangible ways. This word speaks to the motive behind the involvement. Does God want to get to know me because He wants to judge me or condemn me? No! God wants to be intimately acquainted with me so that He can be caringly involved in my life.

In summary, the three Hebrew words tell us that to establish an intimate relationship with someone you must (1) get to know that person, (2) let that person get to know you, and (3) become caringly involved with one another. What a terrific goal for marriage!

What can you do today to begin getting to know your spouse, let him or her get to know you, and become caringly involved with one another?

Intimacy Is to Know Me

O Lord . . . you know me. Psalm 139:1, NIV

The psalmist in this passage is expressing the sheer wonder that God knows him and still loves him. He marvels at how intricately God knows and understands his heart, mind, thoughts, and actions.

Father, thank You for knowing me and my spouse. Give me Your perspective as I admire the beauty of my spouse.

Ephesians tells us that we are God's workmanship, or handiwork, and that He has studied and admired His creation. As our Creator, God knows our strengths, weaknesses, moods, needs, preferences, and desires. He looks at what He's made, and He likes what He sees.

Ephesians 2:10 tells us how God sees His creation. Ephesians says that we are His workmanship, created in Christ Jesus for good works. This word *workmanship* actually comes from a Greek word meaning "poetry." So in essence, we are God's poetry. He made each of us unique, exactly as He wanted us to be.

Your spouse is God's poetry, a reflection of His creativity and handiwork. We would encourage you to spend some time in prayer and ask God to give you His eyes and show you what He sees when He looks at your spouse. Ask God to show you the beautiful intricacies of His design. Ask Him to capture your heart with the beauty of His poetry: your spouse.

This may sound a little weird because we don't often think of our spouse as beautiful poetry, especially when we've been married for a while and the flaws and imperfections seem to overshadow any view of God's masterpiece. But Teresa and I would encourage you to ask God to give you a renewed view of the beauty in your spouse. He knows your spouse intimately and loves His work. Ask Him to give you the same view.

What can you see as unique and beautiful
in your spouse today?

A Pure Choice

Let the husband render to his wife the affection due her, and likewise also the wife to her husband. 1 Corinthians 7:3

David and I married so young that we had no concept of giving to meet each other's needs. We tried to grow up and stay married at the same time. Years later I had become emotionally dead over the hurts that had occurred between us. I didn't feel much of anything for David, much less intimacy.

Thank You, God, for knowing what's best for us and providing instruction in how to keep intimacy in marriage.

One day David asked me how I felt toward him, and all I could say was, "I don't feel anything. I just feel dead on the inside." I wasn't trying to be mean or hurtful. I truly felt numb. I know now that over the years the hurt had accumulated so much that I just stopped being able to feel. My heart for David had almost become anesthetized by the pain from the past. I couldn't feel the positive emotions anymore. I knew I was supposed to feel warm, tender, and affectionate toward my husband, but those feelings just weren't there.

During this period I knew I wasn't supposed to withhold myself sexually from David. In obedience to God and for the sake of our marriage, I had to make sure that our sexual intimacy continued. There were times, though, when it was purely a choice on my part to give. I chose to give to David even when the feelings weren't there yet.

The process of healing the hurts from the past was a lengthy one. And as David and I learned how to heal those hurts, God has honored His promise to bring back the feelings of love and passion. Today, I want sexual intimacy with my husband, and this desire is out of my desire to give and to receive.

What can you do to keep intimacy alive in your marriage, even when times are tough?

Intimacy or Interruption?

You will know the truth, and the truth will set you free.
John 8:32, NIV

Sherry and Mark came to one of our conferences for some marriage enrichment. They were very articulate and intelligent people. They asked to see David and me after the conference for some private consultation.

Father, show me how You want my heart to change so my marriage can become more intimate.

Sherry started by saying that she had heard we had "fixed" other husbands, and hers needed it badly. As we began to explore with Mark, he was barely able to offer an opening sentence before Sherry interrupted him. We attempted to ask Mark how it felt to have his wife interrupt him, but she interrupted again.

After a few minutes of negotiations and guidelines for our discussion, Sherry got her chance to talk about her feelings. She expressed feeling alone in their marriage much of the time. She said that when she came to Mark with her deepest feelings, he was either too busy or too tired to listen to her. She needed his attention and comfort, and he wasn't giving it.

We discussed how the word *intimacy* comes from the root word *innermost* and relates to a vulnerable sharing of one's inner thoughts, feelings, and self. We suggested that both Sherry and Mark needed to feel secure in this kind of sharing, confident that they would find support in one another through listening, empathy, and reassurance.

We identified hurts between Sherry and Mark and helped them through their confession and forgiveness. Sherry became free to listen, and Mark became free to respond with warmth and interest.

Sherry and Mark are like many of us. We may be the most articulate, intelligent people in the world, but without a heart that is submissive to God and to one another, we will never enjoy deep marital intimacy.

What steps can you take today to bring into your marriage
the security it takes to enjoy true intimacy?

Super Marital Bliss?

*If we walk in the light as He is in the light, we have
fellowship with one another.* 1 John 1:7, NASB

I (David) have to laugh when I thumb through some of the marital self-help books. To hear various authors tell it, super marital bliss is available to anyone who wants it—anytime and all the time.

God, help me give up unrealistic notions about marital intimacy and instead consistently live in the light of Your Word when it comes to my marriage.

To be honest, some days I feel lucky if I can pull off being semidecent to Teresa. Maybe I am setting my sights too low, but I tend to believe that the bill of goods many of the marriage self-help books contain is misleading. Super marital bliss is a pipe dream. We will never be completely and constantly intimate with our spouses. That possibility was lost when Adam and Eve sinned in the Garden.

Discouraging? It doesn't need to be. A deep, consistent, intimate relationship with your spouse is possible. The key to this kind of fellowship and intimacy with your spouse is found in today's Scripture verse. It's found in asking yourself, "Am I walking in the light of His Word?" Teresa and I can have consistent fellowship when we both live out the principles of God's Word.

It makes sense if you think about it. We have fellowship when, as Ephesians 4:15 tells us, we speak the truth in love to one another. We have intimacy when we are living out James 5:16, which tells us to confess our sins to one another and pray for one another. We have marital bliss when, as the book of Romans tells us, we show equal care and comfort to one another and accept one another. True intimacy is possible when we are both walking in the light—the light of His Word.

How can you and your spouse make the Word of God
central to the marital intimacy you long to enjoy?

The Two Become One

*A man shall leave his father and mother . . . and
they shall become one flesh. Genesis 2:24*

Our marriage looks a lot different now than it did when we first started out.
Time erodes idealism and exposes the futility of the world's shallowness. It
didn't take us long to see what our sin nature looks like—not only in each
other but in ourselves as well.

*Lord, bind us
together as a
married couple.
Help us to identify
the Scriptures
You want us to
live out so that we
can draw closer
and increase our
intimacy.*

David and I have learned that when we aren't
getting along, it's because we aren't living out a portion of God's Word. We aren't walking in the light
that brings fellowship with one another. When we
have these breaks in fellowship or have conflict, we
spend time alone and ask God what Bible verses He
would like us to be living out.

Many times in the past we've discovered that
conflicts have occurred in our marriage because we
weren't free to live out Genesis 2:24. David and I discovered that it was one thing to physically leave our
father and mother, but quite another to emotionally
leave them and cleave to one another. We left the
panhandle of Texas when we were married at the age
of sixteen, but it has taken us decades to emotionally leave our parents. It
has taken us years to identify the hurts from our childhood and heal them
so that we can be free to become united with one another.

As we have done this, we have seen the ugliness of sin and the beauty
of Christ in our lives. Though we have far to go, God has given us a love for
each other by which we can hope all things, believe all things, and endure
all things.

What Scriptures can you live out in order to increase
your closeness and intimacy with your spouse?

The Intimacy of Romance

I found him whom my soul loves; I held on to him and would not let him go. Song of Solomon 3:4, NASB

"I don't feel anything at all. I just feel numb." Ken and Donna's romance was gone, and mere existence had replaced it long ago. It was a rough journey with their mentor couple, but old wounds were opened up and the painful healing process began. Serious childhood traumas needed attention, but Ken and Donna persevered until, little by little, hope returned.

Keeping romance alive or rekindling it is essential for intimacy and abundance in marriage. At the appropriate time in their marriage journey, we encourage couples to reflect and talk about romance. This helps open up needed areas of vulnerability. We suggest that couples reminisce about their courtship and talk about their first date and early romance. We ask couples to think about the silly, fun times they had together. We encourage them to remember their

Thank You, Father, for romantic love. Help me to be sensitive to my spouse's desires for more romance.

favorite songs, dancing together, and their honeymoon fun. We even suggest that couples ask one another this question: "From your point of view, how could we improve our marriage romance?"

We encouraged Ken to slip a love note in Donna's purse or shop for a personal gift for her. We suggested that he surprise her with flowers or a picnic for the two of them. We encouraged Donna to take the lead in verbalizing love and giving compliments. We asked her to be the first to express affection, to initiate fun activities, and to plan a candlelit dinner at home alone.

As Ken and Donna diligently put old things behind them and pressed on together, they enjoyed new intimacy.

What act of romance can you do today to help keep the romance alive—or rekindle it—in your marriage?

kindness

Pleasant and Gracious Servanthood

Be kind to one another, tenderhearted. Ephesians 4:32

True kindness springs from a tender heart, a heart that has been softened by God's quiet love. Kindness is betrayed by roughness and stoic indifference. It is not genuine when strings are attached, and never does it call attention to itself.

Father, soften my heart that my spouse might see the depth of my feeling through acts of kindness.

In marriage, kindness means doing the *right things*—like bringing flowers and remembering anniversaries—and doing these things with the tenderness of a caring heart. Kindness means having a pleasant attitude when helping your spouse with a project. It means talking to one another with words that are gentle rather than sharp, tender rather than harsh. Kindness means showing mercy and sympathy. It means looking for opportunities to serve our spouse and show him or her tender care.

God showed us the ultimate act of kindness when He stooped down from heaven to serve us in the person of His Son. He has vulnerably revealed the loveliness of His heart by giving Christ in our stead. He used His strength and might for our protection and redemption, but He demonstrated His kindness daily.

We men have believed a lie. Society has convinced us that to be tender is to be weak, that to show kindness is to be less than a man. But the Savior of the universe, who battled through the gates of hell, modeled real manhood for us, and He did it through kindness.

The Savior showed kindness as He knelt before His twelve disciples and gently washed their feet. On the eve of His death, Jesus wanted His last moments with them to include this kind gesture.

May we married people find ways to demonstrate that sort of kindness to our spouses.

In what ways can you demonstrate true kindness
to your spouse today?

Wrapped in Kindness

*As God's chosen people . . . clothe yourselves with
compassion [and] kindness.* Colossians 3:12, NIV

Kindness sees me (David) as Teresa's servant. Today's verse refers to this kindness when it tells me to wrap myself in compassion and kindness. This means I am to "wear" kindness as I go about my day. It is to be a part of all my interactions, conversations, and attitudes.

That didn't sound very appealing to me as a teenage husband. If I was pleasant, it wasn't from serving. And if I had to serve, I sure wasn't pleasant about it. But several years into our marriage, God began to "tenderize" my heart.

Father, wrap me in Your kindness so that I might show the same to my spouse.

God showed me His great kindness through a janitor at the local church. The Lord had begun to draw Teresa back to church, but I was a reluctant attendee. I hadn't been impressed with many of my church experiences, so I walked into church one day and sat in the back row, looking for the other "rebels." Instead, I met Paul that day.

Paul was the janitor for this small local church, and he befriended me immediately. His cordial nature and caring manner attracted me right away. I just liked being around this kindhearted man. I went with him as he did maintenance repairs just so I could be around him. Paul demonstrated the truest picture of a Christian I had seen to that point. He lived out Christ's kindness before me. Because of Paul, I gave my life to Christ.

It's no small miracle that caring for Teresa as I should now seems natural rather than forced. Showing her kindness and serving her is a joy to me, not a burden.

All because God showed me a picture of kindness.

In what specific areas of your married life do you
need to "wrap yourself in kindness"?

Love My Brother?

All of you be of one mind . . . tenderhearted. 1 Peter 3:8

Being kind to one another was a family priority when the kids were small. For example, I (Teresa) taught them to say "thank you" when someone shared his or her toys or when an adult served them at the table. As the kids became teenagers, we seemed to grow out of making kindness a priority. Instead, issues like being home on time, getting homework done, and not wrecking the car became important. The habits of being kind to one another we had developed seemed suddenly foreign during those teen years.

Father, help us to create an atmosphere of kindness in our home.

David and I discussed what we were seeing happen between the kids. During one of our marriage staff meetings, we thought of a plan to increase kindness in our family. We first determined that David and I needed to model kindness to one another. Second, we decided to insist that the kids talk to one another with kind words and respectful tones. We determined to design and follow through with a plan of discipline that encouraged kind words and actions. Then the work began.

David and I worked hard to affirm one another and the kids at dinner. We watched our tone as we talked with the kids and used words that were tender rather than inflammatory. We stopped Eric when he teased his sister about a sensitive subject. We asked Robin to keep quiet if she didn't have anything positive to say about the dinner—or the cook who prepared it. We stopped Terri from criticizing her younger brother and sister, even though they often "got in the way."

The kids are all kind to each other without us having to stand over them. It's a joy to see kindness become a heritage we can pass on to our kids.

In what ways can you, your spouse, and your children demonstrate God's tender love within your household?

Getting the Feeling Back

[He] is able to do exceedingly abundantly above all that we ask or think. Ephesians 3:20

For twenty-plus years of marriage, Joan and Allen had gone through the right motions. They greeted each other with hugs and verbalized their love. They regularly went on dinner dates, and each did special little things for the other. But now the "nest was empty," and both were feeling a little awkward and uncertain. They were committed to each other and committed to show kindness to one another, but there was little emotional involvement.

Father, thank You for feelings. Give me sensitivity to my own feelings and those of my spouse. Let me not be content with kind pleasantries but pursue true emotional closeness.

Joan and Allen thought that this was as good as marriage gets.

Without adequate emotional skills or purposeful development, adults often enter marriage hopeful of deep, emotional closeness but unable to achieve it. If they aren't careful, they can drift apart into their separate worlds. He can get absorbed in his career or hobbies, and she can escape into the world of the children, career, or just endless activity.

It's not enough just to be "nice" in marriage. A marriage isn't successful and intimate just because there are few conflicts. Many couples assume that because they don't fight, their marriage is strong. David and I have discovered that if you aren't purposefully working on increasing your emotional closeness, you will drift apart. Kindness and pleasantries must be accompanied by determined emotional closeness.

Joan and Allen fulfilled the daily duties of marriage and family, but they had lost touch with their feelings. As they learned to sense and communicate their feelings, they were able to express empathy and comfort each other. Their kindness toward each other grew richer and with added feelings. God began to restore their marriage to something beyond anything they had ever asked for or dreamed about.

What can you do today to rekindle the loving feelings you and your spouse once shared?

How'd You Know That?

Love suffers long and is kind. 1 Corinthians 13:4

I (David) don't have one particular hobby, but there are some activities I really enjoy. For example, I like to play golf. I'm not any good at it, and I lose more balls than I care to admit. But I enjoy getting out there and hitting a few. I also like to drink coffee. One of my favorite things to do is go to the local coffeehouse and try all the different blends. And I can sit in Barnes and Noble, drink coffee, and read books for hours. I'm a real java fiend.

God, help me be kind, especially by taking an interest in things that matter to my spouse.

Teresa isn't a golfer, nor does she like to watch others play. One day, though, she asked me, "David, would you like to play in the golf tournament next month? I read about it in the newsletter and wondered if you'd like to play. And if you do, I think I would enjoy going with you." I was sure Rod Serling was going to step out from behind a door and tell me I had just entered the "Twilight Zone."

Teresa likes coffee, but she's content with two cups in the morning and the occasional cup of decaf after dinner. One day, though, Teresa presented me with my very own coffeepot for the bedroom. She said she knew I liked to drink coffee in the morning while I read the paper, so she set up a special coffee bar just for me. It was complete with freshly ground coffee and my favorite mega-sized coffee mug. I was sure I had died and gone to heaven!

Teresa's question about golf and her gift of coffee meant that she had come to make some things important in her life because they were important to me. Her kindness was overwhelming.

Which of your spouse's interests can you take
an interest in today?

In My Hour of Need

Always pursue what is good both for yourselves and for all. 1 Thessalonians 5:15

I (Teresa) was lying in bed with the flu, too sick to get anything done but not quite sick enough to go to the doctor. I had a million and one things to do, and now I couldn't do any of them. I ran over the list of necessary "to-do's" and got exhausted just thinking about them. The kids needed to be picked up from school, and then they needed a quick snack and help with their homework. Then there was dinner to fix and kids to get bathed. A thought ran through my groggy head: *Am I too sick to run away from home—just for a day or two?*

Father, help me to be sensitive to my spouse's needs and to respond with kindness in work and action.

About that time David called from work. He asked how I was doing and if I needed anything right away. I answered "no," but my heart said differently. Without hesitation David offered to pick the kids up from school and get them a snack on the way home. He told me to rest and not worry about dinner, as he would pick up some burgers. He even thought to reassure me that he would be in charge of all homework and bath duty for the evening. He just wanted me to concentrate on getting better, because he was sorry I was sick. I felt better already.

It's the times when David is sensitive to my needs and the needs of our family that I appreciate him the most. His kindness that day spoke volumes of his love for me. I knew he had given thought to what would be good for both of us and our kids.

This, to me, was an example of David showing me kindness through meeting a practical need—the need for rest.

In what *practical* ways can you show your spouse kindness today?

Small Acts of Kindness

*And the Lord's servant must not quarrel; instead, he
must be kind to everyone.* 2 Timothy 2:24, NIV

Teresa and I have enjoyed plenty of special times together—trips overseas, memorable gifts, and a silver wedding anniversary—but the daily "smaller" things are just as important to us.

Neglecting the small things can rob a marriage of intimacy. It's those things that show a husband and wife that their love is a kind love.

*Lord, keep me
from rushing
past the small
expressions
of kindness that
can help keep love
alive and warm.*

For us it's been important to take time for talking and relaxing together. It's been crucial for us to "date" one another, enjoying common interests and weekends away. It's important for us to share feelings, fears, dreams, hopes, insecurities, and joys and to verbalize appreciation and gratefulness to one another on a consistent basis.

We have found it imperative that we meet our spouse's need for affection. In our times of sexual intimacy, we've found it meaningful to give special emphasis to foreplay and sensitive "afterplay." We've both taken turns focusing on giving to our spouse's desires, preferences, and wishes during sexual intimacy.

Finally, for us it's been essential to initiate times of prayer, gentle touch, verbalized love, quiet closeness, and loving glances.

The "big" memories of our marriage seem to remind us that our relationship is forever, that our commitment is sure. But it's the small things that remind us that our marriage is uniquely our own. The small gestures of kindness remind us that our love is truly our own.

What "small" gesture of kindness will you demonstrate
to your spouse today?

Showing the Way So Another Is Secure in Following

Lead me in Your truth and teach me, for You are the God of my salvation. Psalm 25:5

Bob and I (David) were talking about him being open to follow so he could better lead his family. "I'm still searching for someone to whom I can feel comfortable submitting," he said. "Then I'll follow."

That was almost twenty years ago, and Bob still hasn't found anyone he can submit to. His family has suffered because of it. They've been plagued with church conflicts, rebellious kids, job instability, and financial problems.

I'm not sure humbly submitting ever feels comfortable, but it is the key to good leadership.

What do You require of me, O God, but to love mercy, do justly, and walk humbly with You?

God has taught me about leadership through some surprising people. A church custodian during my college years taught me much about the Bible and how to impact people with the Good News of Christ. A loving grandfather showed his rebellious grandson about acceptance, even though I didn't want to learn. Some of the sweetest elderly saints have taught me what it means to lead others toward thanksgiving to God in the midst of terrible suffering. And even our grandchildren have taught me about the nature of a loving God whose very character leads us into relationship with Him.

As I have struggled with my own hesitancies about following, I have learned to be more sensitive when I'm trying to lead. I've learned that leading by example far surpasses leading by manipulation. I've enjoyed the blessing of leaders who know me and want the best for me, contrasted with the disappointment in leaders who just want me to do stuff.

Finally, I've discovered that to lead in marriage must mean I am also willing to follow, willing to follow the God of my salvation wherever He wants to take me.

In what areas of your married life do you need to learn to follow God's lead?

Christ Needed to Be Led?

Then Jesus, being filled with the Holy Spirit, returned from the Jordan and was led by the Spirit. Luke 4:1

Christ being led? What a mystery! The perfect God-man modeled life in the Spirit, showing that He did nothing of His own initiative. Christ modeled for us the humility that is necessary to live the Christian life. He showed us that even He needed to wait before the Father in order to be led. Even He needed to hear from the Spirit and yield to the Father's plans.

Father, thank You that You do have a plan for my life and my marriage. May I diligently seek after that plan.

If Christ needed to yield Himself to the Holy Spirit's guidance, then I certainly do.

There are times when I (David) struggle with knowing what my wife needs. She seems so different from me that my own fear of inadequacy hinders me from giving to her. There have been situations where I've literally sat back and scratched my head, having no clue how to meet her needs. It's at those times that I have needed to ask for the Lord's leadership. I've needed to be led by His Spirit. Day by day I need Him to lead me into wisdom and grace so that I can live out His plan to love my wife as Christ loved the church.

Unfortunately, I often forget about God's available leadership and try to figure things out on my own. I call upon my own "wisdom" and training to get me out of conflicts with Teresa. Instead of calling upon the One who authored the whole idea of marriage, I try to tough it out myself. When I do that, I make a mess of things. But the Lord has been gracious, and when I take the time to seek out His leadership, He always provides. He always shows me exactly what Teresa needs and how I can meet that need.

In what areas of your life do you need to yield to God's leadership?

Are You Willing to Be Led?

*Though the Lord is on high, he looks upon the lowly, but
the proud he knows from afar.* Psalm 138:6, NIV

I (Teresa) teach a seminar titled "Basic Needs of a Man." One point I make in this seminar is this: Men have a basic, God-given need to be the leader in the home.

I'll never forget giving this talk in a large retreat setting. An older woman asked what she should do if her husband wouldn't lead. I asked her, "Are you willing to be led?" Her blank expression and awkward silence told me "No," and I asked her to meet with me privately after the conference.

Father, I humbly submit to You and am willing to hear from You.

I listened to this sweet lady tell me about the many years of frustration and irritation with her husband. After I had comforted her and shared my compassion with her, we sat in silence for a few moments. Once again she asked me, "But what do I do if my husband won't lead?" I asked a second time, "Does your husband sense that you are willing to accept his leadership? Are you ready to tell him you will start letting him be a leader in your home?" At that, she turned her back on me and walked out the door. Her answer to my question was clear.

We all desire to have our needs met, but sometimes we don't want to do our part. God tells us that He looks favorably upon the humble and the lowly. He looks favorably on the ones who are willing to be led, the ones who know they are in need and look to Him to meet that need. But God sees those who are proud and unwilling to be led from a distance. They will never see His face or enjoy His provision.

That's a scary place and a place I never want to be.

What keeps you from humbly following the lead of those
God has placed in your life? How can you change that?

Christ's Example of Leadership

Teach me Your way, O Lord, and lead me in a smooth path.
Psalm 27:11

Virginia and Ned were playing the classic power struggle game. Virginia was the most verbal and sought to control with threats and explosions. Ned was rather quiet and passive. He sought power by procrastinating, escaping into TV or work, or generally avoiding Virginia. They genuinely loved each other and wanted to please the Lord, but they couldn't find His path.

Lord, make me sensitive to Your way so that our marriage path may be smooth.

Ned was shocked when I (David) suggested that maybe Virginia's demands and explosions were just her way of seeking any kind of reaction from him. I suggested that perhaps some of her reactions came from underlying fears about finances and disciplining the children. I proposed that Virginia might need Ned to give caring attention to these things, but she wasn't sure how to communicate those needs. Indeed, after we talked with Virginia we discovered that she was looking for Ned's leadership in some of these areas.

Virginia was shocked when I suggested that Ned's procrastination and escape were his methods of protection. I proposed that Ned might be feeling inadequate in some of these areas but might not know how to communicate that in loving ways. Indeed, after talking with Ned we discovered that he was looking for concrete ways to give to his wife. In some areas he felt quite capable, but in others he felt like he needed extra support.

After asking God to show them how to walk a smooth path in their marriage, Virginia and Ned developed a plan. They agreed upon some parenting guidelines, and Ned began taking the lead in disciplining the kids when he was home. Ned contacted a financial planner, who worked with them on a family budget.

Ned and Virginia were great examples of what can happen when God steps into a relationship and helps establish leadership.

In what areas can you be a better leader for your
spouse and children?

By the Nose or Arm in Arm?

Christ is the head of every man, and the man is the head of a woman. 1 Corinthians 11:3

Men like to joke about marriage. Some of the jokes are funny, but some are just plain cruel.

One joke I (David) frequently hear from men is referring to another man's marriage as "a ring through the nose." When a man gets a good dose of this type of humor, it threatens his ego, so he often tries to present the opposite image: "I run the show at my house, and the little woman does everything I tell her to do." John Wayne rides again.

God, help me to lead my spouse arm in arm, rather than by manipulating or controlling.

These images are disturbing, and they demonstrate how men often miss the point of leading and being led. These images paint a picture of people trying to control and manipulate.

Christ tells us that He is the head of our home. I'm certain that Christ has no part of controlling or manipulating. Instead, He is the head of man so that every husband can be certain that Someone is looking out for his needs. Christ is ready and available to hear about each man's needs and abundantly provide. Christ is ready to protect and guide.

Christ also tells us that the man is the head of a woman. There is no hint of control or dictatorship. Instead, each husband is responsible to provide for his wife, just as Christ provided for him. Because of Christ's provision, each husband can protect, guide, and help make a path smooth.

God's plan for intimacy involves a different type of leadership. It's neither John Wayne-like nor ring-through-the-nose in its approach, but an arm-in-arm style of facing problems together. Each person's view and feelings are equally important, and when one takes the lead, it is a loving action meant to show the way so that the person following has a clear path.

What steps can you take to make sure that your leadership is loving and caring, not manipulative and controlling?

Where You Lead, I Will Follow

I have taught you in the way of wisdom; I have led you in right paths. Proverbs 4:11

"Why won't you let me lead?"

This question has been asked many times in our years of marriage. I (Teresa) have had to learn to allow my husband to lead. David and I have worked on this issue often. Usually, a particular project or family decision preceded our conflict. David and I would discuss our options, and then after I'd had my say, I left the final choice to him. No sooner was the decision out of his mouth than I would criticize him. Bottom line: I thought he'd made a bad choice, and I was determined to let him know.

Dear God, help me not to arrogantly think I have all the answers. Give me a spirit of submission so that I might be led.

I've discovered that David would never learn to be an effective leader in our home if he were not allowed to make choices and even mistakes. He would never be able to lead in our relationship if I didn't keep quiet about the mistakes and take control of my "I told you so" responses.

I've also discovered that David is less likely to be able to hear God's wisdom if he's too busy trying to defend himself, and he's less likely to discern God's clear direction if he feels put down and distrusted. When we have a decision to make, my best contribution is to give David my sincere, gentle input and then back off. He is then able to pray to God unhindered.

God works through David to care for me and the kids. Trusting God to care for me means I must trust David to lead.

What is your reaction when your spouse attempts to lead in the home? How does that line up with what God says it should be?

Leading Your Marriage Affectionately

I am my beloved's, and his desire is for me.
Song of Solomon 7:10, NASB

Touch is one of the most powerful of our five senses, but too often couples deprive themselves of this pathway to closeness. Teresa and I often suggest to couples that they take turns leading one another in nonsexual touching. We suggest that both husbands and wives initiate times when they express their love through the sense of touch. It's also important that both spouses sense the security of shared closeness that doesn't always end with sexual intercourse. Each person must feel secure that when his or her spouse initiates physical touch, he or she is leading toward closeness and intimacy—not necessarily sex. We recommended three "touch exercises" to increase closeness through nonsexual touching.

Father, lead us into the intimacy You desire.

First, *a hand massage*. With palms up, begin tracing lightly your spouse's palm. Trace each finger all the way to the tip, touching each fingerprint in a light circular motion. Trace the inside of each finger, pausing to move back and forth where two fingers join at the palm.

Second, *a footbath*. Take turns washing and bathing each other's feet. Don't talk; just relax. The purpose isn't the washing but relaxing and enjoyment. Use your hands or try a sponge as well. Go slowly and don't rush.

Finally, we suggest *synchronous breathing*. Lie facing each other and look into each other's eyes. Lie close enough to feel your spouse's breathing rhythm. Soon you will find a common rise and fall in your inhalation-exhalation. Alter this pattern by fitting like spoons as you hold one another. Place her back against his abdomen. After breathing is synchronized, close your eyes and just relax, feeling the sensations.

Try some of these exercises or discuss your own. Above all, communicate your desires with your spouse and listen attentively to his or hers. You'll discover more of God's blessing—an affectionate marriage relationship.

Which of the nonsexual touching exercises
will you initiate with your spouse?

love

A Commitment to Doing Good for Another

Love one another, even as I have loved you. John 13:34, NASB

The word *love* is overly used and often misused in our language. We can hear the word *love* used in connection with Mexican food, tennis, and sex. But God's intention for a loving marriage is something sacred and precious.

Father, thank You for Your commitment to love me in spite of my imperfections. Empower me to do the same for my spouse.

True love is an unconditional commitment to an imperfect person. There is no perfect person or perfect marriage, but love means being firmly committed to loving your spouse in the midst of both your imperfections. To love is to delight in your spouse's person and presence—who this person is—not just in what he or she does. It means having a deep, tender affection for your spouse. Love means desiring to be with that person and expressing devotion to him or her. Love is not based on performance or behavior but on your choice to care for your spouse as you have been cared for.

The Father's firm commitment to love us allows me (David) to then love. He made His commitment to me despite knowing all about me. My present failures are no surprise to Him.

How different marriage would be if we lived from this same vantage point of divine love. This is what true love is: a commitment to love with our words and deeds a person who isn't always "worthy" of that love.

The next time Teresa fails me in some way, might God remind me that it's already been taken into account, and that my love is to remain firmly committed to her.

Can you receive and then share God's unconditional love? Such is the only hope for an intimate marriage.

What actions can you take today to show your commitment to love your spouse unconditionally despite his or her imperfections?

Return to Your First Love

Keep yourselves in the love of God, looking for the mercy of our Lord Jesus Christ unto eternal life. Jude 1:21

When I (David) don't feel close to God, it's me who has moved. He's still right where I left Him. God's love is a firm commitment, but I choose whether to abide in its abundance or walk away from it. There have been times when I felt lost, as if God had abandoned me, but those feelings indicated my own separation from Him, not His attitude toward me.

There have been times when my love for the Lord was shaken because of my own sin and rebellion. The love of God and the mercy of the Lord have humbled me at those times. Just like the Prodigal Son, I've made my way back to the Lord—scared, uncertain, and ashamed. And just like the loving father of the prodigal, my heavenly Father has welcomed me back with open arms. When I returned to the love of the Father, it was there waiting for me—generously, abundantly, and without condition.

Lord, stir us often with remembrances of our first love— for You and for one another.

We suggest to couples that they return to their first love for one another. We ask them to spend time reflecting on when they first fell in love. We encourage them to think about the things that originally attracted them to one another and about the little ways they expressed their care and love. We have them think about the enjoyable ways they spent time together.

Returning to these ingredients of "first love" helps many couples renew perspective, gain hope, and move beyond past hurts as they are healed.

I've learned that as I keep remembering the love of God, I am better able to give the love of God. And as I remember the love I first had for Teresa, I am better able to fan the flames of love that have lasted for almost forty years.

What specific things can you do today to renew your "first love" for your spouse?

"I Love You" First

We love Him because He first loved us. 1 John 4:19

David said one day that he'd be glad when I (Teresa) said, "I love you" first. David needed me to initiate statements of love. It wasn't that I didn't love him or that I was afraid to share my feelings with him. I just wasn't used to expressing my positive feelings. When I was growing up, I wasn't taught to share my feelings aloud at all. After I left home for good, I remembered that my mother signed her letters with "I love you," but I never heard her say those words.

Thank You, Father, for expressing Your unconditional love to me. May it free me and enable me to do the same with my spouse.

I can look back and see the change that took place in my life when I first received Christ's love. When I saw how Christ loved me, then I could love myself. The Lord showed me how He loved me before the world began, how He loved me when I was in my mother's womb, how He loved me even when I disobeyed my parents. God loved me when I felt deep rejection from the girls at school. He loved me when, against our parents' better judgment, David and I got married. He loved me first. Plain and simple—He loved me.

When I felt God's tender affection toward me, I was finally able to give to David. Before that I couldn't give that love to David because I hadn't received it myself.

David also helped me by continuing to give to me and express his love for me. He's never loved me conditionally, but rather he's loved me with the unconditional love of Christ. Having received love from God and David, I'm finding it easier to express my love.

What words and actions can you use to initiate
a statement of love for your spouse today?

Coming Out of Hiding

[There is] a time to keep silence, and a time to speak.
Ecclesiastes 3:7

"Nothing's wrong." "It really doesn't matter!"

These are classic lines from a person who hides feelings of hurt, irritation, and unmet needs, but who seethes inside with pain or anger. Rather than "cause problems" or risk rejection, the "hider" seeks to suffer in silence. But when we hide our own feelings and desires, we undermine our own self-worth and sow the seeds for inevitable retaliation.

Often those who've hidden their true feelings for years complain that they can't feel love. Resentments have quenched romance, and bitterness has squelched affection. Much marital pain comes from the mind-set of "I'll not tell you what I need, but I'm angry that you're not meeting that need."

Thank You, Father, that we can openly and vulnerably share our hurts and needs with our spouse.

The wisdom of Solomon says that there are times for silence and times to speak. The appropriate "speaking the truth in love" (Ephesians 4:15) is critical to a deepened relationship. Christ modeled this in the Garden when He vulnerably shared His need for prayer: "Stay here and watch with Me" (Matthew 26:38).

Christ's openness with His needs is an important encouragement. Vulnerability with need is a testimony of trust. When we are secure in our relationship, we are able to tell the other person of our needs, knowing that he or she won't reject us or fail to meet our needs.

We can see in this same Garden account that Christ didn't hide His disappointment when the disciples fell asleep but openly asked them, "Could you not watch with Me one hour?" (Matthew 26:40).

A caring, loving relationship is built on the secure knowledge that if I'm feeling lonely, hurt, or disappointed, my spouse will want to know about it. Then I won't feel the need to "hide."

What steps do you need to take in order to be more open
and vulnerable with your spouse about your needs?

SEPTEMBER

love
mercy
peace
praise
prayer

Bumper Stickers and Love

What a man desires is unfailing love. Proverbs 19:22, NIV

I (David) love bumper stickers. Some of them are genuinely funny. One I saw a few months ago said, "Of all the things I've lost, I miss my mind the most." I can identify. I can also identify with the bumper sticker that said, "I love my wife."

I don't know what the husband's motive was in using the rear end of his car as the place to declare his love for his spouse, but I will assume that he wanted people to know that he was not ashamed to tell others that he loved his wife. Pretty brave guy.

I would like to think that the man's wife feels pleased and secure to have her husband openly declare his love. I also hope that she knows through many other things he does that he loves her deeply.

> *God, I would like my spouse to feel secure in my love. Help me to proclaim my love through my actions each day.*

While I would never think of announcing my love for Teresa on a bumper sticker, I want to declare it in ways that tell her—and others around us—that I love her deeply. The wisdom of Proverbs reminds us that our desire is for the security of love; "unfailing love" it is called. I wonder if Teresa feels secure in my love or if I leave her with doubts.

How about you? Does your spouse feel secure in your love? How do you let your spouse know that you love him or her? Do you say the words "I love you" often, or do you think that if you say them once a week, that's enough? Do you show your love through actions that are meaningful to your spouse? In the next few days, talk to your spouse about these things and learn whether he or she feels secure.

What will you do today to let your spouse—and others around you—know that you love him or her?

A Picture of Giving Love

*Husbands, love your wives, just as Christ also
loved the church.* Ephesians 5:25

I watched as Mr. Lacy looked into the window and checked his reflection. He carefully combed his hair and straightened his tie. He had to be seventy years old, yet he acted as eager as a schoolboy. He was a regular visitor to the local nursing home. He was meeting his wife, a victim of Alzheimer's disease.

*Lord, thank
You for giving
Your only Son.
Teach me to
love my spouse
the way
You love me.*

His wife never spoke much, but it didn't seem to matter to him that he got no response. He still made cheery conversation, read letters from family, sang to her, fed her, and just held her hand.

That's the kind of love God had in mind when He laid out His plan for marriage. Real love is a commitment to care for another regardless of the response, regardless of what is given in return. Christ took human form to demonstrate that kind of love to us—at the cross.

Mr. Lacy is a privileged man who loves his wife in a way the world can look at with a deep sense of longing. He paints for us a beautiful picture of what Christ's love looks like.

When I (David) reflect on Christ's "giving Himself up" for me, I'm often challenged to ask myself what I have given up lately in order to better love Teresa. At times the answers are convicting. I have often been very stingy and shallow in my giving to her.

The Lord has gradually broadened my opportunities to "give up" more of myself, my plans, my time, and my priorities for my wife. The irony has been that the giving no longer feels like giving, as the joy it's brought Teresa has blessed me beyond anything I've given.

In what ways can you "give up" more of yourself
for your spouse today?

Loving Your Spouse with Spirit, Soul, and Body

They shall become one flesh. Genesis 2:24

The Bible contains three different Greek words for love that reinforce for us the dimensions of marital intimacy. We often discuss each of these words with couples who are looking for improvement in their marriages.

Agape is then used to convey God's desire that believers share this love with others (John 13:34). This kind of love is shown through action, commitment, and giving—not through its feeling. It is an expression of God's Spirit and is impossible to produce through self-will. The practical encouragement for couples concerning *agape* love is that each person freely receive it, then freely give it to their spouse.

Heavenly Father, help us enjoy our love for each other so we can testify to Your plan for marriage.

The word *agape* is used in the New Testament to describe the attitude of God toward His Son (John 17:26), toward humanity (John 3:16), and toward those who believe in His Son (John 14:21).

The word *phileo* is distinguished from *agape* in that it speaks of tender affection and represents the emotional aspect of a relationship. *Phileo* love refers to two hearts being knit together in tenderness and mutual companionship. This is the love with which couples affectionately cherish one another. *Phileo* love can be nurtured best by intentionally deepening the relationship through dates, sharing of common interests, getaway times, and other times together.

Finally, *eros* is the word from which the English word *erotic* comes. This love speaks of sensual fulfillment through the physical pleasures of sexual expression. Throughout Scripture God has set up for us the boundary of confining these sexual pleasures to the marriage relationship (see Hebrews 13:4).

What a blessing it is to share these three loves with the person to whom we have committed ourselves for life!

In what specific ways can you express these three types of love to your spouse today?

A Caring Ministry to One in Need

You have heard of the perseverance of Job and seen . . . that the Lord is very compassionate and merciful. James 5:11

Mercy touches us at the point of pain and ministers at a time of loss. Life inevitably brings both, but a deeper tragedy is enduring them alone. Each of us needs the merciful support of others when we are going through hard times.

Thanks, Father, for the blessing that comes from being comforted in mourning.

During life's pain and loss, every part of my (Teresa's) being cries out, "Does anyone care?" Mercy answers, "I care, and I'm here with you." Mercy is most often the comforting support of one's presence during times of pain. It's the reassuring touch of mercy that draws me away from future anxiety and into the security of present love.

Couples often benefit from sharing "pain points" with each other. As they reflect on such times of pain and loneliness, the sensitive comfort and caring touch of a merciful spouse cries out within each of them, "I'm no longer alone!"

The irony of the Lord's mercy is that it is so undeserved. It is particularly ironic that we don't forget His mercy at our point of sin. We might expect God's compassion over life's tragedies or others' sins, given that He is Lord. But what is so startling is the mercy He extends to us even when it's been our own sin that has hurt us. We have a heavenly Father who not only is saddened when our own sin has hurt us, but who reaches down to us in compassion and mercy.

As James says, the Lord is *very* compassionate and merciful. Having experienced the wonder of such love, I can now pass it on to others, including my spouse.

In what specific areas and in what specific ways can you extend mercy to your spouse today?

Unlimited Mercy

God . . . is rich in mercy, because of His great love
with which He loved us. Ephesians 2:4

There can be no mercy "shortage" because God is rich in it. All our hurts, disappointments, and failures combined will never exhaust God's supply of mercy.

All too often the marriage "business" brings together two emotionally bankrupt partners who don't have much to give one another. Consequently, the two people begin a cycle of "taking" from one another, and that brings anger and disappointment to both people. This system of "taking" is often referred to as "codependency." This refers to two people, each overwhelmed with his or her own neediness, trying desperately to take from the other.

Thanks, Father,
for Your unlimited
supply of mercy.

Teresa and I sometimes illustrate this marriage cycle this way: We have two cars at home, and my car is beginning to run low on gas. Instead of going and buying more gas, I siphon gas from Teresa's gas tank and put it into mine. The next day, Teresa notices she is running low on gas, so she does the same thing I'd done the day before: siphons gas from my car and puts it into hers. Guess what happens as this cycle continues over the next few days? Of course we both run out of gas.

This is what happens in the "taking marriage."

The only way Teresa and I can give one another the mercy each needs is to tap into God's unlimited supply. When we approach God seeking mercy, He gives to us out of His limitless supply. We are then free and empowered to shower those around us with His mercy.

Welcome to the kingdom, where God is the God of all comfort, where God is love, where God is rich in mercy.

What specific steps can you take today to make your marriage
relationship a rich supply of mercy for your spouse?

Sharing the Mercy We've Received

Through the mercy shown you they also may obtain mercy.
Romans 11:31

David and I are so grateful to God for showing us mercy throughout the first ten years of our marriage. It was only through His grace that our marriage was able to first survive, then thrive. Our marriage was not made in heaven, but when we received Christ as our Savior, God started to heal our marriage and then use our past to help mend other hurting marriages. Since we've received God's mercy, it's easy for us to give others mercy.

Father, thank You that because of Your mercy, we can show mercy. Thank You for the opportunities to show that mercy to people who need it most.

The apostle Paul gives an important insight into the divine mercy of God, namely that it's contagious. When God touches a few with His mercy, through those few many others are touched by that mercy. It's the nature of divine mercy to produce "cheerful givers"—saints filled with gratitude—who pass on to others what they have received.

One special gift of mercy David and I can give is to minister to pastors, missionaries, and other couples working to serve God. It's very hard to find someone to share your problems with when you're in church-related work. Everyone expects you to bear burdens but not to have them. David and I can show mercy by being available to hear these people's personal problems without their feeling judged.

David and I are grateful for the mercy God has shown us in our marriage and family life. But we are even more grateful for the opportunity to be "cheerful givers" of this grace when we pass it along to those around us.

In what ways and to whom can you and your
spouse pass along God's mercy today?

Mercy from a "Feeling" Heart

[I am] one who by the mercy of the Lord is
trustworthy. 1 Corinthians 7:25, NASB

"My husband has as much feeling as a machine."

"She makes love to me with as much passion as a cardboard box."

These are common complaints from married people in today's world. Couples want to "feel" love but have no idea what those feelings really are.

Our world emphasizes achievement and performance to the exclusion of emotional development. Young children learn to tie shoes and count to ten, but how do they learn how to identify their feelings? Older children begin the treadmill of endless activities, but how do they learn to deal with normal

Thanks, Father,
that You've created
me to feel.

fears and disappointments? Adolescents focus on athletics, academics, or popularity, but how do they learn to heal hurts from normal teen life? Most don't learn these things; instead they get married.

Scripture reveals the Lord as a God who "feels." His heart is touched with grief (Genesis 6:6), disappointment (Matthew 26:40-41), and compassion (Psalm 103:13). How could the God who "is love" not be one who longs to relate to us with love from the heart? And how could this God not want us to relate to one another in the same way?

Our work with couples often has to start with the emotional basics, starting with this one: Feelings are not opinions. For example, "I feel like you're not handling the kids right" is an opinion. But "I feel lonely when we've not had quality private time together" is a feeling. We help couples learn to name their feelings and work on healing unresolved feelings from the past. That way, anger is put away (Ephesians 4:31), fear is cast out (1 John 4:18-19), and mourning is comforted (Matthew 5:4).

When couples take these steps, they can enter into the love of marriage with a merciful heart, just as God intended.

What can you and your spouse do to better
verbalize your feelings?

Have Mercy on Me, Please

What does the Lord require of you but to do justly, to love mercy, and to walk humbly with your God? Micah 6:8

Many Bible scholars refer to Micah 6:8 as the "heart" of the Old Testament—a one-verse summary of Old Testament teaching. Micah's focus is similar in many ways to that in Christ's great commandment as recorded in Matthew 22:37-40. Micah's focus is on the simplicity of relationships. Micah gives us the "vertical" command to "walk humbly with God" and the "horizontal" command to "do justly and love mercy." We see two ingredients highlighted in this commandment. First, to do rightly and justly so that we don't offend or sin against others. Then second, to be a lover of mercy—perhaps particularly as we encounter the offenses and sin of others.

Father, thank You for giving us instruction for all areas of our lives, including our need to show those around us mercy.

We receive great blessing when we apply this call for mercy to our marriages.

We all mess up, and one of our biggest fears is that the person on the receiving end of our mistake will make us pay big-time. It's a wonderful experience when our mistake is met with mercy instead of wrath. We are relieved when, instead of blasting us, the person forgives us and tries to help us learn from the mistake. That's what mercy is all about.

We all make a lot of mistakes in marriage. When we do, we need—sometimes desperately—our spouses to show us mercy. When they do, healing takes place. When they don't, the pain worsens.

Marriage requires a merciful attitude if it is to be successful. With that attitude of mercy, we become what God intended us to be—mature, deeply loving people.

Shown any mercy to your spouse lately?

What can you do today to begin developing a merciful attitude, particularly toward your spouse?

Thanks! I Needed That

Mercy triumphs over judgment. James 2:13

Sue finished the final page of her research paper. She'd been writing in long-hand for a week. She had been afraid that her procrastination had cost her a chance at meeting the deadline, but she had two more days to type, correct, and print out the paper. Sue's husband, Barry, had told her he would show her how to do that as soon as he returned home from his business trip. Sue knew she was going to make it. She would graduate in the spring after all.

Lord, help me to show mercy in my marriage by meeting my spouse's needs.

Sue started thinking about graduation day. She could just see herself walking across the stage in her cap and gown. But her thoughts were interrupted when the phone rang. It was Barry. He told Sue that his trip had been extended to all of the following week.

As Sue heard her husband's words, her fear of not graduating quickly turned into anger. But even as her anger rose, even as she was tempted to lash out sharply at Barry, the Holy Spirit quieted her emotions, and her anger gave way to mercy. Her feelings of judgment subsided, and she spoke merciful words to her husband.

"I'll miss you," Sue said. "And I was particularly hoping for your help on the computer with my research paper."

After a moment of silence, Barry reassured his wife.

"I'll tell you what," Barry said. "I'll call back tonight after my last meeting and take you through using the computer step-by-step. If we need to, I'll call my office and we'll get it typed for you there."

Barry's kindness—the fact that he sacrificed his own time for her—touched Sue. She later realized that this could happen only because she was merciful in her response to Barry.

What can you do today to make sure that mercy
triumphs over judgment in your marriage?

How Do You Feel?

*Should you not also have had mercy on your [brother],
even as I had mercy on you?* Matthew 18:33, NASB

Everyone expresses emotion. Some share their feelings openly, while others hide them. Some seem overly sensitive, while others are unsure of what they feel. Different people often express the same emotion in greatly different ways. Some might express feelings of loneliness by withdrawing in sadness, while others might express those feelings through endless conversation.

*Father, through
Your mercy let
me be aware that
my spouse often
feels pain.*

A major ingredient in relational closeness is the open and constructive expression of emotion. A first step in learning to express emotion to your spouse is to develop an emotional vocabulary. That means putting names to the different emotions we enjoy or endure. In order to establish emotional sharing within marriages, we encourage couples to take turns naming as many emotions as they can.

Why is it important to identify emotions? One reason is that many emotions define for us major emotional needs. For example, very often a person might identify anger as a felt emotion, when in reality this anger might be the sum of feeling unappreciated, rejected, and misunderstood. Feeling unappreciated means we need appreciation, feeling rejected means we need acceptance, and feeling misunderstood means we need understanding.

We need a divine intervention of mercy to empower us in this vulnerable heart-to-heart sharing. Mercy makes our hearts tender toward the needs, emotions, and even failures of another. Mercy allows couples to communicate with one another about their emotions and to act appropriately toward them.

More importantly, as today's Scripture reminds us, God has given each of us a great portion of mercy, and He is very serious in his expectation that we share that mercy.

What can you and your spouse do today to better
communicate your feelings to one another?

Harmony Based on Knowing Another

And His name will be called Wonderful, Counselor, Mighty God, Everlasting Father, Prince of Peace. Isaiah 9:6

For too many years David and I lived with conflict and emotional discord. After we gave our lives to Christ we earnestly prayed that the Prince of Peace would rule and reign in our household. We wanted our marriage and our family to reflect the beauty of His name.

Gradually the Lord began to show us that to have a home of peace means that each of us must prioritize our relationship with God, then give priority to our spouse and family. As David began to prioritize family and marriage over career, many of our conflicts subsided. As I began to prioritize David over ministry, many more of our conflicts ceased. We began to see signs of peace in our home.

Thank You, Father, for sending the Prince of Peace.

To have a marriage that is marked with peace, David and I had to develop a commitment to loving one another in spite of our differences. We had to see one another with the "grace-filled" eyes of our Savior. To have peace, we had to look beyond one another's faults. As David began to see past my faults and love me rather than try to preach at me, the peace of Christ filled our home. As I began to look beyond David's faults and see his need for respect and honor in our home, the Prince of Peace was able to reign.

Finally, to have a home filled with peace we had to face the inevitable conflicts in marriage. The Prince of Peace showed us that to have a home that is free from discord, David and I would have to share the truth with one another in a loving way. We committed to resolve our conflicts—but with words that were gentle, words that were conducive to an atmosphere of peace.

How might you be an ambassador of the Prince of Peace today? How might you bring more tranquillity and peace to your home?

Peace in Spite of Differences

Be at peace among yourselves. 1 Thessalonians 5:13

Peace in the relational sense is the inner tranquillity that springs forth from a common source. Differences between us and others tend to produce anxiety and not peace, and great differences tend to produce considerable anxiety.

Thanks, Father, for the commonality of need, which You wisely use to bind my spouse and me together.

Most of us tend to be threatened by differences between us and others. We feel insecure because we infer that those differences imply that we're wrong, inadequate, or a failure. Such insecurities can prompt great divisions, as well as attempts to change others to make them more like us.

But we believers can rest in a peace that the world doesn't know. This peace comes from the commonality of faith in the One who holds the world and who knows our common human condition. Our common faith, which is grounded in divine acceptance of us despite our imperfections, encourages our acceptance of one another and prepares us to really know one another. This often leads to finding out how much alike we really are despite our differences.

Anxiety or tension over differences pushes many couples apart. Teresa and I differ over punctuality, bedtime, exercise, money, and disciplining kids. Underneath all these differences, however, we share a need for love, attention, and comfort.

We've been amazed to find that we each need encouragement when we're down and support when we're struggling. The more we've recognized how God created us needing a relationship with Him and with one another, the less attention we've paid to our differences. When we came to this recognition, peace began to replace tension. It's a peace that comes in sensing that each of us knows the needs of the other and cares about meeting those needs.

What differences between you and your spouse do you
need to replace with a commonality of need?

Peace within Our Borders

May peace be within your walls. Psalm 122:7, NASB

One side of our corner lot is completely natural, with lots of trees growing all the way up to our deck. However, the landscaping on the side of our home next to the street is unfinished, so it's not the best view from our deck.

David was enjoying being outside one evening when I came out to join him. He'd completely relaxed after work and was at total peace. But I'd been out only a few minutes when I totally ruined his peace by my attitude. I have a tendency to be a person who sees the glass as "half empty." When I came outside, I could see only the things wrong with our backyard. I started complaining over what we hadn't accomplished instead of enjoying what we had.

Father, allow Your love and peace to rule within the walls of our home, so that we may take these things to our "neighbors."

David challenges me to see life in a more positive way. As I do, I find peace.

The psalmist's desire for "peace within your walls" highlights a principle that peace "within" precedes peace being extended beyond. In our ministry, when we talk about Christ's great commandment to love God and our neighbors (Matthew 22:37-40), we often highlight the fact if we're married, our nearest "neighbor" is our spouse.

David and I often say that it seems that Great Commandment love must begin at home. If Christ's love is not working at home, it's hard to take His love and peace beyond our "walls." Establishing peace and love at home continues to be a hard-fought battle—but it's well worth the effort.

Peace is a reward for a positive attitude.

What actions can you and your spouse take today to ensure that peace rules within the walls of your home?

Promoting Peace While Speaking Truth

[Speak] the truth in love. Ephesians 4:15

"Honey, I'm sure you didn't mean it to, but it hurt when you seemed to side with the kids over me when I asked them to get in bed."

Doesn't this seem to be a better way to handle this conflict than saying, "I'm sick of you always siding with the kids"?

Lord, remind me to always speak the truth in love, thus promoting peace in my home.

Speaking the truth without love causes strife within a marriage. But couples can learn to "speak the truth in love," as today's Scripture verse instructs us, thus promoting peace in the home.

Hurts, irritations, and unmet needs are inevitable in close relationships. In fact, closeness actually *magnifies* daily irritations. In the family, admittedly imperfect people are thrust together into close proximity day after day, and that causes stress, which is further intensified at home by the tendency to drop the public "mask" of being nice.

We often encourage couples to make a list of common complaints: too little time together, disagreements over child raising, lack of support in housekeeping, and so forth. Then we ask them to write down what speaking the truth without love might sound like. This part of the exercise tends to be easy since most couples have previously heard truth spoken without love. Now comes the hard part—rewriting the statements of truth adding love. Couples often need help getting started, so we provide a little help, such as:

"I would enjoy it if we might _____."

"It would mean a lot to me if _____."

An expectation of marital intimacy without conflict is unrealistic. But learning to resolve conflict by speaking the truth *in love* actually deepens intimacy and encourages peace.

How might you change the way you speak to your spouse so that you speak truth with love?

A Place of Peace

Let the peace of God rule in your hearts. Colossians 3:15

We have been blessed with the opportunity to do many ministry seminars across the country and overseas. We greatly enjoy doing these things, but I (Teresa) have to admit that I am a little less enamored with the travel than David is.

In spite of the many years we've traveled, I always feel somewhat anxious when we are on the road. It isn't that I think something bad might happen to me while I'm gone. Rather, it's an anxiety born of my being away from home—my place of peace, my place where I feel anchored. No matter how unpredictable my life may be, home always feels stable and good. Often when we are on the road, I tell David I just need to be home and "nest."

God, thank You for marriage, family, and my home. Please help them to be a continual place of peace.

Dorothy in *The Wizard of Oz* was right. There truly is no place like home. I miss it when I am away and am always glad to get home. It is great to return home to peaceful surroundings after a seminar. This sense of returning to my "peaceful" nest is my frame of reference for the "peace of God." When I'm resting in His peace, anxiety is gone and a sense of "welcome" fills my heart. Peace is when I feel at rest, relaxed, and the "peace of God" is when I'm relaxing with Him, resting in the security of His care.

I want my home to always be a place where this incredible peace rules. I know that will happen as David and I rest and rely on our Lord, who promises us a peace beyond understanding.

What can you and your spouse do daily to reinforce
a sense of security and peace in your home?

All for One and One for All

The fruit of righteousness is sown in peace by those who make peace. James 3:18

Ken dearly wanted to go to seminary. It had been his life's dream. Kay, his wife, wanted to help him. So together they planned for Kay to get a part-time job outside the home. The kids would have to be in day care for half-days.

Lord, give me such a longing for peace that I will meet the needs of my spouse over my own.

About halfway through the year, Ken noticed changes in his wife. Kay lost her temper more often, and she looked pale and downcast. Ken knew his wife had a very difficult boss and that she hated leaving the kids in day care. The situation was tearing her apart. Ken knew that his wife came first, and he decided that if God wanted him to continue seminary, He would have to provide funds in another way. Kay needed to quit her job.

God leads us in the direction of His peace. External things may challenge us, but when we're where He wants us, His peace prevails. Ken and Kay had lost that sense of peace. As they prayed together for His direction, each came to express gratitude for one another. Kay wanted to support Ken in this dream of attending seminary, while Ken wanted to provide Kay with a more peaceful daily life.

They didn't have any discernment about what to do, but as they made a commitment to give to one another, they had a sense of oneness and gratitude. They sensed that God was pleased with their care for one another and trusted Him to give additional direction.

The Lord indeed made provision. A week later, Kay was offered stay-at-home work. Now she could quit her job, be home with the kids, and support Ken at seminary.

We enjoy peace in our marriages when we make our spouses a priority, even over other important things.

What steps do you and your spouse need to take today
to bring God's peace to your home?

Words of Peace

*An excellent wife, who can find? . . . She opens her mouth in wisdom,
and the teaching of kindness is on her tongue.*
Proverbs 31:10, 26, NASB

A wife has a special role in contributing to the healthy and positive emotional atmosphere of the home. Teresa often encourages wives to bring up the subject with their husbands with statements such as, "I want to be the wife of a genuinely happy husband, so I'd appreciate your sharing with me little ways I could make you happy." She also sometimes encourages wives to study what makes a husband happy by reviewing Proverbs 31 and 1 Peter 3:1-7.

*Father, give
our marriage
Your peace,
which the world
does not know.*

We often encourage couples who want to establish a more peaceful home environment to be cheerleaders of each other with positive words. We encourage them to send one another off daily with words of encouragement, gratefulness, and affection and welcome each other home with words of empathy, understanding, and tenderness. We tell them to publicly and privately offer one another words of praise.

We believe this is in keeping with what the Word of God tells us about the power of words. As today's Scripture passage indicates, one important aspect of a wife's "excellence" is "kindness . . . on her tongue." Words have the power to instill peace or stir up strife.

A wife of excellence must learn to bridle the tongue and to turn negative comments or criticism into words that edify (Ephesians 4:29). For example, notice the difference between "You care more about your career than you do me!" and "I know you've been very busy with work, and I feel both appreciative of your diligence and lonely without you. I'm looking forward to spending some time alone together soon."

A spouse who learns to speak in a loving manner takes a huge step toward promoting peace in the marriage.

What words of praise and encouragement can you speak to your
spouse today in order to promote peace in your marriage?

praise

Commending Meaningful Contribution

Who is like You, O Lord, among the gods? Who is like You,
glorious in holiness, fearful in praises? Exodus 15:11

The psalmist's rhetorical question is quite fitting: None is like You, O God! Praise has no real definition apart from the wonder of our Creator. He gives the word its meaning and in so doing defines our purpose. We have the privilege to bring forth praise.

None is like You,
O God.
We praise You.

To bring forth praise in a marriage means I must leave behind my negative words, thoughts, or critical attitudes. To praise a spouse means I have to forfeit my role as *complainer, instructor,* or *nag.* To praise my spouse means I must look for opportunities to find value, merit, and commendation. I express gratitude for my spouse and share favorable words that bring him or her joy.

Teresa and I have come to find that if we have difficulty sharing praise with each other, that often means we need to give more attention to our devotional time with the Lord. We've noticed that we can't leave the presence of the Lord with a critical spirit or a negative attitude. Receiving His care for our irritations and reflecting on God's provision for our needs prompts our gratitude for Him. And it seems that the more "vertical" praise we express, the more easily our "horizontal" praise begins to flow. Turning aside to be with Him and experiencing the wonder of a praise-filled heart seems to prepare us for deepened closeness with one another.

Teresa and I have also discovered that as we increase our expressions of praise for one another, God is doubly blessed. He hears our gratitude and receives the glory for His generous provision. But the Lord is also blessed by the unique and miraculous testimony of an intimate marriage. Only God could have brought us from years of just "putting up with each other" to the intimacy of praise for one another!

What words of praise do you have for God? What
words of praise do you have for your spouse?

A Win-Win Experience

A man is valued by what others say of him. Proverbs 27:21

Praise is genuinely a win-win proposition. The recipient of praise feels blessed at having been acknowledged as significant and important. The "giver" of praise is blessed with a grateful heart and guarded from a critical spirit.

In our conferences we often remind those attending that on the first day of Christ's earthly ministry He hears from heaven. He hasn't yet performed a miracle or preached a sermon, but Jesus begins His ministry by hearing words of praise. "This is My beloved Son, in whom I am well pleased" (Matthew 3:17). Christ will be rejected by His own people and ultimately betrayed by His disciples, but

Thanks, Father, for the privilege and power of praise.

He must have drawn strength from the significance of these words—His Father is pleased! The Father's words of praise communicated value to His Son. Our words of praise communicate value, strengthen hearts, and sustain marriages.

Communicating praise to another affirms and deepens the relationship. We often use praise-sharing in our work with couples. Couples tell each other things like, "I feel especially loved by you when _____." This helps give each spouse a better understanding of how the other best "feels" love. Another exercise might sound like, "One of the qualities I admire in you is . . . I saw that quality when . . ." This helps identify specific qualities and concrete examples that are worthy of praise. In each of these exercises we ask couples to face one another, hold hands, and verbalize their response to their spouse. The spouse "receives" the expression of appreciation and acknowledges it positively in some way.

Many couples remark about the simplicity of these exercises and the profound impact on their lives. Each person begins to experience the win-win of praise.

How would you complete the exercises listed above? When will you share these words of praise with your spouse?

Give Him a Break

*If there is any virtue and if there is anything praiseworthy—
meditate on these things.* Philippians 4:8

David and I seemed to be going in two different directions with our finances. I wanted to save more, and I felt David was trying to spend more. One weekend I had been in South Carolina doing a conference and David had been in Tennessee doing schoolwork. We met in Atlanta on Saturday evening to spend the night.

*Lord, thank
You for helping
me change my
thoughts.*

David had thoughtfully made reservations for us at a hotel and carefully planned our reunion. Because David wanted to prioritize my desires, he even made inquiries into the best shopping and "people watching" places in the city. He took great pains to make the time in Atlanta special for me.

Instead of praising him, my first thought was to criticize David for how much extra money we would be spending. Thankfully, God impressed on me that I should consider the praiseworthy attributes of my husband. God prompted me to meditate on the virtuous traits of my spouse. I realized that I needed to praise David for his efforts and his thoughtfulness instead of being so negative. I could have ruined our fun if I'd been critical instead of giving David praise. Even more important, I could have deeply wounded my husband if I had continued to meditate on only the negative things.

One of the lessons I've learned along the journey is to praise David for his "motives" even if I don't quite agree on the "methods." His motive to make the time special for me was worthy of praise, and God challenged me to give it. The more I've learned to praise motives instead of criticizing our different methods, the more God has worked to bring our methods closer together.

Instead of focusing on your spouse's differences or negative traits, what praiseworthy things could you meditate on today? How might you express those things to your spouse?

The Power of Praise

Let another man praise you, and not your own mouth.
Proverbs 27:2

Couples we visit with are often those who have overlooked the power of praise. Wives particularly seem to underestimate the power of their words of affirmation. And men can often appear so aloof or self-assured that you would never think they needed their wives' praise.

I remember Lewis's constant criticism of his wife, Andrea, for how she spent money. He challenged her with questions such as, "Don't you realize how much it costs to live where we live?" and "Don't you understand how expensive it is to send the kids to the school we send them to?"

Guard my lips, Father, that my words might only exalt and edify.

It was obvious to all who knew them that Lewis and his wife didn't lack for money. They had all they needed and more. So was Lewis just "tight" and critical by nature? What was the *real* problem with these two?

I (Teresa) remember asking Andrea, "Who has typically affirmed and appreciated Lewis for his diligence as a provider?" Her answer was insightful. "I'm not sure anyone has," she told me.

As strange as it may sound, Lewis's criticisms of his wife's use of money may have been his cry for appreciation. We encouraged Andrea to consider ministering to this need rather than reacting to her husband's criticism.

Andrea began to express appreciation and praise for her husband's diligence and wisdom, publicly praising him for his faithful provision to the family. What Lewis had really needed all along was his wife's praise. When she began to speak such positive words to him, his criticism stopped and their closeness deepened.

Through his or her words, a husband or wife has a particular ministry in building up his or her spouse.

In what area of your marriage can you change
your words of criticism to words of praise?

Faint Praise

Her children rise up and call her blessed; her husband also, and he praises her. Proverbs 31:28

Isn't it a great feeling to be praised for something you've done? There is hardly anything like it. We all love to get verbal "pats on the back" when we do something well. It's part of how we are made.

God, help me offer praise to my spouse regularly, clearly, and honestly.

Sadly, most marriages are what we call "praise deficient." In most marriages, praise, when it is offered at all, is often faint or "backhanded" at best. We're talking about "compliments" such as, "That dress doesn't look all that bad."

We all need praise to keep going in life. We need someone to notice our effort and talents and give us verbal "strokes." We need praise that is clear, strong, and accurate so we know beyond a doubt that we are being praised.

The accuracy of our praise relates to the genuineness of our words. True praise is not flattery—words of "praise" spoken to another person for our own benefit. Genuine praise is unselfish—an expression of our gratitude for the benefit of another.

One important element in true praise that helps communicate its genuineness is honestly and genuinely "knowing" the person. If I (David) were to praise Teresa for her flexibility, she would either laugh or wonder if I had lost my mind. Flexibility is definitely *not* one of Teresa's personality traits, and it would not be genuine if I were to praise her for it. On the other hand, she would be blessed if I were to express my gratitude for her forgiving heart, commitment to truthfulness, and diligence in fulfilling her responsibilities. These words of praise would affirm to her that I really do "know" her.

Praise your spouse for the good things. Don't let your praise be faint. Make it loud and clear and honest.

What honest words of praise can you speak
to your spouse today?

Words of Refreshment

A wholesome tongue is a tree of life, but perverseness in it breaks the spirit. Proverbs 15:4

Ann's parents had an awful marriage. Her father was weak and her mother was too controlling. Ann felt it was her calling to keep her own marriage from suffering the same fate.

At first Ann's comments to her husband were helpful, but slowly they deteriorated into stinging criticisms. He became weak and withdrawn. Ann and her husband had a real commitment to their marriage, so they decided to seek help. Ann learned that her husband had endured criticism as a child and was dealing with it now as he had then: by withdrawing into his own world.

Father, help me to delight in giving words of praise to my spouse.

Today's Scripture verse reminds us of the power of the tongue. Our words have the power of life and the power to break the spirit. Ann's criticisms were breaking her husband's spirit and pushing him toward withdrawal.

Ann and her husband were feeling the same pain they had felt as they were growing up. They were locked into a cycle of hurting one another in one of the most painful ways possible: in ways they had been hurt before. As Ann criticized her husband, it was magnified by the pain of his father's criticism. As Ann's husband withdrew from her, it touched the pain of her dad's distance.

The power of the tongue to bring life was about to come into play. After participating in one of our couples' "intensive" retreats, Ann and her husband came to see one another's pain, and they offered one another caring words of comfort.

Ann found that it was helpful to start out by giving her husband one praise a day. Soon she began managing more than one. Her husband began responding with more openness, talking with her about his day and his struggles. She started listening more. Soon things started improving dramatically.

If you were to give your spouse one comment of praise today, what would it be?

God Did Good!

He did good . . . filling our hearts with food and gladness.
Acts 14:17

What an understatement it is to say that God did good! He did good because that's His nature. He's not a celestial killjoy but a caring Father who desires not to withhold any good thing from us. His longing is that we might come to enjoy everything pertaining to life and godliness. That includes us enjoying our spouses. Enjoying another person—coming together with another to find a special joy in each other's company—is a special part of God's plan for marriage. God did good when He created your spouse *just for you*.

Thanks, heavenly Father, for being a good God!

It's amazing how many couples have the mind-set that at best marriage is to be tolerated. Coping is the most they hope for, and they believe that they've done great by just somehow staying married.

Into this attitude of mediocrity and complacency comes a God who desires to give life and give it abundantly. This doesn't mean special protection from problems, but it does mean joy, peace, and liberty in the midst of them. Part of His plan for such abundance is the divine relationships through which He's chosen to work: marriage, the family, and the church.

A particular strategy Teresa and I have developed to see God bring forth "His good" each day is to obey Romans 12:15: "Rejoice with those who rejoice; mourn with those who mourn" (NIV). We do that often by inquiring of one another, "Did anything positive and exciting happen today?" We then rejoice together. We also ask, "Did anything sad or disappointing happen today?" and if anything sad or disappointing happened, we mourn together.

Being able to rejoice together and mourn together has helped us to develop an attitude of praise in our marriage. It's an attitude that says, "God, You did good by bringing my spouse to me."

In what specific ways can you celebrate God's
goodness in bringing your spouse to you?

Entreating God for Unity in Marriage

Give ear to my prayer, O God. Psalm 55:1

God's provision for communion with Him through prayer says a lot about His character. He sought us and established this divine channel of prayer. He listens for our cry as a mother listens for her young.

He knows my voice and attends to my cries. Such is my God: a God of loving initiative who seeks me, a God of great sensitivity who listens for me, a God of intimacy who knows me, and a God of grace who attends to my needs.

Thanks, Lord, for the special privilege of sharing together in prayer.

God's plan for marriage is to bring together a husband and wife in order that they might become "one flesh"—spirit, soul, and body. Spiritual oneness through mutual prayer is a vital part of God's plan.

It's not surprising then that the world's order for marriage is exactly the opposite: "Let's be physically intimate, then see if friendship develops. If later it seems important, we will explore our spiritual life." Many couples carry the pain of these misplaced priorities for decades, unaware that God has made provision to restore His priorities. Critical to this restoration process is tapping into the power and potential of prayer.

Prayer should play a vital part in the life of married believers. It's important to pray and entreat God's attention and favor for your spouse. Prayers of thanksgiving can draw a couple together in closeness. Prayers for the children help a couple be of one mind when it comes to rearing their kids. Requesting prayer as one spouse leaves for the office in the morning gives the couple the opportunity to be like-minded during the day.

God is willing to give ear to our prayers, both those said individually and those offered as a couple. We should make sure we take the time to enjoy this wonderful privilege.

At what times of the day and under what circumstances
will you and your spouse share together in prayer?

Prayer Helps Heal Hurts

Pray for one another, that you may be healed. James 5:16

There may be no more powerful healing tool for relationships than prayer. Amid every argument in marriage, couples can find common ground in yielding prayer: "Not My will, but Yours, be done" (Luke 22:42). There's an important healing message as two agree in prayer, declaring their dependence upon their Creator. When couples declare together God's greatness, their pride is shattered and their relationship is healed.

Thanks, Lord, for Your healing plan.

An important dimension of prayer that Teresa and I have found helpful is our prayer together after apologies. James 5:16 gives us a formula for relational healing: First, to confess our sins to one another and then to pray for one another. In His infinite wisdom, God declared an important guideline for healing in relationships—apology followed by prayer.

Recently after hurting Teresa with an impatient, short response, I was convicted to apologize. "It was wrong of me to hurt you with my insensitive response; I'm sure it hurt you. I was wrong; will you forgive me?" We embraced and she whispered, "I forgive you." As we stood there embracing, I whispered a prayer, "Lord I don't want to hurt Teresa with my words or attitude. Change me, Father; make me more sensitive to her. I want to love her better."

The combination of my humble apology and then my request for God to intervene has proven time and again to bring healing in marriage. I've discovered that as Teresa senses my heartfelt understanding of how I have hurt her and then hears my admission of wrong, she feels respected and valued. Then as Teresa hears my prayer to God and request for His power to make necessary changes in me, she feels secure. As I pray the prayer of James 5:16, hurts are healed.

What confession might need to be shared with your
spouse? What prayer might your spouse need to hear?

Someone with Skin On

In their prayers for you their hearts will go
out to you. 2 Corinthians 9:14, NIV

I (Teresa) know God hears me when I pray by and for myself. There are times when I know He wants me to rely on Him alone. But I also know God has given me someone "with skin on" to pray with me and for me.

On an especially hard day, I want David to pray for me. I always feel a lot closer to him when we've prayed. I seem to cope with my situations better when I've had the opportunity to talk to David, and then he leads us in prayer. Our oneness in our home, which comes because we've joined together in prayer, weakens the evil one and his attack on us. When David and I agree together in prayer, I feel I can walk through my trials with the attitude of an overcomer.

Father, thank
You for giving me
someone with skin
on to pray on my
behalf.

God has used our prayer times to help break me of my self-reliance. My tendency is to have an attitude of "I'll take care of it myself, and if it gets really bad, I'll pray." I know this attitude gets me in trouble at times, and I know it's an attitude God has wanted changed. He has used our prayer times to teach me humility and to teach me to be more dependent on Him on a moment-by-moment basis.

God has also used our times of prayer to draw my husband and me closer spiritually and emotionally. David has told me that he's particularly blessed when I ask him to pray with me and for me. He said it meets his "need to be needed" and draws us even closer together.

What specifically would you like your spouse to pray
for when you get together to pray today?

Looking unto Him

My God shall meet all your needs. Philippians 4:19, NIV

Andy and Patti came to us for help during their first year of marriage. Love had already died, and resentments had quenched romance.

During our first session we identified common but painful dynamics within Andy and Patti's relationship. Andy and Patti's expectations of one another were "killing them." Andy said, "Patti expects dinner out twice a week and a $300-a-month clothes budget, so I give it to her whether or not we can afford it." Patti said, "Andy expects sex twice a week and my companionship at company functions, so I accommodate him whether or not I feel like it."

Thanks, Father, for Your provision, which frees me to give.

God has certainly created us with the capacity to bless our spouses by meeting their needs, but our *expectations* are to be directed toward God, not our spouses. God is the One who has promised to "meet all your needs." In His sovereignty, He may seek to involve your spouse in giving to you, but we are not to build our expectations around our spouses.

Andy and Patti were trapped in the painful bondage of trying to "take" from one another. We told them that God's desire, in contrast, was for them to trust Him with their needs, and that they would know they were trusting Him as they began to focus on meeting one another's needs.

Where do I direct my expectations for meeting valid human needs? God often involves others in ministering to my human need, but He wants my faith directed toward Him. Expecting God to meet needs in accordance with His Word will prompt a faith that He can work through others.

Andy and Patti began to give their own needs to God and give to each other.

What can you do today to begin trusting in God
and not your spouse to meet your needs?

The Couple That Prays Together, Stays Together

Is anyone among you suffering? Let him pray. James 5:13

The mystery of two becoming one in marriage is only possible through an intimate relationship with the One who ordained it. Prayer is the avenue of relationship with this One. Marriage was intended to live out of mutual divine dependency. As Teresa and I go to the Lord in prayer and depend upon Him to relieve any suffering, comfort any pain, and meet any need, He provides an unlimited source of love for our spouse. Prayer acknowledges our absolute dependency upon God and draws upon Him as the source of abundant love.

God, help us to take prayer seriously in our marriage.

Teresa and I have also discovered that prayer brings humility to a relationship and increases compassion for one another. As I pray with Teresa, I am reminded of my own need for grace. As we pray together about issues with the kids or decisions in our ministry, I am challenged to humbly acknowledge my inadequacies and submit myself to God's unmerited favor.

Over the years I have prayed for Teresa as well. I've prayed for her as she's dealt with difficult family issues. I've gone to the Lord as friends have moved away or hurt her deeply. It's been those times that the Lord has brought a special tenderness in my heart for Teresa. As I have reflected on her sufferings and asked the Lord to give me His heart for Teresa, I've been overwhelmed with compassion for my wife.

Finally, Teresa and I have found benefit in this simple prayer: "Lord, I want what You want; help me discern it and give me power to live it." Regardless of the issue or the conflict, as we pray this type of prayer together we experience oneness in our desire to know and do His will.

When could you pray with your spouse about an area of struggle? In what area might the Lord want to sensitize your heart as you pray for your spouse?

Whose Idea Is Better?

"For my thoughts are not your thoughts, neither are your ways my ways," declares the Lord. Isaiah 55:8, NIV

Over the years Teresa and I have wasted a lot of time and a lot of words arguing over whose "thoughts" are better. We've had strife over every imaginable marriage issue, including such things as, "There's no gas in my car," "There's no money in my checkbook," and "Why didn't you call and let me know they were coming home with you?"

Father, help my spouse and me to remember to bring issues to You in prayer, trusting You for the best because You know best.

Our list of marital "issues" over the decades is endless, but even though we've been slow learners, we've found a better way.

We begin with the principle that neither of us has thoughts, ideas, and plans that are "best." They may be good, but as today's Scripture passage points out, they are not *His* thoughts and therefore can't be the best. The bottom line is, God's thoughts, ideas, and plans are second to none.

The famed missionary George Mueller prayed this way: "Father, I have my thoughts about this issue, but I want Your thoughts. I don't want to have my own will about the matter—I want Your will." As Teresa and I both prayerfully approach the Lord in that way, He brings us together and causes His ways to prevail.

As we've learned to approach the issues of our marriage in this way, we've not only enjoyed more harmony, but we've also come to appreciate one another's perspectives. I've come to greatly appreciate Teresa's insight into people, her sensitivity to our kids' needs, and many other areas. I would not have come to fully appreciate these strengths in her had we not spent time together seeking God's thoughts, ideas, and plans.

What issues do you need to bring to the Lord
for resolution today?

OCTOBER

prayer
protection
rebuke
reproof
respect
security

Beginning Silently

If two of you agree on earth about anything that they may ask, it shall be done for them by My Father who is in heaven. Matthew 18:19, NASB

Many of the couples we visit with desire a closer spiritual relationship with one another, and they often ask us how and where to start this journey. This seems to be a widespread concern among married people. One recent survey indicated fewer than 15 percent of churchgoing couples pray together. Couples give various reasons for this, such as: "I'm not exactly sure what to say," "I would not pray as well as the minister," or, "I'm afraid my spouse might correct me."

Father, thank You for the power of two people in prayerful agreement. Let it be so for me and my spouse in our marriage.

We suggest that couples begin the journey of learning to pray with one another by starting with an occasional silent prayer together. We recommend that couples spend a few minutes talking about things that matter most—concerns, hopes, dreams, and fears concerning topics such as kids, work, money, or future events. This discussion can take place at the close of what we call "marriage staff meetings" or during the last minutes before sleep.

We suggest that at the close of this discussion, the couple reach over and take each other by the hand—the husband's initiative seems appropriate—and pray together silently for two or three minutes. If one or both spouses is comfortable praying out loud, fine. If not, they can continue to pray silently.

Most of the time couples sense an important spiritual closeness when they pray together, and many report that physical closeness often follows.

Today's Scripture passage makes reference to the Father's response to "two agreeing" in prayer. In light of God's plan for the marriage covenant, there may not be two agreeing any more powerfully than two God already views as one.

What specific steps will you take today to make praying with your spouse more comfortable and fruitful?

Standing between My Spouse and Harm

So will the Lord of hosts defend . . . deliver . . . preserve.
Isaiah 31:5

Isn't it good to have the Lord of Hosts as your protector? Others might be helpful, supportive, and encouraging, but you are promised that with Jehovah you will prevail. Nothing escapes His notice, and no obstacle stands in His way. The sheltering wing of His protection provides safety and security. His mighty hand preserves my life and protects me from the adversary. His strong name is my defense and shield.

Father, thank You for Your protection. I need You at my side to preserve and protect me and my marriage.

This passage in Isaiah reminds me (David) that God is the complete, absolute protector of my soul. As I read this passage, I picture myself in a battlefield under attack from a host of brutal enemies. I am weak, helpless, and exhausted. Just then the Lord tells me, "I am your safe refuge. I am the fortress you can run into and feel secure. I am your defender. I fight in the battle with you. I stand beside you and fight off the enemy's blows. I shield you from their darts and deliver you from their traps. I am your hope for victory. I preserve your life and your health. I take you out of danger and set you in a place of rest. You must fight the battle, but know that I am always here to defend, deliver, and preserve you. You are my child, and I love you."

As I have sensed God's protection, I have been better equipped to give protection in my marriage. Protection means that I work to provide a safe haven and refuge for my spouse and to preserve the love that we share. It means I will never take for granted the gift that God has given me in my spouse.

In what specific circumstances or areas does God provide protection in your marriage? In what areas is He equipping you to provide protection?

Protected by Wisdom from Above

Wisdom strengthens the wise. Ecclesiastes 7:19

The psalmist speaks of my tendency to wander like a sheep, but he tells me that God's wisdom protects me as I choose my steps. God's wisdom protects me from straying as He gives me discernment for daily life. God sees it all—the big picture. He sees the end from the beginning and the last step before I take the first step. Such wisdom gives me something to share as I seek to love this special spouse God has given me.

Father, give me the wisdom of Your Word. Help me to know exactly how to provide Your loving protection for my spouse.

Protection in marriage relates to a growing sense of security in your spouse. It means you have the confidence that your spouse will be there for you to lean on. It means you have the security of knowing that your spouse will defend your reputation or character. Protection means guarding against physical or emotional harm. It means doing all you can to protect your spouse from situations that would lead to emotional pain or stress. Protection means you will do what you can to support your spouse and come to his or her aid.

In order to give my spouse protection, I must have wisdom and discernment from the Lord. His wisdom will help me know the timing and the practicalities of protection. His wisdom will help me know when to step in and when to wait on Him. His wisdom will help me discern how best to defend my spouse and still give grace to others.

Protection is sometimes complicated. That's why I need God's discernment and strength.

In what specific areas will you begin to provide protection for your spouse today? What steps will you take to provide that protection?

Learning to Be Secure

The Lord will preserve him and keep him alive. Psalm 41:2

When our son, Eric, was about five, he went through a fear of separation from us. David and I struggled with just how to minister to Eric during this time, but I also had to deal with a personal issue of my own. I had to come to a place where I trusted God to protect our kids. Up until that time, I had pretty much operated with an attitude of "God gave us these kids, but I'm the only one who can be counted on to protect them." God had to do a significant work in me. He wanted me to protect our kids, but He also wanted me to be free to count on Him to take care of them, too.

Thank You, Father, for walking with us through every event in our lives. Help me to trust You with my spouse and our family.

David and I made a plan. First, we gave Eric plenty of undivided attention when we were home. That told him he could be reassured of our love. Next, we took small steps to encourage Eric to stay with others while we were gone. We first left Eric with his grandparents for the evening. Next, we left Eric with his grandparents for the whole day, then overnight, then for a weekend. Each time we left Eric, we reassured him that we would return quickly, told him how sad we were that he felt scared at times, and praised him for his courage. Slowly God began to restore Eric's sense of security.

I learned some great lessons during that time. First I learned how to help our kids through some times of fear. I also learned that God could take care of our kids and my husband even better than I could. He could and can be trusted to provide loving protection.

What will you do today to give your spouse and children
the assurance of God's and your protection of them?

Overwhelmed and Underprotected

If anyone does not provide for his own, . . .
he . . . is worse than an unbeliever. 1 Timothy 5:8

The pressures of constantly managing their home overwhelmed Alice. Bill collectors called her daily about overdue accounts and bounced checks. The kids demanded her help and attention with activities, homework, and sibling rivalries. She worked forty hours a week and was active in various church activities at night. Any "leftover" time Alice had she spent caring for her ailing mother.

Lord, remind me
of my spouse's need
for my protection.
Let me be a place
of refuge and
safety.

Alice's husband, Sam, couldn't imagine why she was so resentful and uninterested in sex. But as Sam learned what it meant to protect his wife, Alice found more energy, interest, and romance.

Sam began to understand that to protect Alice meant providing support with the kids and taking over the family finances. He learned that for Alice these supportive gestures were crucial to her freedom from exhaustion and crucial to their unity in marriage. Sam began to understand that although Alice was extremely capable and said she was handling everything well, deep down inside she needed Sam's protection. She needed his participation with the kids so that she would no longer feel alone in her parenting. She needed him to take the pressure of the bill collectors and to establish a new system for their family budget. Alice even asked Sam to help her say no when people from the church asked her to take on more responsibility. Sam and Alice agreed that before she took on any more commitments at church, she would discuss them with Sam. They realized that he could protect her by helping her feel the freedom to decline requests without feeling guilty. This step freed up Alice's time and her emotional energy.

Husbands are charged with the huge responsibility of providing protection and support for your spouses. When we take that responsibility, our marriages are more likely to prosper.

In what ways will you protect and support
your spouse today?

Knowing When to Protect

Do not forsake [wisdom], and she will preserve you. Proverbs 4:6

Our two-year-old granddaughter, Madison, needs our protection often. She would stick her finger in the wall socket, fall off chairs, climb in the toilet, and play in the knife drawer if we didn't protect her from doing so. I (Teresa) like taking the role of protector when Madison is at our house.

Spouses also need each other's protection. But sometimes protecting someone can mean loving them enough to stay out of the way and let them do something painful. What they learn will help create wisdom, which works as an internal protection from future harm.

God, give me discernment so I know when to protect my spouse.

There have been times when I have had concerns about David's business deals or the people with whom he's made the deals. I've voiced my concerns in a loving way and then trusted David to God. David has taken my concerns, prayed about them, and then made the decision he thought best. Sometimes my concerns have been right on target, and other times it seems I was worried about nothing. But there have also been times when David wished that he had paid more attention to my wisdom. It's those business deals, though, that God has used to teach David valuable lessons—lessons I don't think he could have learned any other way.

So I will definitely keep Madison from sticking her fingers in wall sockets and playing in the knife drawer because she needs that kind of protection. With David, I will step in the gap between him and danger when my doing so is really best for him. I hope he will continue to do the same for me. At other times, though, I will lovingly stay out of the way and pray that God will use the pain to help him gain wisdom.

How do you know when to step in and protect
your spouse and when to stand back?

Lean on Me

Guard what was committed to your trust. 1 Timothy 6:20

Mark, Lisa, and the boys were invited over to her dad's to celebrate her birthday. They arrived an hour later than expected because of some unexpected traffic delays. Lisa's dad was furious. He never raised his voice or said an unkind word, but even the children picked up on his unforgiving spirit.

God, help me lovingly protect my spouse from harm when it is appropriate for me to do so.

Mark and Lisa apologized and tried to explain, but her father just went about setting the table in cold silence.

Mark was not going to risk the whole evening being ruined. He respectfully told Lisa's father that they would like to stay and celebrate his daughter's birthday, but they would not subject their family to this kind of treatment. Mark suggested that her dad would have to make a choice to talk things over and resolve the issue, or they were going to leave. Lisa's dad decided to talk, and they healed the hurts and restarted the evening on a better note.

As Mark and Lisa returned home that evening, she thanked Mark for being so courageous and bold on her behalf. "It meant so much to me that you would stand up for me," she said. "I love my dad, but I didn't want to spend my birthday being punished for being late. Thank you for taking the initiative to speak up. It gives me great security to know that I can count on you to protect me." Mark reaffirmed his love for Lisa and told her how important it was to him to protect her from emotional harm.

Mark set a great example for all of us in that he had the courage to confront in a firm but loving way.

How specifically might you begin increasing your
protection of your spouse and children?

Protection from Drifting Apart

Guard, through the Holy Spirit who dwells in us, the treasure which has been entrusted to you. 2 Timothy 1:14, NASB

Couples sometimes drift apart after several years of marriage. We like to suggest a few ways couples can preserve the gift of love God has given them.

First, we encourage couples to verbalize—to let their spouse know that they miss them, need them, care about them, and appreciate them. Gentle words are soothing, reassuring, and communicate that "you're special to me!"

We encourage couples to ask one another about the words they speak so that they can speak meaningful words to one another. We also encourage them to ask about their actions. For example, a wife might say: "Proverbs 31 speaks about a wife

Lord, help me be protective of the love we share.

comforting her husband. What can I do to be more comforting to you?" On the other hand, a husband might say: "Ephesians 5 speaks about a husband giving himself up for his wife. How can I demonstrate this to you?" We encourage couples to ask one another about home atmosphere so that their homes can be comforting or relaxing to both spouses, which positively impacts their relationship.

Next, we ask couples to empathize with one another. It is important that both spouses feel the freedom to express frustration, anxiety, or fear. Couples can do that through empathetic words and touch. This shows a person how much it hurts to see his or her spouse sad. We encourage couples to reaffirm their love and concern for one another and to reaffirm their commitment to come alongside and share one another's burdens.

Finally, we encourage couples never to lose sight of the impact small gestures can make in a marriage. We're talking about small gestures such as welcoming your spouse home when he or she has been away, noticing your spouse each evening, making eye contact, and talking about what's important to each other that day.

What steps will you take today to begin protecting
the love you and your spouse share?

rebuke

To Set Straight, Refute Error, Share Truth

My son, do not despise the Lord's discipline and do not resent his rebuke. Proverbs 3:11, NIV

Truth must be shared and embraced if it is to "set us free." Many times the very truth that I (David) need to hear seems unpleasant. That's often an indication that my sin or weakness has been exposed. I may have to hear painful truth as God's hand works to grow me and bring maturity. That's what a rebuke looks like.

Father, thank You for loving me enough to share the truth with me—even when it hurts.

God is committed to the truth and will employ any "instrument" to deliver that truth. Truth came to Balaam from a donkey. Jonah found truth in a giant fish. God gave Peter a dream of "unclean animals" to bring truth. And the Prodigal Son realized truth in a pigpen.

God's rebuke has come to me through disappointment and defeat, through blocked goals and bounced checks, through declining health and sleepless nights. And, yes, it has often come through the loving but firm words of a caring wife.

For me, rebuke has often meant Teresa gently pointing out, for example, that my busy schedule was keeping me from prioritizing our family. She lovingly pointed out that to "give myself up for her," as Ephesians 5 tells me to do, I must be willing to give up my schedule and agenda just to be with her and the kids.

Rebuke has meant that Teresa helped me see that my motives were good when I made the kids destroy their secular music, but that the method provoked them to wrath. My heart was in the right place, but the way I handled the situation damaged the relationship.

Time and again, the Lord has used Teresa to help me see the truth of His Word and to help me recognize my own blind spots.

How will you respond when your spouse lovingly brings you rebuke?

It's Hard to Hear

Open rebuke is better than love carefully concealed.
Proverbs 27:5

Teresa has always been able to speak her mind, and that's why I knew something was wrong when she was so quiet in the car one day. We had embarked on the "Ferguson family home tour," which meant we were traveling the streets of Austin, showing the kids the twelve homes we had lived in when they were growing up. There were plenty of comments like, "Dad, are you sure we lived there?" As we rounded the corner to our current home, Teresa was unusually quiet.

Father, when Your loving correction is needed, involve my spouse in communicating Your truth.

When the kids were settled at home, I asked Teresa what was bothering her. She hesitated, spent a few minutes collecting her thoughts, and then began to tell me: "David, I felt saddened and hurt by some of the memories attached to all those homes. I was struck with this thought: *Why did we have to move all those times?* The answer was, *David thought these homes were good investments.* I began to reflect on how many times we uprooted our family, all in the name of a good investment. It seemed like the main agenda was yours, not the well-being of the family."

Teresa's words stung my heart. We spent a few minutes holding one another in silence, and then I confessed my selfishness. It was true; in those days of moving I had very little sensitivity to the needs of my family. I mainly thought about things that concerned me. I felt deeply grieved for Teresa and the kids but relieved that she felt the freedom to tell me what she was thinking. It felt good to know that she loved me enough to speak honestly.

Intimate relationships exist only in openness and flourish only in vulnerability. Holding back truth for fear of rejection or retaliation has no place in an intimate relationship.

How will you begin responding when your
spouse speaks difficult-to-hear truth?

Rebuke in Times of Emotion

Rebuke is more effective for a wise man than a hundred blows on a fool. Proverbs 17:10

Have you ever been misunderstood? I remember well one incident where David misunderstood me.

We were going to be teaching a Bible study in Dallas, and we were late getting to the airport. I was only trying to help David find the quickest route and the best spot to park the car. But David felt I was trying to take over. After we'd arrived at the airport, we were going to get something to eat, and I started to tell David where to set my luggage. He blew his top and said, "I don't need you to tell me how to go get something to eat!"

Father, when Your truths rebuke us, we may not like it, but Your motive is always for our good.

My feelings were hurt. When we got to our motel room in Dallas, I announced, "David, I don't want to go to this Bible study. Send me home." After David apologized for his part in our conflict, we discussed what had happened that day. I was able to talk to David about my fears relating to all that happened that day: I was afraid we would miss our plane, afraid we wouldn't get there in time to get a good seat or have enough room for our luggage. But instead of sharing those tender feelings, I had tried to control the situation.

Even as David comforted me and told me how he wanted me to communicate my fears with him, I still resisted his care. "I just can't help it," I said. "It's too hard for me to control my emotions." It was at that moment that David talked to me about the truth found in Romans 8:11: "If the Spirit of Him who raised Jesus from the dead dwells in you, Teresa, can't that Spirit be in control of your emotions?"

I had to make a choice between my emotions and the truth of that verse. I chose to go to the Bible study. God was true to His Word: He brought the appropriate feelings as I was obedient to His Spirit.

What steps can you take to make sure you lovingly and properly rebuke one another, even when emotions are high?

Rebuke Is Not Attack

He who listens to a life-giving rebuke will be at home among the wise. Proverbs 15:31, NIV

"Honey, I'm concerned that Robin may have been wounded by your impatience with her as you left for work this morning," Teresa admonished me.

I had certainly been short and irritable as I rushed our daughter out the door that morning, and Teresa pointed it out to me. I didn't like hearing her words. They were painful to hear, but they were true. However, nowhere in Teresa's comments was there a hint of personal attack. Her words contained a gentle, truthful rebuke.

Heavenly Father, bring across my path loving rebuke.

Rebuke must always be distinguished from pressure to perform or manipulation to change. Rebuke always calls attention to a person's behavior, words, or attitude that miss the mark of God's Word. It never contains a personal attack on character. Rebuke is calmly stated and is never said in retaliation or anger. Rebuke always benefits the one who receives it.

Attack comes in many forms, including perfectionism, constant criticism, unreasonable expectations, prideful superiority, endless rules, and social pressure. Rebuke is not about verbal put-downs, sarcasm, temper tantrums, or harsh discipline, and it does not include rejection, silence, or the withholding of love or affection. Rebuke makes use of none of these things, but instead encourages change and ministers acceptance.

Teresa and I have let today's Scripture passage help us determine if our words are truly within the guidelines of loving rebuke. We ask ourselves, "Will my words bring life to the person who hears them?" If the answer is "no," then we make sure we revisit the motives behind our words.

God wants us to grow in wisdom by receiving rebuke, but He also wants us to bring benefit to the person who hears our rebuke.

What steps will you take to make sure your motivation for "rebuke" is as God would have it?

Ready for Rebuke?

Preach the word! Be ready in season and out of season. Convince, rebuke, exhort, with all longsuffering and teaching. 2 Timothy 4:2

Love definitely has its soft side, but let me (Teresa) suggest it also has a sharp side. Deep love means caring enough to set somebody straight when that person has driven off the correct path.

God, help me to discern when and how to rebuke my spouse. Help me to be open to loving rebuke as well.

We don't like this side of love, and we often refuse to acknowledge it as love when we are on the receiving end of it. But it is love. Christ told Peter, "Get behind Me . . ." because Peter couldn't accept Christ's assertion that He had to die (Matthew 16:23). Pretty tough rebuke, but an act of love designed to set Peter back on the right path.

Loving our spouses can mean a tough "setting straight" response to moral error. Doing it right often means making sure you have "taken the log out of your own eye first" (see Matthew 7:1-5).

I've been tempted at times to rebuke David for being too harsh in his discipline with the kids or not patient and long-suffering enough with them, only to have the Holy Spirit prompt me to inspect myself in this area. It was then that I realized that it wasn't time to talk to David about his responses to the kids until I had humbled my own heart concerning my own impatience.

I've been tempted to rebuke David about his tendency to bend the rules and find all the loopholes. And then the Spirit reminded me of my own rebellious attitude toward some of the church leadership and my unwillingness to comply with new church structure. The Lord let me know that it wasn't okay to talk with David until my heart was completely surrendered to Him and His established authorities.

How specifically will you prepare yourself today
to lovingly rebuke and receive rebuke?

Give It to Me Straight

Those whom I love I rebuke. Revelation 3:19, NIV

I (Teresa) remember the outcome of one of our first marital tiffs. After our argument, David stomped out of the room, slammed the door, and sank into bed in an angry slump. I sat on the couch fuming with anger myself. I don't know how long I sat there, but I finally packed up my purse, made a lunch for the next day, and trotted off in a huff to stay with David's grandmother.

David's grandmother lived only a few hundred yards away, so I didn't have to travel long, but I just knew this would show him I meant business. I sat down in the house and waited for David to discover that I was gone then frantically call his grandmother to see if she knew where I was.

God, please help me to accept rebuke from my spouse when I need it.

An hour passed with no call, so I called him. He couldn't believe I was on the phone. Wasn't I in the next room? Wasn't I still out in the living room sitting on the couch?

Even though David and I were only sixteen at the time, he showed some great wisdom that night. He told me that going to his grandmother's home was no solution to our argument. We were family now, and our problems needed to be kept between us.

What he said was true. I know now that his rebuke was said because he loved me and wanted us to make our marriage work. Ties with parents need to be replaced with ties between husband and wife. We need to turn to each other to work things out.

I needed to hear David's rebuke that night, and he was willing to speak it to me in love. Through the decades, we have tried to continue to live by that precedent in our marriage.

What can you do today to set a precedent of willingness to lovingly rebuke your spouse when he or she needs it?

Rebuke from the Scripture

All Scripture is God-breathed and is useful for teaching, rebuking, correcting, and training in righteousness. 2 Timothy 3:16, NIV

Mark and Allissa had made great progress in healing the hurts from their marriage. They had eliminated several major conflicts, and they had restored their friendship. Now they desired to tackle their spiritual closeness.

God, hide Your Word in my heart that I might more fully enjoy You and Your abundance.

Couples often find spiritual closeness through Scripture memorization, focusing particularly on passages dealing with marriage, family, and communication.

We started Mark and Allissa on a joint memory project of ten passages in Proverbs dealing with communication. We encouraged them to choose a consistent time every day to memorize. They shared in looking up the verse in the Bible and reading the context of the verse so that they could have a clearer understanding of the verse as it relates to the thought of the passage.

Mark and Allissa began by saying the reference and then reading the verse itself. They found that the verses normally break down into logical phrases. So as they tried to memorize each verse, Mark and Allissa took a phrase at a time and committed it to memory until they finally completed the whole verse. They quoted and repeated the verse, checking one another as they said the whole passage out loud.

Mark and Allissa began to use their car-pool time together each morning for their memory work. They quickly learned the ten verses we gave them, plus many more. They saw tremendous growth in their relationship because of the convicting power of the Word of God. Both Mark and Allissa described numerous times when they were about to say or do something that would bring harm to their marriage, but the Spirit brought the Word to their minds.

God's Word works like that—it serves to bring necessary rebuke so that marital hurt can be prevented.

What will you do today to start making the memorization of the Word of God a bigger part of your marriage?

Building Up by Exposing Wrong

He who ignores discipline despises himself, but whoever heeds correction gains understanding. Proverbs 15:32, NIV

God's reproof is consistent with His character. He reproves us to keep us on the pathway to blessing. God often "whispers" warning through His still, quiet voice, but He also speaks "audibly" through His Word and almost "shouts" His pleas during many of life's great disappointments. He desires not to withhold any good thing from us as we walk uprightly with Him (Psalm 84:11). He not only promises blessings, but He lovingly reproves us so that we keep walking toward those blessings.

Father, thank You for wanting what's best for me.

As we look through God's Word, it's important that we come to a new understanding of His reproof. When we read one of God's commands, it's important to ask ourselves: "Why is God giving us this warning or this rule?"

Every time you find a command in Scripture, you will see behind it a loving God. He doesn't give us commandments simply because He's into authority and likes telling us what to do. Rather, God has given us His commands in order to protect us. For example, when God tells us not to steal from one another or kill one another, He is doing so because He wants to keep us from getting hurt or from hurting others. God knows that if we disobey His Word, we will suffer the consequences of pain and separation from Him.

Part of God's plan for reproving us is His use of a loving spouse to give correction. Marriage without reproof is an accident waiting to happen. Without the freedom to lovingly speak correction within the marriage relationship, indulgence can go unchecked, selfishness uncorrected, and the entanglements of sin unheeded.

We should all heed the reproof God brings through our spouses, and we should thank Him daily for that part of the marriage relationship.

What can you do today to give yourself and your spouse freedom to reprove one another as it is needed?

Warning Signs

He who refuses correction goes astray. **Proverbs 10:17**

As I (David) have traveled down life's highway, I have come to a fork in the road, where two signs greet me: (1) Receive Reproof, and (2) Go Astray.

Help me, Father, to look beyond others' actions and see Your reproof.

Unlike rebuke, reproof is often not spoken but comes through natural consequences. For example, if I stay up late watching a movie, the natural consequence will be that I am tired at work the next day.

In relationships, the reproof for failing to meet family members' needs may come as they seek to meet those needs through others. A lonely spouse may escape into friendships with others—a natural consequence for the loss of intimacy between a husband and wife. Or a lonely child might seek acceptance with his peers at the price of his personal safety—the natural consequence for the loss of closeness between a parent and child.

If my spouse or child turns to others for what God wants me to provide, then I am at a fork in the road. I have to decide: Will I receive this reproof, or will I go astray? Will I heed God's Word, which tells me to care for my family, or will I continue ignoring their needs? Will I heed God's Word, which tells me to comfort my wife as God has comforted me, or will I continue to neglect and overlook her? Will I accept my children as God has accepted me, or will I continue to base my love on their performance?

There are important relationships at stake on my journey down life's roadway. My relationship with a holy God must be filled with devotion. My relationship with my spouse must be cherished. My relationships with my children must be nurtured. Because of those relationships, there's too much at stake to go astray.

How will you and your spouse respond to the reproofs
God sends your way?

Pushing My Buttons

The king's heart is in the hands of the Lord, like the rivers of water; He turns it wherever He wishes. Proverbs 21:1

Some of God's most effective reproofs come through the circumstances of life. But I (Teresa) often struggle with wanting to point out problems and alert others of their mistakes—as if God had assigned me the Holy Spirit's job.

David often jokes about a man's "macho button." David says that this button is a mystical place inside a man and that recurrent complaining is the only thing that pushes this button. When his wife pushes this button, a man begins to rebel and take on an attitude of "I wouldn't change now even if I wanted to!"

Lord, You can change the hearts of kings and spouses. Keep me still so You can do Your work.

I'm not sure that every man has this button, but I know my husband does. And this macho button often comes into direct conflict with my tendency to point out problems in others. After many spats and outright arguments over this one particular area, I decided to test the principle of letting David endure reproof. I decided that, for once, I'd wait and see if God would use the circumstances of life to teach my husband what I had been unable to teach.

On our way back from San Antonio, I noticed we needed gas and mentioned it to David. He checked the gauge and decided we could go a few more miles. Although I've had a tendency to harp on and complain about David's habit of letting the gas in our car get too low, this time I kept quiet. When we ran out of gas, I calmly picked up something to read and told him I hoped he enjoyed his walk.

I'm glad to say that the theory only had to be tested twice. We've not run out again.

In what specific area(s) do you need to just be quiet and
let God do the reproving in your spouse's life?

Reproof Balances Truth with Love

[Speak] the truth in love. **Ephesians 4:15**

Teresa and I are different in so many ways, including how we handle our inevitable marriage hurts. Teresa tends to speak the truth, but not always in love. On the other hand, my tendency is not to communicate the truth about my hurt at all.

Thank You, Father,
for the balance
Your Spirit brings
to relationships.

In order for us to have an intimate relationship, my wife and I have both needed to change in this area. Teresa has become more loving in how she expresses her hurts, and I've become more open about mine.

I've been challenged to vulnerably express my needs to Teresa rather than expecting her to read my mind and then getting angry when she can't. I've had to let go of my tendency to sulk or withdraw when my needs aren't met. I've needed to say words to Teresa like, "Sweetheart, it would really mean a lot to me if we could schedule some time for us to do something fun together. I love having the kids and grandkids around, but I need some time just with you."

Teresa has been challenged to pray through her presentation of her needs. Instead of saying, "David, why can't you learn to pick up after yourself?" Teresa says, "David, it's important to me to have the living room picked up before our guests come over." I respond much better to that kind of reproof.

Can I openly and lovingly communicate my needs to my spouse as well as others? Can I discuss my hurts? These are crucial relationship issues.

God instituted marriage, the family, and the church. God often desires to involve the meaningful others in my life to meet my needs. My challenge is to speak the truth in love, as Ephesians tells me to do, and then trust God with the results.

In what areas do you and your spouse most need
to "speak the truth in love"?

Let Me Turn on the Light for You

Correct, rebuke, and encourage—with great patience and careful instruction. 2 Timothy 4:2, NIV

We all fall into untruth. It is the human bent to misinterpret, distort, and misperceive reality. Because we are prone to miss the truth, we all need help seeing it. We all need someone who can help us "turn on the light."

Turning on the light is a delicate thing. We can all become defensive when it comes to hearing how we've gotten it wrong. So when we help our spouses into the light of the truth, we must do it with gentleness, sensitivity, and love.

God, help me speak the truth in love so that my spouse is helped to grow.

David has helped turn on the light for me. It's been a painful process, but I needed the light to shine in one of the dark places of my heart, and it's this: I've always had a rather blunt tone about me. I'm a very bottom-line, get-to-the-point, and cut-to-the-chase person. Those are admirable qualities in some situations, but when it comes to relationships, I've discovered that my abruptness and bluntness can be harmful.

After hearing me having a phone conversation with my daughter, David approached me with great sensitivity and love. "Teresa, I know you didn't mean to come across this way, but your tone sounded awfully harsh toward Robin." After careful examination and much prayer, I have come to realize that I need both God and David to help me become more gentle with my words.

David's reproof was painful for me to hear, but it was true. I would have missed the truth about my words had David not illuminated the truth for me.

I'm grateful to have a God—and a husband—who love me so intensely that they are willing to shed light on the dark areas of my life, to speak loving words of reproof when I need to hear them.

What is your response when your spouse attempts to illuminate dark areas of your life?

Give Me Feedback

Whoever heeds correction is honored. Proverbs 13:18, NIV

Dan was complaining to his wife, Audrey: "I just don't feel close to God. I feel like I do all the right things—perfect Sunday attendance, tithing, and membership on several church committees—but it gets me nowhere. When I pray, I'm not sure He really listens."

Lord, help me to receive feedback from my spouse with an open heart.

Audrey lovingly responded, "Dan, close relationships are built by spending lots of time getting to know each other. Two of the best ways I know to do that with God are consistent time spent in Bible study and in prayer. I've been thinking about this too. You know, I wait to have a devotional time with the Lord until chores are done, dinner is over, and the kids are in bed. By that time I'm totally wiped out. I barely have a coherent thought left for the Lord. I think He deserves more than that."

Audrey continued, "As far as spending time in prayer, I heard our ladies' Bible study teacher put it this way: God wants us to share our hearts with Him. He doesn't just want to hear our wish lists or complaints. God wants to spend time being with us, hanging out with us. He wants us to get to know Him, like He completely knows us. He desires our thanks and our praise. He desires our attentiveness and respect."

Dan and Audrey spent a few minutes discussing their perspectives and needed changes. Dan finally concluded, "I think I'm beginning to get it. My attitude needs to change from what can I *get* from God to what can I *give* to Him. He's given me so much already, how can I not express my gratitude?"

Audrey thanked Dan for his receptive heart and praised him for his willingness to receive feedback. Dan was grateful for the loving reproof.

In what areas of your spiritual life or marriage do you think you can use your spouse's feedback?

Watching Your Thoughts and Speech

*We all make many mistakes, but those who control their tongues
can also control themselves in every other way.* James 3:2, NLT

In our work with couples, we see significant growth take place as couples
allow God to change their "self-talk"—the way they talk to themselves. We
encourage couples to take careful inventory of their thought life and the
words that result. It's these patterns of unhealthy self-
talk that can lead to so many unnecessary conflicts
in marriage.

A wife innocently declines her husband's invitation to go for a walk. His self-talk says, "She never
wants to do anything I want to do. She'd go if I were
more important to her. Just wait until she asks me to
do something with her!" His verbal response may be,
"Never mind, I won't ask again!"

*Transform me,
Father, by the
renewing of
my mind.*

A four-step process helps control self-talk and improve communication. First, think before you speak. Just because you think something doesn't
mean you have to say it. Next comes taking wrong thoughts "captive" as you
share them with God. Sharing your thoughts with God helps you express
your feelings and vent any inappropriate emotions and then gives Him time
to remind you of the truth.

Now you are ready to replace these old thoughts with new ones that
more adequately represent the truth: "My wife must be tired or may need
time to relax. She did go to the boat show with me last weekend. That was
clearly something I wanted to do. I know she loves me and thinks I'm important. I can use the time alone to think through some personal priorities."

Finally, you are ready to speak words that edify: "While I take a walk,
why don't you do something you'll enjoy? I'll look forward to our being
together when I get back."

By working through this process, couples have found they "stumble"
less in what they say and provoke fewer conflicts within their marriage.

What areas of self-talk might the Lord want
to change in you?

Conveying Great Worth

Be devoted to one another in brotherly love. Honor one another above yourselves. Romans 12:10, NIV

To respect means to value, to give honor, and to regard highly. It means to convey great worth.

God understands respect. One day soon the Father will highly exalt His Son, giving Him a name above every other name. One day soon, at the name of Jesus every knee will bow and every tongue will confess that Jesus is Lord (Romans 14:11).

Father, help me to give honor to my spouse as well as Your Son.

God also understands disrespect. The Father sent prophets to the children of Israel, but they were mocked. He sent priests to be mediators between Himself and the people, but the people ignored the priests. God sent His Son to be His people's ultimate deliverer, but they rejected Him. He was "despised and rejected" (Isaiah 53:3, NIV).

In marriage, we must also understand respect. Respect takes many forms. Respecting Teresa means asking before I take something that belongs to her and returning something I borrowed. Respect means checking with her before making plans that affect her.

One of the best ways to show Teresa respect is to sincerely confess when I have done wrong. To tell her "I was wrong, and I care about your hurt" conveys that her feelings are important to me. A sincere confession lets my wife know that I regard her so highly that I don't want to leave any hurt unhealed.

We must also understand what respect sounds like. To give respect means talking to Teresa with an appropriate tone of voice—one that is free from sarcasm, haughtiness, or condescension. Respect might include asking her opinion or preferences. It means treating my spouse's choices, schedules, and ideas as valuable and worthwhile.

How can you begin showing genuine respect
to your spouse today?

Respect at Calvary

In honor [give] preference to one another. Romans 12:10

Consider for a moment the respect that Christ displayed throughout the pages of the Gospels. He treated people according to their worth to the Father, not according to their appearance or even behavior.

Think about it. Jesus treated the woman caught in adultery with respect. He never made reference to her being "caught in the act" or to why she stood unkempt and disheveled in front of an angry mob of religious zealots. Christ didn't talk down to the woman, even though the culture of the day would have certainly deemed that appropriate.

God, let me see my spouse according to his or her worth to You.

Jesus treated Zacchaeus with respect. Christ didn't make fun of him for being up in the tree. He didn't tell Zacchaeus how to act or demand that he give back all the money he had stolen. Christ simply invited Zacchaeus for dinner.

Jesus even treated Judas with respect. Even in the midst of His darkest hour, Christ didn't humiliate or shame Judas in front of the other disciples. He didn't berate Judas for being the ultimate traitor. Christ just dipped the bread and gave it to Judas and then said, "What you are about to do, do quickly" (John 13:27, NIV).

How is it that Jesus was able to respond to an adulterous woman, a cheating tax collector, and a betraying friend with respect? Yes, He was the Son of God. But in His humanity, He was able to show respect because He remembered these people's worth to the Father. Each of these three was why the Father sent His Son to die.

We need this same perspective as we relate to our spouses, who are the reasons there had to be a Calvary.

How would you describe your spouse's worth to our heavenly Father? How will that change how you see or treat or speak to him or her today?

Respect at the Family Barbecue

Let the wife see that she respects her husband. **Ephesians 5:33**

This summer we were going to have a barbecue as a family get-together. Several members of the family had arrived at our house, and we were preparing things for the meal. To my (Teresa's) surprise, David suddenly volunteered to grill the steaks. He normally lets me do the cooking, so when he volunteered to help, I doubted his abilities. He hasn't had much practice in the kitchen, so I thought he needed some extra guidance.

Lord, thank You for Your Spirit, who shows me the ways in which I communicate disrespect to my spouse.

Our daughters were in the kitchen with us as David prepared the steaks for the grill. I began to tell David just how to cut the steaks, how they should be seasoned, and even what plate he should put them on. I gave explicit instructions as to how to place them on the grill and then warned against cooking them too fast. David stood quietly at the kitchen counter. As I looked up and saw the look on his face, I knew he was angry. I had blown it. I had wounded him and disrespected him.

I would never consciously tear David down with my words, but that was exactly what I had done that day. I'd shown disrespect for his character and abilities. Worse still, I had done it in front of others.

When I realized what I had done, it saddened me. I'd shown disrespect to David because of my own fears. I had hurt David because I feared what the family would think of the meat. That was too high a price to pay for well-cooked steaks. I took David aside and asked him to forgive me for causing his hurt. I'm so grateful that I became aware of how I wounded David, so that the hurt could be healed and our unity restored.

How will you respond the next time you become aware that you have done or said something to convey disrespect to your spouse?

Respect Motivates

Now we ask you . . . to respect those who work hard among you. 1 Thessalonians 5:12, NIV

During our almost forty years of marriage, Teresa has faithfully built me up in front of our children, family, and friends. I am always secure that when she is with her friends, Teresa doesn't participate in "male bashing" or join other women in disparaging their husbands.

I can always count on Teresa's respect for my perspectives and ideas. When Teresa and I decided to redecorate the living room, she consulted me about the kind of furniture that I would find most comfortable. She asked me what fabrics I liked for my chair, and she asked me what style of chair I would most prefer. I felt so respected when she took the time to understand what I would most like.

Father, thank You for the blessing of a respectful spouse.

Teresa feels free to communicate her own ideas and at the same time not devalue mine. She is careful to include me in discussions about Christmas gifts for the kids and grandkids. Even when she knows what kind of toys would be best or what colors the girls most prefer, she still listens carefully to my ideas and includes them in her decisions.

I'm never afraid that Teresa will put me down in front of others. I don't have to worry that Teresa will tell embarrassing stories about me or point out my flaws through sarcastic jokes. She is careful to poke fun only in areas where she knows I feel secure. She's careful to tell only the stories she knows I'm comfortable with her telling.

This security I feel in Teresa's respect has often motivated within me a renewed faithfulness and dedication in my daily walk as husband and father. Her respect has motivated me to continue working on our marriage and myself.

How would your spouse respond today if you were to shower him or her with acts and words of respect, particularly respect shown in front of others?

R-E-S-P-E-C-T, Tell You What It Means to Me

Honor all people. 1 Peter 2:17

I (Teresa) am convinced that when you put toilet paper in the holder, you should do it so that the sheets come over the top rather than from below. I'm convinced there is a certain way to load the dishwasher so that you achieve maximum efficiency. I am convinced that it is much better to get somewhere early than to get there just on time. I am convinced that it is better to unpack all your things and place them in the drawers of a hotel room than to live out of the suitcase for the entire trip.

God, help me regard my spouse's ways as highly as my own.

While I am convinced of all these things, they are my preferences. However, they are not necessarily David's. It's been a difficult journey, but I have learned that respect means regarding my spouse's needs and preferences just as highly as I do my own. It means I must consider that what is important to me may or may not be of natural importance to David. Even though it's important to me, it may not be all that important in light of eternity. Respect in a marriage also means I may have to give up some of my preferences.

For us, that means I may have to choose what is most important. Do I want David to show me respect by leaving for the airport in plenty of time, or could I choose to respect that he has many details to attend to before we leave for a trip? Do I need David to show me respect by loading the dishwasher a certain way, or could I choose to respect his need to feel appreciated and just be grateful he's helping out at all?

How could you show respect to your spouse by giving importance to his or her preferences above your own?

Practicalities of Respect

*Let each of you regard one another as more
important than himself.* Philippians 2:3, NASB

One general guideline of respect is that before you make a commitment that impacts another person's life, you take the time to discuss it with that person. David and I have learned that it's important to discuss business commitments, trips, houseguests, and major financial decisions with one another, because those things impact both of us. We've even discovered that it's important for us to discuss certain things with our children before we implement them. We discuss family vacation ideas, household responsibilities, and changes of schedule or routine.

*God, make me
sensitive to the
need for respect
in our family.*

We've also learned that it's important to solicit and show deference to other people's opinions. In our home, everyone is entitled to an opinion, regardless of gender or age. We ask one another to share their opinions, and whenever it's possible we try to defer. For instance, instead of telling our kids where we're going on vacation this summer, we'll ask them where they would like to go. Instead of handing down a decision about how we'll spend Thanksgiving and Christmas, David and I will each give our ideas and opinions.

Respect in our home also includes giving honor to one another and to one another's property and privacy. We've had many discussions about taking care of the shirt that you borrowed and filling up the gas tank when you borrow my car. We've learned that it's important to honor others' privacy by knocking before entering a child's room. If David or I request a little solitude, then we work hard to honor that request.

Finally, respect includes honoring one another's time. Habitually being late indicates disrespect for others' schedules. We've found that it's important to call if you realize you're going to arrive later than expected, and we take care to respect one another's phone messages.

In what ways can you and your spouse begin demonstrating respect to one another and to other family members today?

Listening before Giving

He who answers before listening—that is his folly and his shame.
Proverbs 18:13, NIV

Over the years Teresa and I have learned that in order for couples to better demonstrate respect to one another, they need to discuss what that respect looks and sounds like. What communicates respect to one person may not communicate respect to his or her spouse. We encourage couples to discuss what actions and words convey respect for each spouse. We stress the importance of couples really listening to one another when they talk about respect. After all, listening is the first step toward conveying respect.

Father, remind me often of the great worth of Your children, who are joint heirs with Christ. May my attitude and behavior be consistent with this divine calling.

When we work with couples to get them to talk about respect, we use discussion starters such as: "My desire is to respect you, your roles, your decisions, and your leadership, so I'd appreciate it if you would let me know how I can better communicate respect to you," or "How can I better show you how much I value you and honor you as my spouse?"

We also help couples explore meaningful needs that enhance closeness when met. We do that by encouraging each to ask the question, *When do I need my spouse?* The couples then verbalize these needs this way: "It is very special to me when you _____."

As couples learn to listen better to one another, they find increased ability to hit the "target" with their giving. Husbands know exactly how to give their wives respect, and wives know how to show honor. Each is better equipped to esteem the other and less frustrated in his or her efforts to do so.

In what way will you demonstrate more willingness
to listen to your spouse today?

Confidence of Harmony, Freedom from Harm

*They shall be safe in their land; and they shall know that
I am the Lord.* Ezekiel 34:27

God meets our need for security by promising never to leave us or forsake us and by keeping that promise. He always meets our needs for food, clothing, and shelter. He is our ever-present help in times of trouble, and His loving-kindness is new every morning (see Psalm 46:1, Lamentations 3:23). We can count on Him to be faithful and unchangeable—the same yesterday, today, and forever (Hebrews 13:8). He gives eternal security for those who trust in Christ as their Savior. "I give them eternal life, and they shall never perish; no one can snatch them out of my hand" (John 10:28, NIV).

Father, thank You that You can be counted on. Help me to be that same source of security for my family.

As we receive security from God, we are able to give security in marriage. To give security means I (Teresa) live in such a way as to let my husband know that I am committed to him and only him, that I will always be true to our wedding vows and forsake all others.

Security means providing for the financial needs of my family. It may mean operating on a budget, having a good work ethic, developing marketable skills, and providing a secure financial future in case of illness or death.

Security means refraining from making threats to leave or abandon my family. It means committing myself to protecting my family from physical and emotional harm. It means that I refrain from harming my spouse or children in any way. Security means not losing my temper with my spouse or raising my voice to my children. It means being dependable and keeping promises.

An intimate marriage is only possible when both spouses feel confident of a supportive, caring relationship. An intimate family is only possible when all members feel secure.

What will you begin doing today to provide a greater sense
of security for your spouse and for your children?

True Security You Can't Even See

*Keep sound wisdom and discretion. . . . Then you will
walk safely in your way.* Proverbs 3:21-23

Wisdom leads to security? Sounds a little strange. You can't touch, count, or even see wisdom. How could it possibly bring security? It works this way: God knows that as we seek His wisdom and place our trust in what He values, we'll walk on secure ground.

*God, thank You
for Your offer
of wisdom and
the security it
provides. Keep
me from being
simpleminded
and complacent
so that I may live
in safety.*

We've known couples who look to the number of bedrooms and bathrooms in their home as a testimony of security. They have been deceived into thinking that security comes from possessions and social status. But God tells us that's not great wisdom: Let not a rich man boast in his riches. Let not a strong man boast in his chariots. But let him who boasts, boast that he understands and knows God (see Jeremiah 9:23-24). God wants us to realize that riches and possessions fade away, but that He can provide true safety from harm.

Teresa and I know couples who have relied on their "immunity" against divorce because of their sexual passions, great connection, or attractiveness. They have been deceived into thinking that security comes from physical attraction or appearance. But God's wisdom says, "Charm is deceptive, and beauty is fleeting" (Proverbs 31:30). God wants us to realize that beauty and human passions will fade, but He can provide unfailing love.

The first chapter of Proverbs reminds us that the voice of wisdom calls out to us. She has an incredible promise for us: "The waywardness of the simple will kill them, and the complacency of fools will destroy them; but whoever listens to me will live in safety and be at ease, without fear of harm" (verses 32-33).

In what specific areas of life do you need to feel more
secure? How might your spouse help meet those needs?

NOVEMBER

security
service
support
sympathy
teaching

My Idea of Security

Shall I not seek security for you? Ruth 3:1, NASB

My (Teresa's) feelings of security do not come from David's installing burglar alarms, putting better locks on doors, or doing other things to keep me from bodily harm. To me, security comes when David makes sure the lights are off, the alarm is set, and the locks are locked at night. Security to me is more related to his thinking of me.

Father, my security must be in You first, and then I'll trust You to involve my spouse as You may desire.

For many years I tended to associate security with the things my dad did for us when I was a child. David and I went through a lot of conflict over this issue. I caused David a lot of pain because I expected him to meet my security needs by doing the things Dad did. Dad could install locks, fix anything that broke, and do preventative maintenance on every imaginable household item. But David, by his own admission, lacks mechanical "genes." For example, he once tried to change the car's oil but ended up draining the transmission.

David took my insistence that security meant him doing all the mechanical things as criticism, as my seeing him as inadequate. Only as the Lord took us into a deeper understanding of one another and of what security truly is could I see where I had been wrong and begin to change my expectations. I realized that I can't expect David to be my dad. I need to sense that he wants to give me security.

From time to time I need to let David know what he can do to help me feel more secure. Most of the time it's just "being with me" in some emotional way. I can't expect him to know everything I need. Only when I express my needs can he fulfill them.

What can you do today to communicate to your
spouse what you need to feel more secure?

Only a Rough Exterior

Who can find a virtuous wife? . . . The heart of her husband safely trusts her. Proverbs 31:10-11

Men are typically conditioned to act tough, to resist emotional expression, and never to admit weakness. All of these behaviors hinder intimacy. Underneath this exterior image is often a fearful, insecure husband needful of a wife's reassuring love.

I (Teresa) have the God-given privilege of providing a safe haven for my husband. This special ministry of safety for my husband has included being careful to accept David's insecurities and fears. I've learned to hold my tongue when I discover an area of weakness or inadequacy. It's at those times that I must be careful not to belittle, judge, or dismiss David's fears. He needs my words of acceptance instead of my rejection.

Father, thank You for helping me provide a safe place for my spouse.

I have also learned that I create an atmosphere of safety for David as I give him the freedom to share his fears without reacting with my own. There have been times when I have squelched David's vulnerable sharing because of my own fearful reactions. ("I'm sorry you're having trouble with your boss, but we can't afford for you to lose your job right now!")

My own fears don't have to go unnoticed. Just as it's important for David to share his fears, it's important for me to share mine. I've learned to trust the Lord with my security and at times share openly with a trusted friend. I've learned that I have to trust God to bring maturity into David's life and to carefully discern when or if it is appropriate to share my insecurities with David.

Finally, I've discovered that as I listen to David express his fears, my role is to provide reassuring love. David needs to hear words like, "Sweetheart, I want you to know that I am committed to loving you no matter what. We'll work this out together."

How can you increase the "emotional safety" in your home?

My Copilot

His heart is established; he will not be afraid. Psalm 112:8

I am convinced my wife has "stealth" capabilities when we go shopping. We can enter a department store at the same time, walk into the same section of the store, and she disappears. She's there, and then she's not there.

God, thank You for blessing me with a copilot.

Until I find her, I don't feel quite right. My copilot is missing, and I'm a little panicked. Here I am in a shopping center, alone! It's like being in enemy territory without an ally.

Marriage is supposed to be like that. We are supposed to feel somewhat uncomfortable when apart from our spouse because he or she is our copilot while we are down here on earth. We fly the same plane together, and there is less security in flying alone.

As today's Scripture passage suggests, God is in the "heart-establishing" business, bringing the calming security of confident trust. In marriage, our spouse is one through whom He desires to work in order to establish this foundation for blessing. God wants to involve you in providing stability for your spouse. God wants to reassure your spouse that he or she doesn't need to be afraid of the bumps along the journey because—beyond any doubt—he or she is not alone.

The next time you find yourself without your copilot, pick up the phone and call. Let your spouse know how much you miss him or her. Say you're looking forward to being together because things just aren't the same when he or she is not around. Give your spouse the security of knowing that you think he or she is important, thought of, and deeply cared about. Announce that he or she still melts your heart and lights your fire. Look for ways to help "establish" the heart of your spouse.

How can you bring more stability or a more
firm foundation into your marriage?

The Security of Being "By Him"

The beloved of the Lord shall dwell in safety by Him, who shelters him all the day long. Deuteronomy 33:12

When our children were babies, each of them had a special something to take to bed for security. It may have been a blanket, a favorite doll, or a pacifier. At night when we heard crying or restlessness, we knew there was a good chance it was because the baby's prized possession had fallen out of reach. As soon as we returned it to the child's reach, he or she settled back down and fell asleep. Apparently our children needed the security of their important possessions being *with them*.

Thank You, Lord, that I am secure in You. Help me to create a safe place in my marriage.

Today's Scripture verse references the safety and security that comes from being close to God, from being *by Him*. The presence and proximity of our God is an important principle of security. We not only need the Lord's presence, we need Him in close proximity—*by us*.

In marriage it works the same way: There are repeated times—times of sorrow and rejoicing, adversity and success—when we need our spouse *by us*.

We also find in today's Scripture the importance commitment plays in dwelling in safety and security. How long will the Lord be *by us*? "All the day long" is His answer in this verse.

Remembering all this made me (Teresa) think of David and how he gives me security. His physical presence and commitment to me reassures me that I am loved and safe. I still have that security.

Because God knows your need for security and wants to meet it, He desires to create in marriage a safe haven away from the outside world. Marriage is to be a place where we can be *by one another* and *by Him*.

What can you begin doing today to make your marriage a haven of security?

Free from Fear of the Future

God has not given us a spirit of fear. 2 Timothy 1:7

If our fears are not from God—as today's Scripture tells us they are not—then they must come from the enemy, the one who steals, kills, and destroys. He's called the "father of all lies," and underneath the fear we feel, we can find the lies of the enemy we are believing.

Manifest Your love through me, Father, that it will cast out all fear.

Imagine hearing the words "You'll never change" or "We'll never get any better." Each of these statements points to fear about the future, and each is based on the lie that we can see into the future and know what is going to happen to us.

Fear of the future robs couples of the fulfillment of the present. In an effort to free couples of this fear, we often encourage couples to address their fears openly through verbalizing, prioritizing, and mutual accountability.

First, we teach verbalizing skills as a means to deal with fears and security. One of the spouses may say, "Honey, what have you been worried about or fearful of lately?" This kind of communication helps establish a basis of security within a marriage.

Second, we challenge couples to make sure they consistently prioritize their relationship through regularly scheduled couple dates. This means doing something for fun together—without children (that's family time), and without friends (that's social time).

Third, we encourage couples to develop mutual accountability. We encourage them to say things such as, "What irritating things have I been doing lately? I want to work on changing them." Each spouse listens attentively without being defensive, prays about what is shared, and then makes needed changes. A willingness to consider a spouse's wishes for change helps deepen security in the relationship and also helps expel fear.

What fears do you and your spouse have that need to be cast out of your marriage? What steps will you take today to cast them out?

Giving to Each Other

Through love serve one another. Galatians 5:13

True "serving" springs forth from a selfless, loving motive. There's much labeled as serving in our day that is not. Activity that calls attention to oneself is not serving. Involvement in "helping" others as a social opportunity to be well thought of is not serving. Giving to others less fortunate from a guilt-ridden heart is not serving. "Caring" for another so that he or she will care for you in return is manipulating, not serving.

Father, thank You for choosing to serve me through the gift of Your Son.

The empowerment of true serving comes from the mysterious word *agape*. It is translated as "love," but it is a unique love that comes from above. It could be argued that it is only through the grace of such love that we can be motivated to serve.

Teresa and I spent a lot of empty years in our marriage supposedly "giving" to one another, only to find that our motivation was "giving to get" and "I'll meet your needs if you . . ." This pattern began to change—not because we negotiated a settlement to our conditional love but because we each began to encounter anew His unconditional love for us. We were each in our own way affected more deeply by how the Savior in His love had served us. Such love began to change us, our relationship with Him, and then our marriage.

Serving another comes from the overflow of a heart filled with the wonderment that the carpenter from Nazareth has served me. He who had everything left it all in my behalf. He who could have called ten thousand angels to rescue Him at the cross chose instead to stay there so He could serve me.

May the awe and wonder of His love prompt me to lovingly serve others around me, including my dear wife.

What truly loving acts of service can you do for your spouse today?

Christ: Our Role Model

The Son of Man did not come to be served, but to serve.
Matthew 20:28

What a role model! If there was ever one who deserved special treatment, it was Christ. But His focus wasn't on what He deserved. His focus was on who He was and all that was His. From this identity and inheritance, a life of grateful giving sprang forth.

Teach me, Father, who I really am and what I've really received.

As our Scripture reminds us, Christ came to serve, and His upper-room meeting with the disciples was a classic example of His calling to serve. During dinner, only hours before His own betrayal and arrest, He takes a towel and a basin of water, and He begins to wash the disciples' feet. The Bible says that when He had finished washing all their feet, he exhorted them (and us) to do likewise.

I (Teresa) have always wondered how long it took to wash twelve disciples' feet. However long it was, it seems to me that in the face of all that lay ahead of Him, Jesus was wasting His time washing feet. But the Savior saw this as one of the most important lessons in servanthood He could give.

We see in this passage Jesus' prompting to serve others coming through the security of His identity. John 13:3-5 records that "Jesus, knowing that the Father had given all things into His hands, and that He had come from God and was going to God," rose from dinner and began to wash their feet.

I wonder if this would work for me. I wonder if fully understanding who I am in Christ would cause my heart to overflow with grateful giving. I wonder if fully appreciating my inheritance in Him would prompt me to care for others. God says that I am His beloved child, blessed with everything pertaining to life and godliness. I guess we'll see if that prompts the miracle of serving others—beginning in my marriage.

When will you set aside time to reflect on what you have received so that you will be motivated to serve?

When Is It My Turn?

It is the Lord Christ whom you serve. Colossians 3:24, NASB

David used to walk in the house from work with his hand up, as if he were holding a cup. That was his way of saying, "I need a cup of tea. I've had a really hard day."

In marriages today, where both spouses frequently work, the wife may feel like asking, "When will I be served? I've had a hard day too."

Whether David and I are counseling the husband, the wife, or both, we always tell people that *someone* in the marriage needs to start lovingly serving the other, trusting God to meet his or her own needs in the process.

Father, each of us must give an account to You only for ourselves. I want to be found faithful in serving my spouse.

The encouragement to serve our marriage partner comes from knowing whom we're really serving. Paul reminded the Colossians that they were to do everything "heartily," as if they were doing it for the Lord, for it was He whom they served (see Colossians 3:23). Likewise, as we serve our spouses we're also serving Christ. Maybe it's part of Christ's teaching that when we've done it for the least of these, we've done it for Christ (see Matthew 25:45). This possibility should further motivate each of us to serve our spouses.

Let's consider a few of the practicalities of serving another.

First, I need to give even when my spouse doesn't give to me, simply because God has already given to me. Second, I must serve my spouse lovingly and with joy, not with anger and resentment. Third, when I find myself growing weary in serving, I need to lovingly communicate my needs to my spouse, then trust God with the results. I can count on God to work in my spouse's life or to minister to me through avenues of His choosing.

What can you do today to start making service to one another the rule and not the exception in your marriage?

Free to Serve

What I will to do, that I do not practice. Romans 7:15

When we were first married, Teresa needed me to lovingly "give" to her, but it didn't often happen. I made many apologies and recommitments, but they were short-lived. I identified with the apostle Paul in Romans 7:19: The good I wanted to do, I didn't do.

Father, thanks for freedom from condemnation.

My problem was that I wasn't "free" to serve. Unresolved issues in my own life held me captive in selfish preoccupation. God began a slow but productive liberating work within me, and freedom to serve and give to Teresa followed.

Intimacy involves the freedom to share all of yourself—body, soul, and spirit—with your spouse. A wife needs a husband who is growing in this freedom and who encourages her in this freedom as well.

One aspect of this freedom involves dealing with the "accuser," who brings accusation and judgment against us. This evil one brings accusations against us such as, "You are a terrible father" and "Would a real Christian do what you just did?" This accuser used the guilt I felt over the wrongs I'd committed toward Teresa and my family to attack my worth and value. This condemnation stole my hope of change, leaving me with feelings of failure as a husband, father, and Christian man.

I'm grateful to report that the Holy Spirit began a miraculous work within me. I still remember the joyous day the Lord seemed to say, "David, I know you have done many things wrong since I first brought you into My kingdom. I want you to realize that when I first saved you, I knew you would sin in these ways. But I chose to save you anyway."

At that moment I was free from condemnation. And I was also free to serve my wife and family as God wanted me to.

In what specific ways do you need God to free you
to serve your spouse and children today?

Green-Stamp Service

*With good will render service, as to the Lord,
and not to men.* Ephesians 6:7, NASB

Have you ever found yourself "green stamping" your spouse? By that I mean doing something for him or her while internally deciding that you are owed for your "act of service." I'm not proud to admit that I (Teresa) do that at times.

It sometimes happens as I'm doing the laundry—not one of my favorite chores. As I sort through the dirty clothes, run them through the washer and dryer, then fold them, I begin to think, *David had better appreciate this, and he'd better show me his appreciation by . . .*

God, help me to develop a servant's heart toward my spouse.

Sometimes I catch myself thinking that way, and the Holy Spirit convicts me of my selfishness.

We freely choose to "serve" in marriage, yet sometimes we think we are owed some kind of payback when we do. The human bent is to do things in order to get some kind of payoff. But marital intimacy is destroyed by a "green stamp" mind-set.

We should always seek to serve, not to be served. The apostle Paul encourages our service to be motivated by "good will" and not by what we can receive in return. The principle of "good will" refers to concern for the benefit of another first. Paul reminds us that our serving is not for ourselves, but for others and for the Lord.

God reminded me of this one day when I was in "green-stamping" mode. I was keeping mental score, and David was way behind. Then the Lord brought this thought to me: *Teresa, this is not about you. It's about Me and how you can join Me in loving your husband through serving with a pure heart—a heart that seeks nothing in return.*

In what areas of service have you been "green stamping" your spouse? What steps can you take to make sure you don't do that?

Aspirin, Anyone?

If anyone ministers, let him do it as with the ability which God supplies, that in all things God may be glorified through Jesus Christ. 1 Peter 4:11

Interesting marital dynamics surface when a husband or wife gets sick in some way. Does the one who is sick want to be waited upon and "babied," or does he or she want to be left alone to suffer?

Lord, help me to know myself and then ask how I can best serve my spouse's needs. Give me patience and discernment in this area.

Teresa and I had considerable conflict over the issue. Each of us would try to guess what the other might want during times of illness, but it didn't help. One of us would do for our spouse what we might want him or her to do for us in that situation, but that rarely hit the target. I think we both were shocked at times to find that neither of us really knew what the other needed, and we had not communicated our needs to the other.

Both of us have been through times of martyrdom where we asked ourselves questions such as, "Is this what I really want, or is this what I think I'm supposed to want?" We have also fallen into the trap of not knowing exactly what we need, then becoming angry when we don't get it. We've come to find that it can be tough to figure out our own needs and desires. But only after we learn what our needs really are can we lovingly communicate them to one another.

God began to challenge us to sort through our own confusion about our needs before attacking each other for not meeting them. He then showed us both that being a good servant means listening to the needs of our spouse.

As we've gone through this, we've learned how to better serve one another—in sickness *and* in health.

What needs of yours have you not communicated well to your spouse?
How can you begin to better let him or her know of those needs?

Serving Each Other

We should serve in the newness of the Spirit. Romans 7:6

Mutual giving is one of the goals we work for in our ministry with couples. As each marriage partner finds freedom and motivation to serve the other, intimacy follows. Caring for another during life's endless demands is what having a servant's heart is all about. Caring for our spouse means serving him or her in daily life, not necessarily just in the "big things" that confront us.

Father, free us for serving each other.

We encourage couples to ask one another about their desires and wishes, to ask how they can better honor one another. We teach them to listen attentively to the answers, then lovingly give.

Next, we might challenge the couple to talk about decisions. We tell them how important it is to communicate how much they need and value one another's wisdom and how they want to be more sensitive to one another's opinions. Then we challenge them to talk about how they can better support one another in this area. This helps to bring more oneness and less tension into the decision-making process.

We also try to remind couples not to sweat the small stuff and to let one another make decisions and even mistakes. We encourage them to let him miss an exit off the expressway or pick a restaurant with a long waiting line, or let her verbalize "wild" ideas without shooting them down.

Today's Scripture passage provides additional insight into a life of serving: It is that serving comes in "the newness of the Spirit." Using a contrast with the bondage of law, Paul in essence speaks of fresh "evidence" of the Holy Spirit's work we should expect. If the more *internal* evidence of the Spirit is such things as "love, joy, peace, [and] patience" (Galatians 5:22, NIV), then the *external* evidence might be seen in serving others.

Have you seen much evidence of the Holy Spirit in your marriage lately?

In what small, seemingly insignificant ways can you serve
your spouse daily?

Helping Carry Burdens

Aaron and Hur supported his hands, one on one side, and the other on the other side; and his hands were steady. Exodus 17:12

The armies of the Lord prevailed against the enemy as Aaron and Hur provided support. Joshua led the Israelites into battle as Moses stood with the staff of God outstretched over the valley below. As Moses lifted up the staff, Joshua and the Israelites prevailed, but when Moses grew tired and lowered the staff, the enemies prevailed. Although no one made a plea for them to come, Aaron and Hur noticed the need, took the initiative, and came to render support.

Help me, Lord, to lift up my spouse in every way he or she needs it. Make me sensitive to each and every one of his or her needs.

True support means noticing needs, taking initiative, and quietly giving of oneself—oftentimes without being asked. It took me (David) several years to move past seeing only my needs to noticing Teresa's. But in recent years, we have enjoyed excitement and fulfillment as I have noticed her needs, taken initiative, and given her support.

An obvious principle in today's Scripture passage is that the one who is overwhelmed when left alone can be victorious when supported. Had Aaron and Hur left Moses to bear the weight of the staff alone, he would have collapsed, and the people of Israel would have suffered certain defeat.

God made us to need the support of others. In the marriage context, God has bound two people together so that each needs the strong, loving support of the other.

Countless homes have been torn apart when husbands and wives have had to bear their burdens alone and without support. Support is not standing at a distance giving advice. Rather it's hands-on time when we urge our spouses to allow us to bear their burdens with them.

In what areas of your marriage or role as a parent do you most need the loving, strong support of your spouse today?

The Joy of Mutual Support

It is more blessed to give than to receive. Acts 20:35

One of the ways Teresa and I support one another is through giving to each other. God has graciously shaped us in this area because we spent the first years of our marriage taking from each other rather than giving. We thought it was more blessed to receive, and each of us sometimes demanded certain things from the other. But slowly we have seen that God's lavish giving to us— especially through His Son—is the model He wants us to have in our marriage.

Lord, thank You for giving so lavishly to us. We receive Your love and want to give it to our spouse.

Teresa and I have learned that God wants us to support each other through the gifts of our time, attention, comfort, appreciation, and a whole host of other things. When I see Teresa carrying the burden of anxiety or busyness, I can come alongside her, get under the burden with her, and help her shoulder it by listening to her anxiety or by helping her prioritize her schedule. I can give her reassurance of my love for her and of God's perspective of her value.

Giving to one another characterizes a healthy relationship. Both of us have received God's abundance, and we now "freely give" (Matthew 10:8).

It has been almost humorous to find that sometimes Teresa and I compete for the chance to give and serve. It hasn't always been that way, but it's a joy to see the blessing of mutual giving. For many years I would never have understood or believed that it was better to give than to receive, but it really is!

Think about your marriage. Are you supporting one another by giving each other time, attention, respect, value? When you give to your spouse, you make him or her more complete, more whole.

How can you help carry your spouse's burdens by giving
to him or her?

With Me Always

I am with you always. Matthew 28:20

I (Teresa) was going to be giving a new message to a women's conference in the Houston area, and I was nervous about it. Giving new messages does that to me.

Father, thank You for giving us Your spirit to support us.

Since I couldn't fly to the retreat grounds, David had volunteered to drive me to the conference. We were almost an hour down the road when I went to pull out my new messages to review for the weekend and realized I'd left them on the desk back home. David was so supportive. He offered to take me on to the retreat, then return to Austin and get my notes.

I've never felt so much support from anyone as I felt from David that day. It felt so good to know that he would go out of his way for me. His support was an example to me of how I could be a support to him in the future.

Over the centuries, today's Scripture passage has provided reassurance and support to countless numbers of God's people. Christ makes no promise of shelter from pain or strife or from the aftermath of sin, but He promises that "I am with you always." It's the assurance that I'm not alone, that Jesus is with me, that brings me hope and courage and empowers me. Such are the blessings of the support my Lord has promised me.

I am with you always. It's this testimony of security that is portrayed on a human level in our marriage commitments. As we promise to be with our spouses "for richer, for poorer; in sickness and in health; until death do us part," we are saying that as long as we have breath, we will be with this person always.

That is what security in the marriage relationship is all about.

In what specific ways will you show your spouse Christlike love and support today?

The Miracle of Mutual Support

Bear one another's burdens, and so fulfill the law of Christ. Galatians 6:2

In today's Scripture verse we see the command to bear one another's burdens. But this is more than a command. It is a wonderful privilege to bear the burdens of those around us.

God didn't intend that some of us be just "bearers" and some of us be exclusively "bearees." We have the opportunity to bear the burdens of others around us—the common life struggles of sadness, defeat, temptation, and despair—but we also have the privilege of allowing others to bear our burdens. We can easily grow weary in doing good when we're always "bearing" and never allowing others to bear our burdens.

Lord, heal my spouse and me and free us for mutual giving and support in our marriage.

This truth argues loudly for the vulnerability that is vital in an intimate marriage. This vulnerability is manifested in a willingness to admit need, share struggles, and receive support. Couples can journey through healing hurts, gaining freedom, and finally mutual giving—each spouse joyfully giving to the intimacy needs of the other.

Teresa and I have commented often during our nearly four decades of marriage that it's been by the grace of God that both of us haven't "fallen apart" at the same time. I've had times of transition and uncertainty in work and ministry, and these things have given rise to self-doubt and "faith stretching." Teresa has been there to bear my burdens, provide encouragement, and give me companionship in my faith journey. At other times, Teresa has grown very discouraged—seemingly hopeless—over the kids' discipline and over her weight. God has taught me what support looks like. I've learned that my passive disinterest wasn't it. Over the years I've learned to help bear Teresa's burdens by having a listening ear and a caring heart.

In what specific areas do you and your spouse need
to begin showing one another mutual support?

Learning to Drive

*Come to Me, all you who labor and are heavy laden,
and I will give you rest.* Matthew 11:28

Can you imagine going to England for the first time and having to learn to drive on the left side of the road? Can you imagine what it would be like to approach a busy, downtown intersection in London—driving on the "wrong" side of the road?

God, help me to support my spouse in learning how to be an intimate partner.

God seems to teach me (Teresa) a lot when David and I travel overseas, and our first trip to England was no exception.

My first driving experience in London was insightful. David was really the one driving; I just filled the air with my advice, warnings, and panic. David is actually a great driver, and he had driven in London several times without me.

The problem that surfaced was my need to be in control. Every time David turned into the "wrong" lane, I panicked. I lost any sense of control, and my insecurities surfaced. But the Lord gently pointed out, "Teresa, the issue here is not David's driving. It's your fearful tendency to control things."

Marriage can be like learning to drive on the left side of the road. We are learning a whole new set of "driving" skills.

Because marital intimacy is so difficult to learn, we need to support one another and not tear one another down. Most of us feel pretty lost and awkward in our efforts to learn intimacy, and we don't need someone putting us down or criticizing us. In fact, the more we feel put down, the less we want to try to be close.

Support your spouse. Your spouse is learning to drive on the left side of the road and will need a lot of your love, understanding, and patience.

In what areas of the marriage relationship do you
most need your spouse's support today? In what areas
does he or she need your support the most?

I'm Falling

My yoke is easy and My burden is light. Matthew 11:30

Jill had worked for and prayed for the promotion for ten years. At last, her husband had been chosen as the vice president of the biggest computer company in their city. They had made sacrifices along the way, especially in family time. But it had been worth it, hadn't it? An accumulation of possessions and countless vacations were the rewards of their sacrifice and hard work.

Lord, give me the sensitivity I need to share in my spouse's struggles and burdens.

Then their world came crashing down. Their sixteen-year-old son was arrested for breaking into a pharmacy. He was looking for drugs. Jill and her husband were thankful when he was given two years of probation and enrolled in a drug rehab program.

Not long after that, Jill's husband came home early one evening to talk to her. God had convicted him of how out of balance his life had become. He wanted to quit his job and find a less-demanding position—maybe in a smaller town. He wanted to start all over and get control of their life again. But he wondered if Jill would support his decision. Would she help him learn how to be a husband and a father again?

How could Jill refuse? She loved her husband and her family. She supported him with all her heart.

A powerful way we bear burdens for others is to be reminded that Christ's "yoke is easy." It is a great ministry to encourage one another to seek for Jesus' "light burden." We all face stressful situations in life, but God leads us in the direction of peace and grace—just like He led Jill's husband. Jill provided her husband the support He needed to take on that lighter burden.

In marriage, we all need to do exactly as Jill did.

What can you do today to give your spouse support in taking on the "lighter burden" God may want him or her to take?

Bearing the Load

Share each other's troubles and problems. Galatians 6:2, NLT

Our tempers can often flare when we reach overload. But supporting our spouses by helping bear their burdens helps reduce tension in our lives, encourages mutual sharing, and magnifies feelings of love.

Father, sensitize me to my spouse's warning signs of overload. Bring me alongside to lovingly help.

When our kids were very young, Teresa learned that I got overstressed when I was put in situations where I had to referee conflicts between her and the children. She learned that she provided support in that area by seeking to talk to me about these things privately—away from the kids.

I learned that Teresa was vulnerable to stress over her eating and weight. I learned that I could provide her support in this area by helping her plan out meals, by eating more at home, and by occasionally joining her on her walks.

In our "preventative marriage work," we help couples develop strategies for handling the inevitable stress of marriage and family life. We do that by helping couples determine which things bring overwhelming stress to each partner. Then we discuss ways each person can help reduce the stress in his or her spouse's life.

When you feel the approach of marital conflict, it's a good idea to ask yourself, "Is my spouse reacting this way because he or she is feeling overwhelmed?" If that is the case, then address these feelings with understanding, empathy, and support. It is helpful in these situations to ask your spouse to communicate ways you can protect him or her from feelings of stress.

Another dimension of support is to have times of "escape." This means lovingly insisting on and then supporting your spouse's occasional "escape" into something fun and relaxing—for example, lunch with friends, reading a book, or window-shopping.

Finally, couple prayer times are important. After talking to your spouse about an area of concern, hold hands and pray.

What are the signs of emotional overload your
spouse shows during times of stress?

Identifying with Each Other Emotionally

Jesus wept. John 11:35

Throughout the Gospels we see a picture of an emotionally involved and sensitive Savior. The Son of Man is there to enter into the emotional pain surrounding the death of His friend Lazarus (John 11:1-44). He's available to minister in the midst of the loneliness of a tax collector (Luke 19:1-9) and the rejection of a leper (Luke 17:11-19).

But why does Jesus do this? Why does He take the time and emotional energy to share in the hurts and disappointments of others? It's not His divinity that requires such involvement, but rather His humanity. And if He is to be our great high priest, then He must enter into our emotional world of joy and pain, victory and defeat, celebration and grief.

Father, lead me into my spouse's emotional world.

The word used most often in the Gospels to describe the heart of Jesus is the word *compassion*. He would look upon the sick, lame, hungry, and rejected and be "moved with compassion." He wasn't moved to give advice or sermons, but compassion. We see the power of this compassion in today's Scripture text, which tells us how Christ shared in the pain of Mary, whose brother had died. Imagine that! The shortest verse in the Bible—and likely one of the most familiar—tells us of a God who cries out in grief.

We are called to do that in our marriages. However, many couples in marriage difficulty are there because they have, for prolonged periods of time, remained detached and withdrawn from their spouse's pain. They may have analyzed, avoided, rationalized, or blamed—but they have resisted *entering into* the emotional pain of their spouse.

Our ministry journey leads couples to the point where they can hurt for one another, where they can have genuine sympathy for one another in times of pain.

What can you do today to begin genuinely sharing in your spouse's emotions?

The Mystery of Oneness

All of you be of one mind, having compassion. 1 Peter 3:8

Harmony and sympathy come from a sense of feeling connected—emotionally bonded and attached—to another person. We are to enjoy that kind of closeness within the marriage relationship. It is that closeness that allows us to share in our spouse's emotions.

Thank You, Father, for the mystery of two becoming one in marriage.

Scripture speaks of Christians being part of one body with Christ as the head and with the Holy Spirit connecting us to one another (see 1 Corinthians 12). We care for one another, and therefore we sympathize when another is sad or hurt.

If we could see into the spirit world, we would likely see each believer "attached" by the Holy Spirit to the head of the church, Jesus Christ. When one part of the body suffers loss, betrayal, or pain, the head is moved with compassion. Then the Holy Spirit touches other parts of the body, moving them with compassion for the hurting.

What if this happened consistently within the marriage relationship? We believe that is how it should be. We are to have this kind of sympathy within marriage as well. The Bible says that in marriage "two become one" (Genesis 2:24). As this oneness deepens, each spouse becomes increasingly sensitive to the emotions of the other. Being understood and identified with emotionally are key ingredients to marital intimacy.

This mystery of connectedness is one of the key reasons we do most of our marriage ministry in sessions with both spouses present. We believe we can help each marriage partner better with the "other half" present. It's also our view that God intends for each spouse to play a vital role in the work of healing and restoration and that a spouse's verbalized sympathy and appreciation will mean more to the spouse than ours will.

What can you do today to promote emotional oneness
within your marriage?

I Want My Mommy!

No one comforts me. Lamentations 1:21

The preschoolers in Bible study were out on the playground when one little girl nicked her finger. It was a very minor injury, and one of the teachers tried to tell her that she wasn't hurt badly and that her finger would quit hurting soon. But the child didn't believe it, and she kept crying.

I (Teresa) picked up this little girl and started talking to her about her finger and how bad it must have hurt. I asked her if she wanted her mom, and she responded with an anxious, enthusiastic "Yes!" We talked about how she wanted her mommy until her mother came. Then the little girl was fine.

Lord, thank You for Your compassion and for making marriage a source of care and compassion.

We are not often taught how to give sympathy, but we all need it. Sympathy has nothing to do with facts or reasons. Sympathy is talking to me about my pain. We adults can be just like the little girl with the nicked finger—we just want sympathy from the one we love.

There's really only one thing any of us wants to know when we're in pain, and that is, "Does anyone care?" And if there's no one there to care for us, the pain is worse. If someone is there but doesn't offer empathetic care, we are still not comforted in our pain.

Today's Scripture passage is a lot like our cry when we are alone in our hurt: "No one comforts me."

One of the potential benefits of marriage is the certainty that our spouses will provide sympathetic care when we are hurting. It's great to know that if we are hurting and the rest of the world looks on with indifference, our spouses will care and give us the sympathy we need.

What specifically can you do and say today to provide your spouse the sympathy he or she needs during times of pain?

Not Satisfied with Just Coping

If you do well, will not your countenance be lifted up?
Genesis 4:7, NASB

Philip came for marriage help—by himself. He described symptoms of depression, all of which were related to his marriage. He was embarrassed at being depressed and at having marital problems. He believed that because he was a Christian, he wasn't supposed to have these kinds of problems. But he was tired of pretending, tired of "coping."

Thanks, Father, for Your promise of abundance.

Many couples are like Philip. Amid religious expectations, they struggle just to cope with their marital problems. They pretend all is well, while their lives at home are a mess. They wonder how they can expect to walk in God's forgiveness while harboring anger and bitterness. When a person's home life differs from his or her spiritual values and teachings, feelings of inadequacy, guilt, and condemnation are often added to the pain of loneliness, rejection, fear, anger, or bitterness.

We helped Philip to explore his unresolved anger. He had not found it helpful simply to commit himself to not being angry with his wife. With every new commitment Philip made came new hopes on his wife's part—hopes Philip dashed at his next outburst. We helped Philip identify the hurt behind his anger, and we involved his wife in a meaningful time of forgiveness and comfort. She was able to express compassionate care for the hurt in Philip's life—some of which had nothing to do with their marriage. Philip was able to listen more attentively as his wife communicated the hurt she felt as a result of his anger. Healing was underway, and coping began to give way to abundance.

Philip and his wife learned an important lesson about the expectations we should have for our marriage, one of them being that we shouldn't merely cope with the problems in our marriage; rather, we address them and work to solve them.

What areas of your marriage have you been "coping with"?
What steps will you take today to solve your problems?

I Feel Your Pain

You had compassion on me. Hebrews 10:34

Teresa is not fond of high places, and that's been challenging during our marriage travels. It's hard to cross the Grand Canyon, traveling from one side to the other, without crossing the bridge. It's hard to enjoy skiing without going up high mountains.

In addition to the obvious challenges, the family's response to Teresa's fears has been unintentionally painful. At times the kids have teased her and made fun of her. On other occasions, I've offered many irrelevant, rational arguments such as, "How are we going to go up the mountain without getting up high?" Teresa was always a good sport about her fear of heights and the family's lack of support, but God was concerned about her.

God, help me walk inside my spouse's shoes and sympathize with his or her pain.

Several years ago as the Lord began to teach us the significance of the first human crisis: "It is not good that man should be alone" (Genesis 2:18), He reminded me of how we had treated Teresa. He also reminded me of my own response to a recent medical emergency with our grandson. I felt out of control, powerless, and very small in the midst of that hospital hallway. God impressed me with these thoughts: *David, Teresa's been a good sport through all the teasing about her fears, but she's been very much alone. Could you tell her how sad you feel when you think about her feeling afraid on top of that mountain, because you remember feeling afraid too? Could you tell her you hurt because she had to face her fears alone? Could you reassure Teresa that you will be more sensitive because you have identified with her emotions?*

God reminded me that day of His tender compassion for Teresa and shared some of that compassion with me. He allowed me to sympathize with Teresa so that she didn't have to be alone.

How can you express sympathy and compassion
for your spouse today?

I Hurt When You Hurt

*You have delivered . . . my eyes from tears, and
my feet from falling.* Psalm 116:8

I had just dropped David off at work, and my kids were in the front seat. I had entered the intersection to make a left turn onto our street. Out of the corner of my eye I saw another car enter the intersection on my right. The man driving the car didn't see us. We could only watch as he ran his car into mine.

God, help my spouse and me to understand each other's feelings.

Almost in tears, I got out to look at the damage. The man in the car admitted his carelessness and apologized for running into us, but all I could see was the bashed-in car door. And even though the accident wasn't my fault and even though no one was hurt, I felt as if I had let everyone down.

With the police on their way to the scene, I called David. He was there quickly and came running to give me a reassuring hug. He knew I was feeling bad about what had happened, and he offered me encouragement. He reminded me that the accident wasn't my fault and that the kids and I were more important than any damage to our car. Before it was all over, David's sympathetic reaction made me almost glad the accident had happened.

While I deeply appreciated my husband playing the role of "deliverer" that day, God is our ultimate deliverer, and sometimes His deliverance comes during times of loss, uncertainty, and pain. It's at these times that He brings us comfort, dries our tears, provides reassuring security, and "keeps our feet from falling."

The marriage relationship gives us the privilege of joining God in providing our spouses comfort and reassurance when they need it. It is our calling—our privilege—to give our spouse sympathy in times of pain or stress.

How specifically will you give sympathy when your spouse
is faced with pain, stress, or disappointment?

Family Night "Feeling Project"

*They made an appointment together to come to sympathize
with him and comfort him.* Job 2:11, NASB

It's not uncommon for us to encounter couples who struggle in their marriage because of a lack of emotional closeness. One of the first challenges we face in these situations is to help these couples develop a vocabulary of feelings.

It's impossible to be vulnerable and to communicate feelings when you don't know what to call them. It's tragic that in a culture that stresses education, so many people miss out on what we call "education of the heart."

*Lord, thank You
for emotions and
for how they can
bind my family
together.*

We recently worked with a couple who needed some of this kind of education. We encouraged Don and Margaret to begin by drawing up a "feeling chart." They purchased a piece of poster board and divided it into two columns—one for positive feelings and one for painful feelings. Don and Margaret's entire family were then to name as many of their feelings as possible. After a few nights of developing a "feeling vocabulary," they were ready to move on to communicating their feelings.

Don and Margaret and their kids were now ready to take turns talking about events that happened during a given day and how these events made them feel. Each family member talked about a positive event and positive feeling and then a negative event and feeling.

We recommend this project for families who wish to learn to better communicate their emotions with one another. It makes a major impact on a child to hear that Mom feels anxious or angry, and it can do the same for a child to hear that Dad feels lonely or sad. When that happens, family members conclude that it's okay to have feelings and that it's okay to talk about them.

What will you begin doing as a family to better
communicate your feelings and emotions?

teaching

Constructive Life Instruction

Teach me Your way, O Lord. Psalm 27:11

I (David) have gratefully learned to pray the psalmist's prayer "Teach me Your way" when I'm faced with crucial decisions or struggles in relationships. God has brought tremendous relief as I've prayed the psalmist's prayer when "my way" has clearly been the wrong way.

Lord, I want to know Your ways, but I also want to know You.

By far, the best result from my "psalmist prayers" has been the sweet intimacy with our Lord. I've discovered that just as it's important for me to want to learn His ways, He longs to teach me. The Lord wants me to be in on His plans and His desires. He doesn't just want to teach me His commandments so I'll shape up. He doesn't have a checklist of lessons that I've got to pass. The Lord wants to teach me His ways because He longs for me to know Him better.

It's important to notice that the psalmist offered his prayer only after he had recounted his intimate relationship with the Lord. The writer reflects on God as his ultimate source of well-being and salvation. He reflects on their intimate relationship as they dwelt in the house of the Lord together. The psalmist wanted to know the ways of the Lord because he felt confident of the Lord's agenda. The psalmist also knew that God longs to teach us His ways because He wants to share His life with us.

That's the kind of God we serve—One who wants to know us and be known by us, One who wants to teach us His ways because He wants an intimate relationship with us. That kind of God is easy to serve. That kind of God I can love—and I'm ready to listen.

How could you spend some time getting to know the ways of the Lord today—letting God share Himself with you?

Cart before the Horse

Let the word of Christ dwell in you richly in all wisdom, teaching . . . one another. Colossians 3:16

I (David) can distinctly remember when God used today's Scripture passage to teach me a life-changing lesson on what to do with His Word. Too much of my training and too many of my mentors had encouraged me to look in the Word for what "those" people need. The Holy Spirit clearly convicted me with the verse's exhortation to "let the word of Christ dwell in *you*"! I needed to focus more on the Word for *me*, not the Word for *others*.

Bring us often together, Father, around the truth from Your Word.

The Spirit caught my attention as I read the word *dwell*. How was I to let the Word of God reside, live, or dwell in me? I had memorized Scripture for years and preached sermons on every book of the Bible, but I wasn't sure that the Word lived in me. The Spirit of God prompted these thoughts: For God's Word to dwell in me, I must be living it out. It must have made an impact on my behavior. For God's Word to dwell in me, it must so permeate my being and dwell in my heart that it changes my life.

The Lord's final challenge stopped me cold. The order of words in the Colossians passage seemed important. Before I could teach someone else with all wisdom, I had to have the Word of Christ dwelling in me. In other words, before I was equipped to teach anyone else, God had to do a work in my life and change me. I started thinking about how many times I stood to teach compared to how many of Christ's words were living in me. My heart was humbled.

My words of instruction sound much different now. I now share with Teresa and with others what God has done in me as I have lived out His Word.

Which of Christ's words does He want to see dwelling in you today?

Get Out Your Pad and Pencil!

My son, do not forget my teaching. Proverbs 3:1, NASB

David's spiritual gift is teaching. He loves to study, prepare, write, and then teach what God has shown him. He especially likes to teach at home.

When the kids were young, David tried to "talk" to them about issues in their lives that needed correction. Instead of being concise, he "taught" them. Rather than a clear yes or no, he gave three points, each of them with considerable explanation. Sometimes that was helpful to our children, but sometimes it brought on memorable moments of humor in our family.

Lord, thank You for a spouse who has a desire for Your Word.

One day in one of our family times, the kids asked David a simple question that required a simple answer. When David started into a long answer, one of the kids burst out, "Oh no! Get out your pad and pencil. Dad's gonna teach!" We all laughed together that day, and our child's words that day became a humorous—and oft-repeated—way for the kids to remind Dad that they needed an answer and not a lesson.

We've laughed often at what our children said that day, but our family and friends all admire and appreciate David's ability to impart God's Word. My husband's ability to teach has been a great comfort to me. I've known I could always turn to him to find out where to go for answers in God's Word. We've enjoyed wonderful times together seeking God's direction by exploring a wide range of topics.

I can tell you from personal experience that it is a great blessing to have a spouse who is willing to take the time to teach from the Word of God. This has been a blessing to me and to our children over the years.

How will you respond when your spouse takes
the time to teach you and your children?

Teaching about Worth

I, therefore, . . . entreat you to walk in a manner worthy of the calling with which you have been called. Ephesians 4:1, NASB

"How can I get my wife back?" Allen asked in our first meeting together. He and his wife, Jeannie, were struggling, and Allen sensed her pulling away from him.

Teresa and I had known Jeannie for several months. I remember her words to us: "I've just needed Allen to accept me the way I am, to quit trying to make me like him." She explained that Allen, who was not a Christian, tied his own sense of worth to his accomplishments. And he as much as told Jeannie that she wasn't worth much if she didn't accomplish certain things.

Lord, teach us that our worth is found in You, not in what we do.

Jeannie not only didn't need Allen's pressure to make her into someone she was not, but she also needed him to stop trying so hard to make himself feel worthy through his work and activities. She needed Allen to "be" someone—an accepting someone.

The Scripture passage from Ephesians is a great reminder that the Christian life is a "walk" and a lifestyle, not a to-do list! Like Allen, many people assume that they need to "do things" in order to be a success. But they often find that working too hard hinders relationships with others. Intimate relationships are founded on first being accepted, loved, and valued.

Over time, Teresa and I had the privilege of leading Allen to the inexpressible joy of knowing Jesus Christ. At first he struggled with the fact that he could do nothing to earn Christ's love but needed instead simply to receive Him. As Christ taught Allen about His acceptance, Allen was able to pass on that acceptance to Jeannie. And she came back to a strong relationship with her husband.

How can you find your worth in Christ? How will you show your acceptance to your spouse today?

DECEMBER

teaching
tolerance
training
trust
understanding

How Are Your Grades?

In your teaching show integrity, seriousness and soundness of speech that cannot be condemned. Titus 2:7-8, NIV

I (Teresa) recently recalled how our children would come home from school with fantastic report cards. When they brought their report cards home, the kids wanted to know how I was going to reward them. They would suggest things like new cars or a trip to Disney World. We would typically negotiate their reward— I thought a trip to the local pizza parlor would be enough.

God, help me lovingly teach and learn from my spouse.

There are plenty of positive aspects to this focus on academic achievement. I know it made me ask myself a question: "Do I as a wife pay as much attention to my role as a spouse as my kids did in their role as students?" Answering that question meant considering my actions and attitudes, my initiative and respect. Also, as our Scripture passage notes, I needed to consider the issue of my *conduct*.

When our kids excitedly showed us their good academic marks, they—particularly our son, Eric—often didn't want us to see their grades for conduct. I found it to be that way in my spiritual life, as the Lord challenged me about my conduct, my lack of reverence, and the "soundness" of my speech. I realized I needed to make some changes.

This also got me to thinking about my "report card" as a spouse. If marriage were held in a classroom, how would I be graded? What would be my mark, for example, in Intimacy 101? What would be my mark for conduct?

In the classroom of marriage, sometimes we teach our spouses, and sometimes our spouses teach us. All the time, God is the senior teacher. He's the One who gives us the ultimate instruction—and the ultimate rewards for how we conduct ourselves.

In what area or areas of marriage do you need to work to "bring up your grades"?

Learning through Examples

Speak the things which are proper for sound doctrine. Titus 2:1

We were having dinner with some dear friends when I (Teresa) complimented Andrea on her talk that morning at the Bible study. She downplayed what she had done. Bob, her husband, interrupted with, "Now, honey, I think you should accept Teresa's compliment." Andrea looked back to me and said, "Thank you, Teresa. That's so nice of you to notice."

God, help my spouse and me to learn from other couples and from other avenues You may choose to use.

Bob then explained he was helping Andrea learn to accept praise. When someone complimented Andrea, Bob would lovingly and gently remind her to graciously accept the praise.

Since I oftentimes struggle with receiving compliments, David and I decided to adopt the same strategy. It wasn't long before we began to see just how often I stiff-armed compliments. Soon we found ourselves passing along through example what we had learned from our friends about how to accept praise.

David has helped me in this area (and others) by reminding me of "sound doctrine." I was impacted in this part of my life by David's reading Romans 8:32 to me: "He who did not spare His own Son, . . . how shall He not with Him also freely give us all things?"

God applied this verse to my reluctance to receive praise by softly telling me, "Teresa, since I have given you Jesus, wouldn't I also want to give you a few compliments through those who know you and love you?"

God can teach us through a lot of different avenues, including the examples of others. Our friends taught us something important through their actions toward each other. David also taught me to embrace important truth from Scripture.

What are you teaching other couples who are watching your marriage?

What avenues of teaching is God using with you and
your spouse? What is He trying to teach you today?

The Teaching Power of the Word

Man shall not live by bread alone, but by every word that proceeds from the mouth of God. Matthew 4:4

We often recommend the memorization of 1 Corinthians 13 for couples who desire to deepen their spiritual growth together. This "Love Chapter" is filled with God's teaching on the characteristics of divine love, and hiding it away in your heart helps make the reality of it a lot closer. Couples also benefit from memorizing Scripture passages that speak directly to their needs. Not only individual verses, but large passages of Scripture are important. We recommend Matthew 5–7, John 15, Romans 5–8, Colossians 3, Hebrews 12, and James 1.

Nourish me with the truth of Your Word, O Lord. Make me a doer of that Word and not just a hearer.

We also encourage couples to "personalize" the passages they read and memorize. God delights in hearing His own Word, especially when we use it to express to Him our own desires and emotions. To do this, take the sections you memorize and add personal pronouns wherever possible.

Turning Scripture passages into mental pictures helps us to visualize the truth and turn memorization into meditation. Choosing to dwell on scriptural pictures of God's truth can give us sustained victory in our thought life. We can learn to build these mental pictures into key truths by rehearsing in our mind what patience or kindness might look like. This helps remind us of what true love is.

An additional dimension of blessing from our meditations on God's Word is its impact on the heart of the One who wrote the Scriptures. Imagine what it does to the heart of God to see His children not just being *hearers* of the Word but *doers* also. As our Scripture passage encourages, we should live out every word that proceeds from Him.

How can you and your spouse make memorization and personalization of Scripture a bigger part of your relationship?

tolerance

Patient Endurance of Another's Humanness

*Walk . . . with all lowliness and gentleness, with longsuffering,
bearing with one another in love.* Ephesians 4:2

Tolerance relates to putting up with another person's obvious humanness and bearing with his or her imperfections. To express tolerance demands setting aside a self-centered focus and adopting instead a God-centered perspective. God sees each of us as very different, absolutely unique, undoubtedly imperfect, but divinely created.

Thank You, Father, for Your powerful example in putting up with me.

To express tolerance means I must "suffer long" with my spouse and "put up with" his or her humanness. I must bear with my spouse's flaws and peculiarities with a good attitude. I must be free from resentment as I show tolerance toward my spouse. I must show humility and gentleness instead.

Tolerance relates to patiently enduring my spouse's differences in preference and habits. I must be patient if I like crunchy peanut butter and she insists on smooth. I must be patient if he's a night owl and I'm at my best at dawn. Tolerance also relates to patiently enduring my spouse's weaknesses. I must suffer long even if I always put the car keys on the designated key hook and yet my spouse can barely find the car. I must maintain a good attitude even when I have a great sense of direction and am quite adept at reading a map and yet my spouse can't find his or her way out of a paper bag.

Finally, tolerance relates to God's choice to bear with me and my sin as He sent His Son to die. God endured my humanness as He gave up His Son on my behalf. He daily endures my imperfections and suffers long as I struggle to live a life that is pleasing to Him. Tolerance is a gift I have been given. I am challenged to give what I have already received.

What issues might you overlook today that have previously been
a "big deal"? How might you show tolerance for your spouse?

Grace Is Tolerant

For by grace you have been saved. Ephesians 2:8

"How can I put up with his sloppiness?" "How can I keep overlooking her being late?"

Couples in our marriage seminars often ask how they can possibly tolerate their spouses' faults and weaknesses. In response to that, I (David) often think to myself, *You can give up on them as soon as God does—never!* Who among us has not benefited from our Creator's gracious tolerance? This gift frees us to accept and love others unconditionally. It frees us and motivates us to give our spouses the kind of acceptance and love we have received ourselves.

Thanks, Lord, for Your tolerance and acceptance of me.

The miracle of our salvation comes from the wonder of divine favor, which we receive in the form of God's abundant grace. "While we were still sinners" this grace made us recipients of Christ's love (see Romans 5:8). This love was not extended *after* we stopped sinning, but *while* we were still in sin. When we are filled with gratitude for such grace, it flows naturally from us toward others.

This unconditional love from God frees us from having to perform in order to please our spouses. Having partaken of God's grace, I'm genuinely free to give to my spouse. As Jesus said, "Freely you have received, freely give" (Matthew 10:8).

Having received what I could not earn and did not deserve, I'm free from the fear of never having it and free from the fear of ever losing it. This liberty of gracious acceptance builds intimacy—intimacy with God and with my spouse. In this freedom, tolerance of my spouse comes easily.

How and from where specifically can you find the motivation
to tolerate and accept your spouse, despite his or her flaws?

I'll Not Be Your Mother!

How can you say to your brother, "Brother, let me remove the speck that is in your eye," when you yourself do not see the plank that is in your own eye? Luke 6:42

One of David's "sins" is being late. He's been late ever since we were first married. I used to get so upset over his lateness that I'd be uptight and cranky before we even left to go somewhere. When we arrived, I'd be embarrassed and feel I needed to make excuses for us.

God, as You see the need to change my spouse, teach me to step aside and allow You to make those changes.

In time I began to see that my attitude over David's lateness was a sin against God. I began to see my responsibility in allowing David's actions to cause me to sin. When I examined the "plank in my own eye," I became more tolerant of what I had seen as David's "sin."

The irony of the wisdom in today's Scripture passage is that the more I focus on my own "plank," the more God frees me to lovingly and gently point out my spouse's "speck." When I owned up to my sinful attitudes and actions concerning my husband's lateness, I was able to be more gentle and loving when I pointed out to him why we needed to make more of an effort to be on time to appointments. It worked, too!

Over the past few years, David has changed to the point that he's rarely late and often pushes *me* some to be on time. Obviously, the Holy Spirit's conviction in David's life was much more effective than mine.

It is so freeing now to realize I'm not responsible for my husband's actions. When I nag about his being late or try to cover for him, I'm actually mothering. And God didn't call me to be a mother to David. He called me to be a wife.

In what areas of your spouse's life have you tried to be more of a parent than a marriage partner?

Can I Resent Tolerating You?

Bear with each other and forgive . . . one another. Forgive as the Lord forgave you. Colossians 3:13, NIV

The Lord is the ultimate example of tolerance. He who is perfect, holy, and complete puts up with me, who is imperfect, sinful, and incomplete. God doesn't resent tolerating me. He doesn't pout and act like a martyr while He waits for me to "grow up." He's kind, gentle, patient, and loving. It's as if He is patient because He knows I'll "arrive" one day—even if it is in the world to come.

I wonder if I (David) could have this same kind of attitude toward my spouse, realizing that when Jesus appears, she shall be like Him. Knowing that, can I tolerate Teresa's imperfections as God has tolerated and continues to tolerate my own?

Lord, thank You for bearing with me in my imperfections.

Teresa and I have been challenged to tolerate one another over the years in a variety of areas. My lateness, procrastination, and moodiness have prompted many retaliations from Teresa. Her bent toward control, speaking before thinking, and self-reliance have been the subject of many of my complaints and frustrations.

Whether it's because the years have taken their toll or because of a lack of success in trying to change one another, our focus has shifted dramatically. The past decade has brought to each of us this new question: "What would God like to do in my life in the face of my spouse's shortcomings?" Such a question has intensified the work of Christlikeness in each of us. God is well pleased with this work.

It seems like the more I've grown to understand and appreciate God's tolerance of me, the more tolerance I've had available for Teresa.

I guess that's what tolerance of one another in a marriage relationship is all about.

What do you think God wants to do in *your* life—
in the face of your spouse's shortcomings?

Bite Your Thumb!

Love suffers long. 1 Corinthians 13:4

When I (David) was a kid, my family would go on vacation by car. Some of the trips were long ones, so my parents put a cooler of soft drinks in the car to keep my brother and me pacified during the trips.

God, help me to endure patiently what is difficult or challenging about my spouse.

The problem with giving us the soft drinks was that we often drank so many that we needed to go to the bathroom every thirty minutes or so. On one trip we boys were raising a fuss because we needed to stop for another bathroom break. My dad finally turned around to us in the backseat and with a grin on his face said, "Bite your thumb!" Dad was telling us that we were going to have to endure the discomfort until he was ready to stop.

In marriage, we are often required to endure—to patiently tolerate an annoying habit or personality characteristic in our spouse. Since everyone has different quirks and imperfections, we all need to receive tolerance from our spouses and to show our spouses tolerance in return.

Teresa and I have found one practical strategy to help us suffer long with one another. It starts with each of us making an honest evaluation of some of our own shortcomings. For example, I know I'm withdrawn, often a procrastinator, and sloppy when it comes to details. This step helps take my focus off my spouse's shortcomings.

Next, we identify strengths God has given to our spouse, which helps us focus on strengths and not on weaknesses. Teresa's strengths are that she is outgoing, quick to act, and thorough with details.

Finally, we share appreciation with one another by affirming one another and trusting God to change anything He may want to change in us as individuals.

What might you begin doing today to make yourself
more patient and long-suffering with your spouse?

I Love You Anyway!

Uphold the weak, be patient with all. 1 Thessalonians 5:14

I (Teresa) am not at all good with directions, and I can't make heads or tails out of a map. Therefore, it's easy for me to get all turned around and lost. My only hope of finding my way around is to orient myself to a familiar shopping mall. David, on the other hand, always seems to know intuitively where he's going.

God, please help my spouse and me to be tolerant of each other's shortcomings, no matter how irritating they may be.

Recently David and I remodeled our house, and we needed some new ceramic tiles. We headed out to the tile store, and I promptly got lost looking for it. I'd been to the store once before, a couple of weeks earlier. I didn't remember exactly where the complex was, but I was sure I'd recognize it when I saw it. We tried one complex, then another. "Maybe we could go just a little farther," I suggested.

After I had driven in circles at least three times, David began teasing me a little. He did not attack my character or me personally. Instead, he suggested that we call the business and get directions. In doing this, he showed me considerable tolerance. When we finally found the store, David still had a good attitude, and we enjoyed our time together picking out tile.

I believe that it's part of God's plan that tolerance can be "pulled off" only as patience is being perfected. Our Christlikeness is a high priority to the Lord, who is working to perfect us so that we can be His Son's bride.

God uses our spouses—their imperfections, their quirks, their shortcomings—as tools to perfect us for that very purpose.

How can you begin changing your response to
your spouse's shortcomings today?

Building Tolerance through Gratitude

Forget none of His benefits. Psalm 103:2, NASB

Frances and Derrick were impatient with each other. They lacked any tolerance for differences of perspective or opinion between one another.

Remind me often of the special blessing I've received in the gift of marriage.

We worked with them on several underlying issues in their marriage, and then we addressed their lack of tolerance for one another. I (David) told them that husbands and wives can develop tolerance through focusing on their spouse's strengths. For example, I told them, if I focus solely on Teresa's faults, my patience will be thin with her. Conversely, deepening my gratefulness for my wife's strengths helps me look beyond irritations and weaknesses.

Frances and Derrick discussed some of the benefits of having a grateful heart. They noted that gratitude guards us from a critical, negative attitude and a judgmental spirit. They also realized that expressions of gratitude can encourage others to continue in "good deeds." Finally, they acknowledged that gratitude, when expressed to God, is an important element of worship.

As Frances and Derrick began applying these insights to their marriage, we encouraged them to rediscover areas where they appreciated one another. We also challenged them to revisit the things that originally attracted them to one another. Additionally, we challenged them to try to discover new things to appreciate about one another and to reflect on how those strengths bring balance to their marriage.

The principles of remembering benefits and expressing gratitude have their foundation in today's Scripture passage. We should ask ourselves often if there are blessings and dimensions of grace that we've come to take for granted. Then we need to pause to reconsider our blessings and give worship to God for them.

As we allow our hearts to be filled with gratitude, we will tolerate—even joyfully accept—our spouses and their imperfections.

What qualities in your spouse can you be
appreciative of today?

Modeling God's Way of Facing Life

Everyone who is perfectly trained will be like his teacher.
Luke 6:40

Ever wonder why people are so often anxious? Anxiety is common in individuals and in marriages today. There are many reasons for this, one of which is the fear of inadequacy. I (Teresa) feel inadequate when I face issues or decisions I don't know how to handle, and anxiety results. When I'm put on the spot and have to deal with certain challenges in life and draw a blank, anxiety rises within me. And when I feel anxious, tension, anger, and conflict often result.

Thanks, Lord, for Your Word and my spouse's strengths, which help train me for adequacy in all things.

"Training" can address the anxiety I feel over my inadequacy—inadequacy in handling certain discipline issues with the kids, inadequacy in certain social situations, inadequacy in my marriage, inadequacy in my service to God.

In today's Scripture passage, Christ reminds His disciples of the power of our *influence* on others. It would be Christ's *training* of His disciples that would prepare them to lead His church. Their training would be comprehensive, covering all the subjects they would need to know about after He returned to the Father. Jesus knew they would encounter skeptics, rejection, legalists, and demons, so He wanted to train them how to handle these things. The disciples would *study* home life, giving, kingdom life, and Christ's future return. They would come to find Christ throughout the Old Testament Scriptures, and many of them would help complete the Scriptures as the Holy Spirit directed.

Christ's objective in this training was to give the disciples a sense of adequacy. It's this adequacy that ensures that the workman need not be ashamed, handling adequately the word of truth (2 Timothy 2:15).

Training in adequacy, whether at home or in His work, is vital.

What will you and your spouse do today to address any feelings
of inadequacy in your marriage, in your role as parents,
and in your personal ministry?

Avoiding the Blame Game

If you bite and devour one another, beware lest you be consumed by one another! Galatians 5:15

Many couples pressure each other by playing what we can rightly call the "blame game." It goes something like this: "I wouldn't be so critical if you'd quit watching so much TV," followed by, "I wouldn't watch so much TV if you'd be more affectionate."

We're grateful, Father, that You've given us instruction for our marriage.

In this destructive "game," each spouse *pressures* the other to act in certain ways. For example, wives pressure their husbands to "do" more around the house, and husbands pressure their wives to be more receptive sexually.

Marriage and family life suffer dramatically from the pressure to perform. This pressure often comes when emotional or relational needs are unmet within the marriage. When this happens, affection is withheld and emotional distancing takes place. Demanding, controlling, and taking soon replace grateful giving. Love becomes conditional, and the marriage is robbed of God's intended abundance.

This is a common marital problem, and many couples need to be trained not to resort to that kind of pressure within their marriage.

We often ask couples in our conferences, "How many of you, when you stood at the altar to get married, had actually ever seen an example of the intimate, abundant marriage you longed for?" Sadly, most who respond report that they had never seen a marriage like that. For these people, marriage can be a little like the blind leading the blind to a destination they've never seen. No wonder there's so much strife and pain in so many marriages!

God's Spirit comes to train us in His way—the way of giving, accepting, and loving our spouses as He Himself has given to us, accepted us, and loved us.

Now doesn't that sound a lot more fulfilling than a marriage in which both people constantly pressure one another to perform?

In what areas do you and your spouse pressure one another to perform? How can you change this pattern?

Training in the Trials of Life

He who has begun a good work in you will complete it. Philippians 1:6

I (Teresa) love this definition of *training*: "Journey with me to model God's way of facing life's issues." David and I have both been in training throughout our marriage. It seems that when one of us is going through a lesson from the journey of life, then the other is there to model stability or provide comfort and encouragement. When I'm in the midst of one of life's trials, I have confidence that David will go through the trial with me.

Thank You, God, for causing all things to work together for good—even the mistakes we make in our marriage.

In the midst of these kinds of trials, one critical question many couples forget to ask is, "What am I in training for?" An athlete who constantly trained but never competed would likely lose interest, and a musician who constantly trained but never performed would likely lose motivation. Both need to know what motivates them. As God works through our marriage journey to train us in righteousness and Christlikeness, we need to ask ourselves, What is the end purpose of this journey? Here are two answers to that question in mine and David's marriage:

To bring praise to Him for His gift of grace.

For God to use our marriage as a witness to others—our own children, our family, our friends, our coworkers, and others.

Our marriage has in many ways been a journey in training others how not to make the mistakes we've made. We've often wondered why God has brought us down the paths He's chosen to bring us. But we always understood when we got to the end of those paths. We have learned that God can be trusted. Through our journey, He has expanded the impact of our ministry beyond our wildest dreams. He has used it to touch countless homes and lives.

What specific useful lessons have you learned in the journey,
lessons God can use in the lives of those around you?

A Trained Heart

Solid food is for the mature, who because of practice have their senses trained to discern good and evil. Hebrews 5:14, NASB

Today's Scripture verse tells us that training takes practice. It involves some progress and some defeat. At times this may mean taking two steps forward and one step back. Realizing this need for practice helps me (David) develop patience—patience with myself and patience with others who themselves are still in training, including my spouse.

Train my heart, O God, to discern You and to truly know my spouse.

This passage also implies that there is a depth of training and that my senses can be trained in discernment. This is different from training for a sport or hobby and different from job training. This is training within the human soul that sensitizes my heart to the things of God. When I train in this way, I become aware of His concerns, I share in His burdens, and I am attuned to His caring. And it's here that sensitivity to my spouse originates, as from my "trained" heart spring forth awareness, concern, and caring.

It's this testimony of a "sensitive" heart that we see Christ living out all through the pages of the Gospels. On one occasion He speaks of saying and doing only that which He receives from above (see John 5:19-20). On another He speaks to the issue of discernment: "As I hear, I judge; and My judgment is just, because I do not seek My own will, but the will of Him who sent Me" (John 5:30, NASB).

Christ's example of a sensitive heart toward His Father and toward those around Him is the example I should follow as I "train" to serve Him and to serve my spouse and family.

How, specifically, can you begin accepting the "training" of God for your ministry and for your marriage?

The Narrow Opening

*God disciplines us for our good, that we may
share in his holiness.* Hebrews 12:10, NIV

A man watches a cocoon as the newly formed butterfly inside painfully and tediously tries to force itself through a narrow opening. Thinking he will help the butterfly, the man enlarges the opening, and the butterfly emerges quickly and easily. But because the butterfly was released from the cocoon too soon, it fails to develop properly—and it dies. It never becomes the butterfly it was meant to be.

Marriage has its own "narrow opening," doesn't it? Many difficult situations arise, and we are often tempted to solve them superficially and quickly—or avoid them altogether—rather than go through the pain of working through them. That is why many couples never develop into awe-inspiring, functioning "butterflies."

*God, help us
to face head-on
the difficulties
in our marriage.
Help us resist
the urge to take
the easy way
out.*

God wants to use our marriages to turn us into beautiful butterflies. Our marriages are often times of painful training that prepare us for flight. Anytime we refuse to go through the narrow openings of difficulties, we are costing ourselves the ability to learn to fly.

Marriage has the power to chasten us, to discipline us, to train us. The everyday nature of marriage gives us no room to wear masks, to hide who we really are. We bump into each other's flaws and shortcomings, and we end up frustrating one another.

The next time you find yourself in a difficult situation in your marriage, step back and ask God if He is chastening you, if He is trying to teach you something. Then listen, accept His training, work through the issue, and refuse to rush the process. Resist the urge to make the "narrow opening" larger. Let the training process take its course.

How might God be using a difficult situation in your
marriage to chasten you, to train you? What will you and
your spouse do to allow Him to complete His work?

Boot Camp

*May the God of peace . . . make you complete in every
good work to do His will. Hebrews 13:20-21*

One couple we knew described the first seven years of their marriage as "the great tribulation." David and I knew well what they meant. The early years of our marriage were, to put it mildly, very difficult. We were attempting to mature into a loving couple, and we thought that loving each other would come naturally. When it didn't, we did our fair share of finger-pointing and blaming. Of course, finger-pointing seemed almost appropriate when we were sixteen. But when we were still doing it at thirty-six, the problem seemed more acute.

*God, thank You
for using my
marriage to train
me to be more
loving.*

The early years of marriage can feel like military boot camp. The pain and stress can be intense. Some of our early training included facing the shocking reality that without Christ it's impossible to live marriage as intended.

David became a Christian at age twenty-one, and after that came training in what it meant to have the anointing of the Holy Spirit on our lives and to have God's Word as the foundation of truth for living. Next came dealing with the pervasive and subtle hold that selfishness had on our lives. Brokenness before the Lord and one another brought miraculous healing to our lives. Pain was everywhere, but a "completing" work was underway.

God uses our marital pains and hurts to train us to be truly loving people. Marriage is a training ground for the refinement of our character. God wants us to let the hardships increase our tolerance and strength.

Marriage doesn't bring happiness every day, but if we remain teachable, it will bring maturity.

What specific lessons have the trials in your marriage
taught you? What positive changes in your character
have come from these times of pain?

Life Training from Goal Setting

Chastening . . . yields the peaceable fruit of righteousness to those who have been trained by it. Hebrews 12:11

Because of our lack of goals, vision, or direction, David and I endured much chastening early in our marriage. We were, as the Word says, "cast to and fro," arguing over every imaginable decision. We had conflicts over decisions having to do with how we should invest our time, effort, and money, over participation in certain activities, and over what causes or projects we should support.

Heavenly Father, guide us in setting goals for our marriage.

Without established goals, competing choices often bring confusion and conflict within a marriage. But with clearly defined and documented goals, decision making can be greatly simplified.

The process we came to follow is this simple one: We developed clearly written goals in eight areas of life—spiritual, personal, marital, family, ministry, educational, vocational, and financial. We then established plans to address each goal within given time frames.

We broke our plans down into quarterly objectives, then discussed our progress on selected goals at our weekly marriage staff meetings. Our progress encouraged us, and it also gave us a framework for evaluating other decisions and priorities.

We now have a framework for deciding how we will invest our time and energy. If a given "opportunity" will help us meet one of our already established goals, we have the freedom to say yes. If it will not, then we pass on the opportunity.

We often recommend that couples begin setting goals annually. Usually a series of one-year goals works best. Longer-range goals, such as buying a house, should be addressed but broken down into what can be accomplished in a year. Many couples use the week between Christmas and New Year's as a goal-setting time. Others use the beginning of each school year as their time to set goals. The important thing is to begin setting goals.

In what areas of your marriage do you and your spouse most need to begin setting goals?

Committed Confidence in Another

The heart of her husband safely trusts her. Proverbs 31:11

Walk up to the edge of the light before you and then take one step into what you can't see. This is a good way to illustrate trust.

Trust is never based on having all the answers or knowing all the facts. It's not having a "dead cinch." Trust is based upon some answers and some facts, so it's not "blind faith." But it's not really trust when we see and know everything ahead of us. For example, we trust God having never seen Him. We trust His Son from reading of Him. And we trust His Spirit though we cannot touch Him.

What a joy it is, Father, to have a spouse I can trust.

So it is with relational trust. I (David) trust my wife not to knowingly betray me, even though she can, in her humanness, hurt me. I trust my spouse with my most secret thoughts and feelings, believing she'll keep these things between us. I trust my spouse with my deepest inadequacies and fears, confident that she'll protect me and never exploit me. Such trust touches the depths of human intimacy.

Teresa and I have learned to trust one another's motives, even though we may have been hurt by the methods. We each learned to affirm the other's motives, even as we may have communicated disappointment over methods. It might sound like, "I know you didn't mean to, but I felt disrespected when you seemed to take the kids' side against me."

Such vulnerability maintained our trust level while giving us freedom to deal with the issue of our "methods." This helped us keep our trust in one another at a healthy level.

That has been a huge key to keeping our intimacy growing.

What will you do today to express your trust
in your spouse?

I Am That I Am

*Believe in the Lord your God, and you shall
be established.* 2 Chronicles 20:20

The great I AM of Scripture promises us a firm foundation. When Moses stood at the burning bush and asked God who he should say sent him to deliver Israel, Jehovah's answer was, "I AM WHO I AM" (Exodus 3:14).

This name offers insights into the issue of trust. The first I AM is in a future tense, loosely translated as, "I am the One who will continue to be." The second I AM is in a past tense and is loosely translated, "I always have been." In effect, the Lord was saying, "I will continue to be who I always have been."

*Father, thank
You for Your
unchangeable
nature.*

God's unchangeable nature—His consistency—prompts trust within us. He has been there for us mightily in the past, and He can be trusted to be there for us in the future.

Trust can be seen as a strong foundation upon which to build an intimate and abundant relationship. Brick by brick, we can build the foundation with these aspects of trust:

- I trust you to want my best.
- I trust your words to be filled with truth and gentleness.
- I trust you to rejoice with me when I rejoice.
- I trust you to mourn with me when I mourn.
- I trust you to care when you've hurt me.
- I trust you to apologize when you've been wrong.
- I trust you to initiate caring expressions of love.

And on and on it can go—trust built upon trust.

God gave of Himself to establish with us a relationship of trust. Since He did that, does it not follow that He wants us to have the same kind of relationship with one another?

What can you begin doing today to build a foundation
of trust in your marriage?

Trusting Unconditionally

My heart trusted in Him, and I am helped. Psalm 28:7

I (Teresa) have come to realize that I've wanted to trust David with only the areas in which he's proven trustworthy. But trust is like love—it can't be conditional. Trusting David out of my feelings is wrong. I have to believe the best of him. I don't believe David ever consciously tries to hurt me, so when I withhold my trust, I've already judged his motives.

Father, only as I keep my eyes on You and trust You can I totally trust my spouse.

The times when I've been challenged to trust David in a deeper way or to trust him after a time of pain have been difficult. Everything in me wants to protect my heart and run from discomfort. My only source of help has been the trustworthiness of our heavenly Father. God has reassured me that I must trust Him first. I must trust the Holy Spirit to get David's attention, work on his heart, or work on mine. The results have been amazing. When I have placed my trust in God's ability and His timing, I've been helped every time. Have things always gone my way or happened as I expected? No, but the Lord has been faithful to provide for my needs.

As I take practical steps to trust David, I have to remember the positive (not just the painful) parts of our marriage. I have to tell myself the whole truth about my husband and then choose to believe the best. Has David hurt me? Yes, but he's also been faithful and trustworthy. As I remind myself about the positive times as well as the painful, I am free to believe the best about my husband.

Trust doesn't always come easily, but trust can be gained by choosing to believe in our spouse and think the best.

After placing your trust in the Lord, how will you choose to believe the best about your spouse?

Are You Free to Trust?

Blessed be the . . . God of all comfort, who comforts us.
2 Corinthians 1:3-4

Troy's earliest memories were of acting silly to gain his drunken dad's attention. Ann's parents both worked, so she had felt neglected. She tearfully described feeling closer to her housekeeper than to either parent. Neither Troy nor Ann had really learned how to trust. Instead, both had become performers so that they could gain approval and acceptance. Their performance journey had made them both successful but emotionally distant.

O God, help us to share our pain and to comfort one another amid it.

Sadly, Troy and Ann weren't unusual in how they sought acceptance and love. Many people set out to "earn" love and approval through performing. A child might seek attention in a positive way by excelling in academics or athletics, or in a negative way through disruptive behavior. A spouse who feels neglected or rejected may try to gain acceptance through increased activity and self-improvement programs, or by complaining, blaming, and acting out. In each case, the message is the same: "Notice me! I'm important!"

Troy's childhood embarrassment and Ann's childhood neglect brought them years of understandable sadness, aloneness, and pain. Could they trust anyone to care about such pain? It was liberating and touching to see them contemplate the possibility that the God of all comfort was saddened, hurt, and moved with compassion over their pain. They began to express gratitude in prayer, thanking Him for caring. Their ability to trust was being established. Next, God would involve them in a ministry of giving His comfort to one another.

As Ann and Troy grieved together and comforted each other, their trust was awakened as they found they had a caring God and a caring spouse.

What will you do today to give your spouse the assurance
that you truly and unconditionally care for him or her?

In God We Trust

A wicked messenger falls into trouble, but a faithful ambassador brings health. Proverbs 13:17

"I don't trust you any farther than I can throw you!"

Some of us feel this way about our spouses. Marital trust is such a delicate thing. It can be destroyed gradually, by many small wrongs, or instantly, by one huge wrong.

God, help me put my complete trust in You, and help me trust my spouse to You.

Given that all of us are imperfect and none of us is totally trustworthy, how do we build trust within our marriages? We start by totally putting our trust in God. We must realize that God is worthy of our complete trust. Then we must learn to trust our spouses, knowing ahead of time that as human beings they will to some degree fail us. We need to remember that we will fail our spouses as well, but that we can have enough trust in each other to "glue" the relationship together in times of failure. When our spouses fail, we need to turn to God for help, as our ultimate security is in Him and not in our spouses.

An excellent goal for any marriage journey is to be "faithful ambassadors," as today's Scripture passage puts it. The testimony of our deepened trust speaks loudly about the One who is at work to knit our hearts together. In an age of cynicism and skepticism, the faith-filled marriage is a powerful ambassador for Christ, as it calls attention to the health of our relationship and to the One who is making it healthy.

So trust God with it all, and trust your spouse to Him. You will find that trust to be a building block for true marital intimacy.

In what specific areas of your marriage do you need to trust God better? What steps will you take to build that trust?

Blessed Assurance

Love . . . bears all things, believes all things, hopes all things, endures all things. 1 Corinthians 13:4-7

In an age of expendable relationships, marriages that "bear all things" are a rarity. Tragically, "bearing little" is the norm, even in most marriage relationships.

David and I have commented often that had we not moved away from our hometown, we might not have made it as a married couple. A key reason was the prevalence of fragmented relationships that surrounded us. There was no evidence of "bearing all things" in the marriages that served as our models.

God, help my spouse and me to grow in our trust of each other and to remain committed to building that trust through good and bad times.

Recently some good friends of ours shared with us their burden for three couples living near them in their apartment complex. One unmarried couple lived together, too afraid of commitment to get married. Another couple, married for two years, had recently separated for four months and had just gotten back together. Still another married couple was trying marriage for the second time. Each of these couples seemed to have the impression that marriage is expendable. That created a lack of trust in each of the relationships.

A lack of trust will destroy any marriage. You need to be able to depend on the commitment of your spouse. Yes, David and I have deeply hurt each other, and we will probably hurt each other again in the future. But we don't give up in the face of our pain. We are committed to keeping our marriage commitment. Neither of us will be leaving.

David and I are in our marriage for the long haul, no matter who does what to whom. When the hurts occur, we will do what needs to be done to heal them, then move on. That trust keeps our marital intimacy growing and thriving.

What will you and your spouse do today to build one another's assurance in your commitment to your marriage?

Building Blocks of Trust

My dear brothers and sisters, be quick to listen, slow to speak, and slow to get angry. James 1:19, NLT

Teresa and I often point out to couples that building a relationship involves being vulnerable and discussing a growing number of topics. Unfortunately, however, many couples develop a list of off-limits topics—topics such as emotions, money, in-laws, sex, driving, golf, and so on. As this list of off-limits topics grows, marital distance widens and a shaky marital foundation soon becomes evident.

Father, help my spouse and me to deepen our relationship by broadening the array of topics we can talk about.

To address this issue of "off-limits" topics and to encourage deeper trust in relationships, we challenge couples to communicate with one another about intimacy by asking this question: "What changes can I make to improve our intimacy?"

We also challenge couples to talk about confidentiality within their marriage so that each person is secure that the thoughts and feelings he or she communicates to the other will be kept within the confines of the marriage relationship.

Finally, we ask couples to consider the kind of support they will give to one another as they work to improve their intimacy. We ask couples if each of them can count on the other to be empathetic and supportive, or if they will "shoot down" one another's ideas and negate one another's feelings.

These ingredients encourage vulnerability as trust is deepened and a growing list of topics opens for discussion. Once couples have taken these steps, they can begin communicating what topics they want to open up for discussion. They can do that by writing down the following sentence: "I think I might enjoy our being able to discuss more about _____ _____." They then exchange these lists and begin including one of the topics in their "marriage staff meetings."

When couples begin adding to the topics they can discuss, they find that their closeness is increased as communication opens up.

What topics do you need to open up for discussion
within your marriage?

Knowing without Judging

Apply your heart to understanding. Proverbs 2:2

Understanding is a matter of the heart, just as knowledge is a matter of the head. To understand is to know intimately in experience; it is to become deeply acquainted with. Understanding begins with God, who knows all intimately. Many may look on the outside, but God looks on the heart. The psalmist speaks of His knowing my steps before I take them and my words before I speak them. He formed and fashioned me in my mother's womb and knows the number of my days in this life. He knows the intentions of my heart and the inner struggles of my flesh. And still He loves me. He's known me and not judged me. He knows my future failures and has not rejected me.

Father, create that same understanding between my spouse and me.

No greater testimony of "understanding" can we find than the Word becoming flesh and dwelling among us (John 1:14). This is about God being with us, as us! Christ could have come to earth, died on a cross to pay for our sins, and then immediately returned to glory. He didn't have to stay for a week, a month, or a year, and yet He lived on earth for a lifetime. He lived so that He too could endure grief, sorrow, hurt, and disappointment. He wanted to live as we live because He wants us to know that He understands. Such understanding is additionally miraculous in that even though He knows us, He has not rejected us but welcomed us. He has not come to judge us based upon His understanding, but rather to love us.

Our challenge is to apply our heart and our effort toward that same understanding for our spouse. We must come to know our spouse deeply and still offer love and acceptance.

How might you come to understand your spouse
more deeply?

Understanding the Eternal

May the Lord give you understanding in all things. 2 Timothy 2:7

Today's Scripture passage gives us an exciting prayer about entering into God's understanding. Paul prays for young Timothy and asks that Timothy will have understanding "in all things." Now that's an exciting prayer!

Only God knows all. He is intimately acquainted with everything in the past, present, and future. He reveals Himself as eternal in our temporal world. So to gain His understanding in all things will include a glimpse of His eternal perspective.

Lord, we need Your eternal view of life so we can place priority on things that will last forever.

Think about a couple walking through a maze made of hedges. The husband and wife can see only the path ahead of them. They try one way, only to find a dead end. But imagine if the couple could have a bird's-eye view of the maze. They could see the beginning from the end, the dead ends from the fruitful paths. That's what God's eternal perspective is like. He sees and understands it all.

Grasping and embracing God's eternal perspective will help us understand many things about our lives. To gain that perspective and understanding, we must read His Word, listen to Him in prayer, and be willing to follow His directions.

God will also help us understand what, from His perspective, is truly eternal. God is eternal, so our relationship to Him is very important. Scripture is eternal, so we commit ourselves to studying and memorizing it. People are eternal, so we invest ourselves in our marriages, our families, and our friendships. By contrast, material things are not eternal, so we should spend less time, energy, and money on grasping for them.

How does this understanding of God's perspective help you invest in things that are eternal? How does understanding the eternal help guide your marriage?

What will you do today to replace your focus on things that don't last with a commitment to what is eternal? How will you express that in your marriage?

Why Won't You Fix It?

Who is wise and understanding among you? Let him show by good conduct that his works are done in the meekness of wisdom. James 3:13

Frustration rose in me (Teresa) every time something in our house needed repair or I wanted to start a home project and David wouldn't help. I wanted us to work on projects together, but he always wanted to hire someone to do it. I couldn't understand this.

David and I have had some of our most painful conflicts over David's not wanting to help me hang pictures or wallpaper. It was easy for me to conclude that if David didn't care to help hang a picture, he didn't care about me. Even though I now see how such thinking was irrational, at the time the pain of it was very real. David would respond to my accusations that he didn't care by saying that I took things too personally and that I blew things out of proportion. It took us much discussion to come to resolution and closure on this issue.

Lord, help me not to compare, but to love my spouse in an understanding way.

David finally told me one night that he felt inadequate in the "how-to" area. I began to see that he wasn't just trying to get out of the work, and I came to a better understanding of my husband. As David communicated with me, I also began to realize that I had been comparing him to my father, who could fix everything. I was judging David, which wasn't fair.

David and I had many extended discussions about my expectations and his perceived inadequacies. I was able to offer my husband comfort, and David was able to better see my need for his care in many areas. The communication we shared in this area brought us closer together on many levels.

What steps can you and your spouse take to better understand one another's needs and areas of inadequacy?

Oh, I See What You Mean!

Understanding is a wellspring of life to him who has it.
Proverbs 16:22

After many failed attempts, Orville and Wilbur Wright finally flew successfully in December 1903. They excitedly telegraphed their sister Katherine, "We have actually flown 120 feet. We will be home for Christmas." She took their telegram to the local newspaper editor. He read it and said, "How nice. The boys will be home for Christmas."

God, help me to understand my spouse in the deepest possible ways.

The editor totally missed the point.

Do you find yourself "missing the point" in your marriage when you listen to your spouse? When you hear, "I've had a really rough day, especially when I went to the shopping mall," do you say, "Oh, you went to the mall? Did you get that shirt like I asked you?"

Marital intimacy means listening to your spouse at the deepest level possible. It means hearing his or her deepest feelings, concerns, hopes, and fears.

Teresa might say that I've been "slow to break" in missing the point. In breaking me of so often missing the point of what Teresa was saying to me, the Lord brought me to a painful realization: The root of the problem for me was my own self-centeredness. I was so focused on my agenda, ideas, plans, and needs that I was insensitive to others.

God pointed me to the Christ of the Gospels as an example of someone who never "missed the point" when He talked to those around Him. He listened to people with selfless, sensitive, attentive, and caring ears. That's the kind of love our Lord had for those who came to Him.

And it's the kind of love I'm to have for those around me, particularly my spouse.

How can you begin to be a better listener, to make sure you "get the point" when your spouse communicates with you?

Walk Around in My Shoes for a While

Each of us should please his neighbor for his good, to build him up. Romans 15:2, NIV

John was happily married, with a loving wife and children. He had been a Christian several years, and life was good. One morning, however, a young man called him at his office, claiming to be John's twenty-year-old son. The young man explained he had been adopted as a baby and had for the last two years been searching for his biological parents. He asked John if he would be willing to meet him.

John was stunned. He never knew that his high school girlfriend had been pregnant when they broke up. Now all he could think about was whether or not this would destroy his marriage. He promised his newfound son that he would call later with the decision about whether or not to see him, then hung up. After much prayer and counsel from a trusted friend, John told his wife the whole story.

Thank You, God, that marriage is a place where pain can be shared and understanding can be offered.

Without hesitation, John's wife threw her arms around him and said she understood all the pain he must be going through. She told him that she loved him and would support him. His wife's understanding response caused his love and respect for her to grow.

Today's Scripture passage introduces us to the principle of "the good of others," a fundamental part of Christ's ministry. An attitude that puts the good of others first is critical evidence of God's *agape* love.

John's wife exhibited this kind of love in a unique way as she supported her husband even though he had difficult news for her to hear.

That is the kind of love we are to extend to our spouses. It's a love that understands and accepts, a love that makes us willing to walk around in our spouses' shoes for a while.

In what specific areas do you need to be more understanding of your spouse?

Does Anyone Understand Me?

Do you not yet understand? Matthew 15:17

We often ask married people who really "knew" them as they were growing up. Very often the sad and tragic answer is that no one really got to know them well. Life went on and surface issues were dealt with, but no one really entered their world and got to know them. This is what understanding is all about. Each of us needs people we care about to understand us.

Father, lead us into the depths of understanding each other.

The power of marriage is that through divine understanding we can so "know" one another that God restores the loss we've suffered.

Even in today's Scripture passage there seems to be a sadness in the Savior's heart as He asks, "Do you not yet understand?" One of the deep longings of His heart is that those He is talking to might have understanding. I (David) am sure Teresa has thought those same words, if not actually said them: "David, do you not yet understand *me*?"

In our journey to better understanding each other, Teresa and I have focused on several practical issues. In an effort to better understand what each of us finds important, we ask one another about opinions, ideas, and dreams. We care about feelings of all kinds—joy and hope, sadness and anxiety. We accept these feelings and don't judge them. We empathize with each other's feelings and don't analyze them. We explore childhood reflections.

This communication gives Teresa and me insight into our lives' "journeys." It also helps us understand some of our needs, and possibly some of our hurts. Finally, this allows us to accept weaknesses—to cut each other a little slack when it comes to imperfections.

This is what true understanding within a marriage looks and sounds like.

What steps can you and your spouse take to better communicate your feelings to one another?

Fellowship, Friendship, and Passion

They shall become one flesh. Genesis 2:24

In our training, teaching, and writing, we refer to God's plan for marriage intimacy as the freedom to share all of oneself with one's spouse—spirit, soul, and body. It's our prayer that your marriage be challenged by the mystery of God's plan for two becoming one. From the opening chapters of Scripture, He had a plan for marriage, and much of that plan can be seen in the mystery of oneness.

It's our hope that you walk as:

Father, bless our journey together. Thank You that because of Your provision we are not alone.

- Two saints sharing fellowship
- Two recipients of transforming grace living in the awe and wonder of being loved by their Creator (John 1:16)
- Two mere humans experiencing together the inexpressible joy of being children of God, partakers of the divine nature (2 Peter 1:4)
- Two friends of Christ who deeply know one another and know the One who has called you into eternal life (John 15:15)
- Two aliens walking in this world, but not of this world (1 Peter 2:11; John 17:16), laboring together as ambassadors for Christ, being transformed together into His image (2 Corinthians 3:18; 5:20), longing together for His return (1 John 3:2).

It's our prayer that you become very best friends—two hearts stirred to cherish each other, experiencing together life's joys and struggles. It's our desire that you enjoy the specialness of two lovers sharing passion, physical excitement, expectation, and arousal prompting a desire to become "one flesh."

We pray that you will be able to experience oneness in every aspect of your marriage, giving glory to the One who created it. And finally, it's our earnest prayer that you be able to give testimony that you are *never alone!*

How would you rate the intimacy in three dimensions of your marriage—spirit, soul, and body? How could you bring more "oneness" to each dimension?

About the Authors

DAVID AND TERESA FERGUSON, married for more than thirty-five years, are the directors of Intimate Life Ministries, which serves thousands of churches and ministry leaders worldwide with a message of how to deepen intimacy with God and deepen relationships in marriage, family, and the church.

Early in David's ministry, he, like so many other people in Christian ministry, tried unsuccessfully to achieve balance between ministry and family demands. Out of an intense desire to honor God and minister to the needs of his family, he rediscovered a biblical principle that transformed his life, his family, and his ministry to others. He writes about that journey in his book *The Great Commandment Principle* (Tyndale). For the past twenty years David and Teresa have been sharing that message in print and through ministry retreats, media, and speaking engagements around the world.

In this book, David and Teresa bare their hearts and show how God transformed their empty marriage into one in which they not only meet each other's needs but also become vibrant partners with God in loving the way He loves.

David's graduate work in theology, counseling, and social sciences focused on the Great Commandment principle and its impact on relationships, ministry, and culture. David has earned a M.Ed. from Southwest Texas State University as well as a Ph.D. and a Litt.D. from Oxford Graduate School. He is a member of the Oxford Society of Scholars. David and Teresa have collaborated on the writing of several books and articles. They live in Austin, Texas, and have three adult children—Terri, Robin, and Eric.

About Intimate Life Ministries

Who and What Is Intimate Life Ministries?

Intimate Life Ministries (ILM) is a training and resource ministry, head-quartered in Austin, Texas, whose purpose is *to assist in the development of Great Commandment ministries worldwide,* ongoing ministries that deepen our intimacy with God and with others in marriage, family, and the church. Intimate Life Ministries comprises:

- A network of **churches** seeking to fortify homes and communities with His love;

- A network of **pastors and other ministry leaders** walking intimately with God and their families and seeking to live vulnerably before their people;

- A team of **accredited trainers** committed to helping churches establish ongoing Great Commandment ministries;

- A team of **professional associates** from ministry and other professional Christian backgrounds, assisting with research, training, and resource development;

- **Christian broadcasters,** publishers, media, and other affiliates, cooperating to see marriages and families reclaimed as divine relationships;

- **Headquarters staff** providing strategic planning, coordination, and support.

How Can Intimate Life Ministries Serve You?

ILM's Intimate Life Network of Churches is an effective ongoing support and equipping relationship with churches and Christian leaders. There are at least four ways ILM can serve you:

1. MINISTERING TO MINISTRY LEADERS

ILM offers a unique two-day "Galatians 6:6" retreat to ministers and their spouses for personal renewal and to reestablish and affirm ministry and family priorities. The conference accommodations and meals are provided as a gift to ministry leaders by cosponsoring partners. Thirty to forty such retreats are held throughout the U.S. and Europe each year.

2. PARTNERING WITH DENOMINATIONS AND OTHER MINISTRIES

Numerous denominations and ministries have partnered with ILM by "commissioning" us to equip their ministry leaders through the Galatians 6:6 retreats along with strategic training and ongoing resources. This unique partnership enables a denomination to use the expertise of ILM trainers and resources to perpetuate a movement of Great Commandment ministry at the local level. ILM also provides a crisis-support setting where denominations may send ministers, couples, or families who are struggling in their relationships.

3. IDENTIFYING, TRAINING, AND EQUIPPING LAY LEADERS

ILM is committed to helping the church equip its lay leaders through:

Sermon Series on several Great Commandment topics to help pastors communicate a vision for Great Commandment health as well as identify and cultivate a core lay leadership group.

Community Training Classes that provide weekly or weekend training to church staff and lay leaders. Classes are delivered by Intimate Life trainers along with ILM video-assisted training, workbooks, study courses, etc.

One-Day Training Conferences on implementing Great Command-ment ministry in the local church through marriage, parenting, or singles ministry. Conducted by Intimate Life trainers, these conferences are a great way to jump-start Great Commandment ministry in a local church.

4. PROVIDING ADVANCED TRAINING AND CRISIS SUPPORT

ILM conducts advanced training for both ministry staff and lay leaders through the Leadership Institute, focusing on relational ministry (marriage, parenting, families, singles, men, women, blended families, counseling, etc.). The Enrichment Center provides support to relationships in crisis through Intensive Retreats for couples, families, and singles.

For more information on how you, your church, or your denomina-tion can take advantage of the many services offered by Intimate Life Min-istries, write or call:

Intimate Life Ministries
11615 Angus Road #203
Austin, TX 78759
1-800-881-8008

Or visit our Web site at www.greatcommandment.net

Do-able. Daily. Devotions.

START ANY DAY THE ONE YEAR WAY.

For Women

The One Year®
Home and
Garden
Devotions

The One Year®
Devotions for
Women

The One Year®
Devotions for
Moms

The One Year®
Women of the
Bible

The One Year®
Coffee with God

The One Year®
Devotional of Joy
and Laughter

The One Year®
Women's
Friendship
Devotional

The One Year®
Wisdom
for Women
Devotional

The One Year®
Book of Amish
Peace

The One Year®
Women in
Christian History
Devotional

For Men

The One Year®
Devotions for
Men on the Go

The One Year®
Devotions for Men

The One Year®
Father-Daughter
Devotions

For Families

The One Year®
Family
Devotions, Vol. 1

The One Year®
Dinner Table
Devotions

For Couples

The One Year®
Devotions for
Couples

The One Year® Love
Language Minute
Devotional

The One Year® Love
Talk Devotional

For Teens

The One Year®
Devos for Teens

The One Year®
Be-Tween You
and God

For Personal Growth

The One Year®
at His Feet
Devotional

The One Year®
Uncommon Life
Daily Challenge

The One Year®
Recovery Prayer
Devotional

The One Year®
Christian History

The One Year®
Experiencing God's
Presence Devotional

For Bible Study

The One Year®
Praying through
the Bible

The One Year®
Praying the
Promises of God

The One Year®
Through the
Bible Devotional

The One Year®
Book of Bible
Promises

The One Year®
Unlocking the
Bible Devotional

TheOneYear.com

CP0145

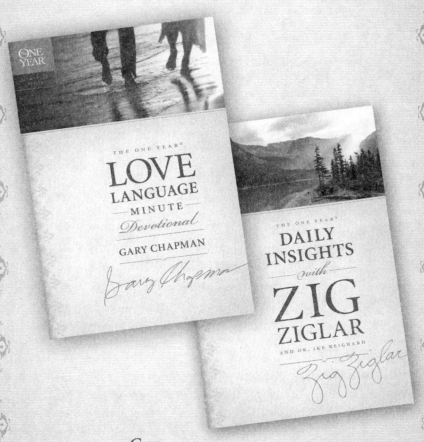

Teach Truth.

MEET JESUS EVERY DAY THE ONE YEAR WAY.

For Kids

The One Year®
Devos for Girls

The One Year®
Devotions for
Boys

The One Year®
Devotions for
Preschoolers

The One Year®
Devotions for
Kids

The One Year®
Sports Devotions
for Kids

The One Year®
Mother-
Daughter Devo

The One Year®
Children's Bible

The One Year®
Josh McDowell's
Youth Devotions

Called 2 Love
A 40-Day Journey into Marriage Intimacy

Using the power of story, the authors lead couples along their own journey to better know and care for each other. An excellent resource for couple mentoring, small groups, and premarital counseling.

Write your own relationship story as you learn how to experience love that lasts.

Called 2 Love:
Like Jesus

An anthology of teachings and practical exercises from notable followers of Jesus

Explore the transforming power of your call to love, like Jesus loves you. Also included are practical devotionals to deepen your love of the Lord followed by loving family, friends, and those who need Jesus.

Powerful, practical experiences in how to live out your faith in all relationships.

Called 2 Love
The Uhlmann Story:

A journey of self discovery and joy-filled connection

Married for more than 50 years, Steve and Barbara continue to see relationships as the way to reveal Jesus to the people around us. In their new book, *Called2Love: The Uhlmann Story*, they share the principles of love and change that transformed their lives.

This heartfelt revelation will guide couples into healthy change that brings healing and true intimacy. – Drs. Les and Leslie Parrot